EXTINGUISH INTERPERSONAL CONFLICT FIRES!

Are you a conflict fire "starter" or "fighter?"

EXTINGUISH INTERPERSONAL CONFLICT FIRES!

How to Resolve Disputes and Enhance Compatibility in Relationships

A Holy Spirit Inspired "Reconciliation Manual"

Bridget U. Bazunu

Bridget U. Bazunu

Extinguish Interpersonal Conflict Fires!

Published by: Jesus Crusaders Publishers, Orlando, FL

Unless otherwise noted, all Scripture quotations are from the King James Version (KJV) and New King James Version of the Bible (NKJV). Emphasis on Scripture is author's own.

Library of Congress Control Number: 2020905955
ISBN 978-0-9712225-3-3

Printed in the U.S.A.

For worldwide distribution

Dedication

I Dedicate This Book to:
The Supreme God; whom I owe my life and all.
Abba Father, You are the reason I live. I exist exclusively
to worship you, give you pleasure, render you glory,
and show forth your praise.

Acknowledgements

My heartfelt thanks to:

The Almighty God – *"In You I live, move, and have my being."*

Mr. S. E. Aihebhoria – Papa, your benevolence, venturesome faith, love for humanity, loaded vision, and zest for God and life will always enthrall me.

Mrs. Comfort I. Aihebhoria (of blessed memory) – Sweet Mother, Gentle, Devoted, Altruistic, Virtuous, Unassuming. Your love and patience will perpetually sculpt me.

Anthony – My undiluted Honey, Lover, and Soul mate. Your unconditional love and validation will always exhilarate and complete me. Daily, may we sculpt and paint our own "Paradise" to portray the multifaceted nature of God, in the name of Jesus.

Antoinette – Purpose-driven, God-seeker, Facilitator, Beauteous, Valuable treasure. Aaah! May your love, charisma, and empathetic virtues continue to impact the world.

Alven and Bridgette – Innovative, Graceful, Faith-propelled, Exquisite gems. Ahh! God-chasers, Music lovers. Continue to inspire humanity with your fervor, geniality, and musical genre.

Anthony Jr., Man of God – Precious, Peculiar, Catalyst. Your artistic gifts in poetry and music are idiosyncratic, philosophical, and inspirational. May your soothing and restorative melodies galvanize others into seeking God, in the name of Jesus.

Micah – Delightful, Bubbly, Anointed Prophet created to transform generations and advance God's kingdom.

My Siblings, Anointed Fathers and Mothers in the Lord, Mentors, Friends, Partners, and Protégés – God will count your love, prayers, inspiration, and support as righteousness.

You are highly favored, divinely covered, and sealed by the blood of Jesus Christ. Remain superabundantly blessed. I love you all.

Table of Contents

Introduction

The Purpose of This Book

Welcome to "Interpersonal Relationships Boot Camp" – a restorative enchiridion designed to give you the tools to avoid or manage conflict, restore harmony, produce qualitative change, and catapult valuable relationships to new heights.

Formal and informal relationships play a pivotal role in society. Thus, we must measure ourselves by a holy standard and follow biblical protocol to be wholesome people.

Relationships should be a safe harbor, not a war zone. However, many are in dire straits because people are growing colder daily. *"And because iniquity shall abound, the love of many shall wax cold" (Matthew 24:12).* Often, we use anger, bitterness, and hostilities to burn down our alliances. Relationships go up in flames when we choose pride, anger, self-idolatry, impenitence, and resentment over reconciliation.

Often, we gravitate to people more than we crave God. We are broken emotionally but yearn to mend others. Rather than let God heal us, we pressure others to soothe our pain and restlessness. We excuse ourselves but put others through the wringer. We resist change but long to fix and control others. Why would others change when we are as culpable as they are? Only when we accept responsibility will they follow our example.

This pragmatic book will empower you to identify and root out personal blind spots and hang-ups that are conflict triggers. Discover how to implement relationship roles, build social skills, improve compatibility, resolve interpersonal feuds, and cultivate healthy soul ties and rapport with others.

Learn how to spot, avoid or exit dysfunctional relationships. Combat "conflict fire with fire" against demonic forces. Strengthen familial, professional, social, and spiritual bonds. The book stresses why we must secure relationships on the bedrock of Scriptures - the only navigational system that can steer them in the right direction.

"Lord, But How?"

The birth of this book is an amazing testimony of God's infinite wisdom. The Lord directed me to write a biblical deconfliction manual specifically designed to empower married couples to harmonize their differences and build healthy and long-lasting relationships. So, I hit the ground running and titled the book, "Defuse Marriage Conflict Bombs!" *How to Avert or Extinguish Conflict Fire Explosions and Embrace Reconciliation.* However, the more I wrote, the greater I saw the need to generalize and craft it into an interpersonal relationship book that everyone could benefit from besides couples. But the Lord did not release me to take a different turn. My finite mind could not comprehend why I should focus only on marriage when I could universalize it for both formal and informal relationships.

The yearning to write it my way intensified my restlessness. I knew that there was a great need for a biblical conflict resolution manual for all relationships but did not want to have to write it from scratch. Even if I did, I had no clue how it would all come together. Nevertheless, I decided to trust God, finish the book, wait for His next move, and see how He would pull this off.

Shortly, after I published the marriage book, the Lord said, *"Now you can customize it for other interpersonal relationships."* *"Lord, but how?"* I asked bewildered. *"This will be extremely hard – if I have to do this all over again for a different audience."* I grumbled, grasping my greatest fear. However, He began to show me how. It was unbelievable! Not in a million years would I have cognized His divine strategy had He not revealed it to me. He made it so much easier because I did not have to start afresh! Instead of the one marital deconfliction book, here is another transformative one for different relationships. Phew! Blessed be the name of the Lord!

You will discover that some paragraphs, passages, and sentences in this book are word for word like the original version, "Defuse Marriage Conflict Bombs!" Whereas in other places, I simply customized it for other relationships whenever possible. Also, I added new materials, Scriptures, and revelations.

Prayer Points

All the chapters are loaded with powerful prayer points designed to stir the reader to pray, not take over the leading of the Holy Spirit. Feel free to modify them as He gives you unction and utterance.

It is always wise to start prayer with praise and worship to usher in the presence of God (Psalm 100: 2, 4 -5). Daily, utilize Psalm 51 as a prayer for forgiveness and cleansing for yourself, family, and relationships. Forgiveness brings breakthroughs. Always apply the blood of Jesus Christ on yourself and household before and after prayer for divine protection. Also, bring the blood of Jesus against any demonic re-groupment, reinforcement, retaliation, or counterattack before and after prayer.

Insert the names of those you are praying for, especially at the beginning of prayer or whenever necessary. Prayer is more effective when you identify the person or people that you are asking God to touch. However, as you proceed, you can use, "I," "we," "us," "our," "her," "his," "she," "he," and the like in place of those you earlier identified.

We need to rejoice in the hope that we have in Christ, be patient in times of trials, and continuously pray (Romans 12:12). As we pray fervently with faith, God will heal our relationships and turn all impossibilities into breakthroughs and miracles. Now, let's roll up our sleeves and get to work

CHAPTER 1

Conflict Fire Starter or Fighter?

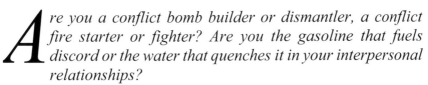

When we nag, harbor resentments,
shift responsibility, disparage others
or lie to one another, we are
gathering wood to start a conflict
fire or fan an existing one.

*A*re you a conflict bomb builder or dismantler, a conflict
fire starter or fighter? Are you the gasoline that fuels
discord or the water that quenches it in your interpersonal
relationships?

It is unfeasible to be gasoline and water simultaneously. Regardless of whether you are in a love, professional, spiritual, familial or platonic relationship, you have to decide if you will let God use you as a vessel of peace or let the devil use you as a conduit for conflict.

Who Referees Your Fights?
Who umpires your responses when you and your friends, kinsfolk, colleagues, fellow believers or neighbors are at loggerheads – the Holy Spirit or the devil? Who you allow to referee your fights can make or ruin your alliances. While the Holy Spirit will coach you to conciliate your disparities, the devil will find deceptive ways to augment them.

1

Do you listen to the dictates of the flesh or the Spirit?
Does argument turn you on?
Does quarreling give you an abnormal high?
Are you a querulous or peace-loving person?

Are You a Querulous Person or Peacemaker?

"As charcoal is to burning coals, and wood to fire, so is a contentious man to kindle strife" (Proverbs 26:21). Take the following quiz to identify if you are a grouchy person or a conciliator. When you have conflict, do you:

- Argue to get attention?
- Want to be right or get your way?
- Shift blame to avoid accountability?
- Always want to have the last word?
- Lose control when you are angry?
- Find it hard to forgive or allow the sun to go down on your disagreements with others?
- Delay reconciliation or allow dissension to linger after an argument?
- Use malicious words or retaliatory behavior to get back at others?
- Find it difficult to relinquish your rights for the sake of peace or the good of a relationship?
- Pick at old wounds, dig up skeletons from the past; spew unrelated unresolved issues or utilize others' vulnerability and candor against them?

A "Yes" answer to any of the above questions suggests that you are a "conflict fire starter." You are a troublemaker given that your answers are symptomatic of one with a tetchy spirit. Pray that God will deliver you from a cantankerous mentality.

When you indulge in any self-seeking behavior, you are gathering lethal ammunition to ignite a "conflict fire" or fuel a current one. Over time, your grumpiness will set off a conflict bomb that might blow up your relationships. You may try to excuse your behavior:

"I am only reacting to Jeremy's behavior!"

"My sister, Phoebe, makes me so mad!"

Well, you have no control over Jeremy or Phoebe's actions. However, you can manage yours. By countering his or her behavior, you are only drenching the "evil coals" of discord with more fuel to keep it aflame. Pacify your anger, cool off the temperature of distressing emotions, intercede for the purported offender, and absolve offenses so that God will get the glory. *"It is honorable for a man to stop striving, Since any fool can start a quarrel"* (Proverbs 20:3).

Conflict "Fire-fighters"

Peacemakers are spiritually minded individuals and conflict fire combatants. They manifest the dictates of the Spirit, not flesh, walk by faith, not sight, and live by truth, not emotions. When we sow peace to thwart discord, we are conflict firefighters. People that eschew arguments or have a teachable, forgiving, forbearing, and compassionate spirit are conflict fire extinguishers. Often, they eagerly walk in love, extend forgiveness, and elect to be the water that cools off any conflict blaze in their interpersonal relationships.

Peacemakers recognize the value of divine relationships and will bend backward to protect them. They do not collaborate with Satan to burn down valuable ties or burn their bridges behind them, given that they recognize the ramifications of crippling godly alliances that have been preordained to enrich their destinies.

Indeed, peacemakers have character deficiencies like everyone else. However, they choose to continually abide in Christ so they may be the vessels through which His love flows. When we allow the love of God to flow through us, we can live affably with crabby folks and win them over with divine love. Those who encounter us daily must also encounter God by how we relate to them.

Conflict "Fire-starters"

Cantankerous people are conflict fire starters. They are carnally minded, apathetic, self-righteous, grouchy, unforgiving, insolent, paranoid, unappeasable, and easily offended. They continuously drip with hostility and make a storm in a teacup when riled. Like a ticking time bomb, the slightest thing sets them off. Curtailing them is like trying to restrain the wind. *"A continual dripping on a very rainy day And a contentious woman are alike; Whoever restrains her restrains the wind, And grasps oil with his right hand" (Proverbs 27:15-16).*

Often, when people refuse to resolve their differences or let go of offenses, they ignite a conflict inferno or use their unresolved anger, disappointments, and vindictiveness as weapons to build a conflict bomb. *Are you gathering woods to start a conflict fire or building a conflict bomb with your bitterness?*

When we insist that a relationship should be on our terms, confute personal responsibilities, highlight our differences or engage in anything that will cripple meaningful associations, we are conflict arsonists. We are stacking up "coals" to start a firestorm or inflame an existing one.

Often, the obliteration of a relationship begins when a sequence of deleterious behaviors is left unchecked. They can build up over time and evolve into a heated conflict conflagration. Each unwholesome action can have a ripple effect and set a relationship ablaze. When we use anger and control as bargaining chips to exploit our formal or informal ties, we are gathering "parched wood" to set them afire. When we deride others or invest little or nothing in their lives, we are empowering the devil to entangle us and those we love in his web.

Quarrelsome people are drawn to conflict like a magnet. They dread serenity and always battle others. Like a merry-go-round, they are always starting, ending or exacerbating an existing conflict. When unresolved hostilities evolve into a caustic row, they would rather trade punches than humble themselves. Such impious conducts only flare-up more

4

antagonisms. The same energy that is used to ignite a conflict fire can be used to build a reconciliation altar.

Resolve to be a "conflict firefighter" that douses fiery arguments as well as a "climate controller" that regulates the temperature of your relationships. Develop interactive or interpersonal skills to avert and resolve feuds. Always allow the Holy Spirit to have the last word and promptly reach out for reconciliation – when there is a misunderstanding. Utilize the word of God to conciliate your incompatibility issues and relinquish your rights for the good of the relationship.

- **Scriptural Confession: Psalm 51; Matthew 18:18**
- **Praise and Worship**
- **Prayer Points**

1. Abba Father, I repent of animosity, ingratitude, cantankerous attitude, and insolent behavior from the past and present, in the name of Jesus.
2. Oh God, *"create in me a clean heart." "Renew a right Spirit within me,"* in the name of Jesus.
3. Let the blood of Jesus purge and cleanse me.
4. I bind every power inciting conflict in my life and relationships. I paralyze and evict you out of my life and relationships, in the name of Jesus.
5. Let every seed of pride and the works of the flesh in my life, informal, and formal relationships wither and die, in the name of Jesus.
6. I bring the blood of Jesus against the principalities and powers that are bringing warfare into my life and relationships, in the name of Jesus Christ. I paralyze you and cancel all your demonic activities, in the name of Jesus Christ.
7. I use the blood of Jesus Christ to destroy every root of confusion, misunderstanding, and strife in my life and relationships, in the name of Jesus.
8. By the blood of Jesus Christ, let every arrow of strife, confusion, warfare, fear, and division fired into my life and

5

relationships backfire and go back to the sender, in the mighty name of Jesus Christ.

9. Let the fire of the Holy Spirit consume whatever is in me (anger, pride, fear, resentments, and the like) that may be evoking conflict, in the name of Jesus.
10. Oh God, do not let Satan find anything in me that he can use to incite conflict in my life and relationships, in the name of Jesus.
11. Every plan of the enemy to destabilize my life and relationships shall come to naught, in the mighty name of Jesus Christ.
12. I take divine insurance in the blood of Jesus Christ against strife, misconceptions, division, pride, and anything that is unlike God within and outside my alliances, in the name of Jesus.
13. Apply the blood of Jesus Christ on yourself and thank God for the victory.

Make This Declaration

By the blood of Jesus Christ, I refuse to buy into any seduction of the devil. I refuse to be argumentative or hypercritical of those whom I am connected to, in the name of Jesus. Instead, I choose to sow peace, love, appreciation, and gratitude in their lives, in the name of Jesus Christ.

CHAPTER 2

"Lord, don't You Care if We Perish?"

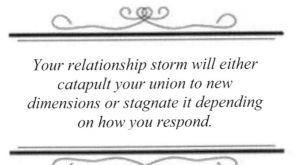

*Your relationship storm will either
catapult your union to new
dimensions or stagnate it depending
on how you respond.*

T he disciples were amazed that Jesus was able to sleep tranquilly while trying to navigate their boat through a storm. As they observed Him, they cried out, *"Lord, how can you nap serenely in a problematic time like this? Don't you care if we perish?"* (See Mark 4:35-41.) Despite the sticky situation, He expected them to utilize their faith to calm the storm. However, they responded with fear, doubt, and unbelief.

Your relationship storm will either catapult your close or distant associations to new dimensions or stagnate them depending on how you respond. Obedience or obduracy determines how long a conflict storm lasts in relationships.

"Lord, Where are You When I Need You?"

Are unmet needs, irreconcilable differences, and incompatibility issues rending your relationships to shreds?

Do you feel despondent because of shattered ties with those you care about?

7

Are you on the verge of throwing in the towel because your relationship with a friend, child, sibling or boss is no longer a safe harbor but a combat zone?

How the disciples reacted to a storm is how we react to impediments. Perhaps, like the disciples, you are asking, *"Lord, where are you when I need you?"* He is always with you. You may not feel His presence because you are numbed by discord. Your heart may be throbbing with apprehension, hurt, and animosity. Notwithstanding, you must yield to Him and respond with faith rather than react with fear to encounter His *"fullness of joy."*

We are all guilty of unbelief and hung up about our ideologies – how God should identify with us, how we should relate to Him, deal with others, and vice versa. When we superimpose our viewpoint on Scriptural prescription for relational growth, we would barely discern Him – even if He were supping with us on our dinner table. Many of us are so undiscerning and deeply preoccupied with self-idolatry that we would not recognize the Lord if he were to visit our homes. Many have utilized their unbelief and ingratitude to silence or chase Him out of their relationships.

Our humanity causes us to wallow in skepticism and query God during crisis even though we are conflict fire kindlers. It is natural to feel disheartened in tumultuous times or when encumbered by circumstances beyond one's control. You may be disillusioned because a relationship that matters to you is caught between the devil and the deep blue sea. Nonetheless, God will never desert you. *"When you pass through the waters, I will be with you; And through the rivers, they shall not overflow you. When you walk through the fire, you shall not be burned, Nor shall the flame scorch you"* (Isaiah 43:2).

Hold on and follow the footsteps of "The Master Builder" of harmonious relationships. He will protect His purpose and will not let your agenda override His. He expects you and the other person to renounce self-centeredness and reconcile your grievances so you can begin to love, fellowship, and trust again. We cannot always have things our way like we do at *"Burger*

King" or *"Subway."* We must align our conduct with His character.

"Lord, why are My Relationships Falling Apart?"

How do you respond or react when your relationship with a peer, family member, neighbor, business associate, Church member or spouse is blazing with conflict inferno? Perhaps your relationship vessel needs an oil change or a tune-up. Often, disagreements erupt when people in a union are striving to give or get from each other, what only God can give them. When you attempt to reap what you have not sowed or withdraw what you have not deposited, your "relationship bank" will run a massive deficit. Be willing to sow yourself, give more than you take, and renounce selfishness to avert sinking deeper into the quagmire of conflict. Only when we empty ourself of offenses and daily pursue peace can we skillfully ride the waves of life.

"Lord, how can you sleep peacefully when those that matter to me are about to capsize?"

Are you frightful and incredulous like the disciples, wondering how the Lord can nap so serenely when your relationship with a friend, colleague, neighbor, spouse, child, relative or Church folk is on fire? Perhaps, He is because He expects you to use reconciliation to empty the excess water in your *relation"ship."* The issue is not how He responds to your situation, but your obedience.

Who or what opened the door to your conflict storm?

What is the storm in your relationship exposing?

What steps are in place to surmount it and seal the cracks in your relationship yacht?

Are you allowing God to use it to build your spiritual stamina and enlarge your capacity to love?

Are you receptive to the "message" the storm is transmitting vis-à-vis your relationship, or are you blind to the truth?

Every storm is a classroom. What are you learning from it?

Every storm has a voice. Every problem is a sifter. It sieves out the worst and leaves the best or the *crème de la crème* in you.

Also, it exposes the depth of your foundation, love, and commitment to God and others. Your relationship storm will either catapult your union to new dimensions or stagnate it – depending on your response. You decide the duration of a conflict storm. While obedience mitigates and shrinks its length, disobedience elongates it.

"Bridget, I wish you knew how big my storm is!"
God is much bigger than all the cyclones in the world combined. I would rather go through a storm with Jesus snoozing in my vessel than set sail without Him. Yes, it is better to experience an interrelationship blizzard with the Lord seemingly silent in it than navigate a seemingly enchanting course without Him.

We take refuge under the shadow of God's wings and are secure about our safety because we are in His will. Daily, we ride each wave by faith, *"deny ourselves, take up our cross, and follow Him"* obediently. Faithfully, with one act of love, tolerance, and forgiveness after another, we steer *"this baby"* on the *"straight and narrow"* course. Regardless of whether He rebukes the storm slowly or swiftly, *"all things will work together for our good" (Romans 8:28)*. Oh, how we desperately need Him whether He is seemingly awake or asleep! We cannot plot a harmonious course without His wind on our sails as we navigate this exhilarating escapade of a lifetime.

"Lord, how can you be silent when my interpersonal ties are blazing with conflict fire?"
"Gabriella, my daughter, has been acting up lately. Brandon hates me and his dad! Granny Mae is upset because she feels neglected and won't talk to me! Plus, I have to deal with those selfish people at work and Church! I am so stressed trying to hold everything together! Don't You care if we perish?"

"Where is your faith?" (See Luke 8:25.)
Is it hiding in your insecurities, discord, self-centeredness, anger, pride, unbelief, discontentment, ingratitude, unhealed wounds,

impatience, finger-pointing, resentment, power struggle, numbed emotions or fear? Perhaps the hullabaloo in your relationships may have muzzled it. Find and utilize it to rebuke the wind! The Lord is counting on you to use your faith, benevolence, and gentleness to oust the wind. He wants you to forgive and settle your differences. Lash out and bombard the devil, not those you care about. Use your spiritual weapons to throw him out of your vessel. Since Jesus, the Creator of the heavens and earth is in your relationship yacht, the devil cannot sink it! Fear not…for how can he submerge the Lord of Hosts? Keep your chin up and utilize your faith to disarm the menace of conflict.

- **Scriptural Confession: Pray Psalm 40:13-17, Mark 4:39, Philippians 4:7**
- **Praise and Worship**
- **Prayer Points**

1. Heavenly Father, please forgive me for blaming you for my problems and the consequences of my choices. I repent of my sins and ask that you wash me clean with the blood of your Son, Jesus Christ.
2. Let the blood of Jesus Christ close every access door that may have been opened through disagreements, disobedience, witchcraft, rebellion, and ancestral curses, in the name of Jesus.
3. Lord, help me to identify what gave access to the "conflict storm" in my relationships.
4. Let the blood of Jesus close devilish doors in my life and seal every crack, in the name of Jesus.
5. Father, dominate my heart, revive my faith, use this storm to build my spiritual stamina, and enlarge my capacity to love others, in the name of Jesus Christ.
6. By the blood of Jesus, I command every storm ranging in my life, family, and relationships to cease, in the mighty name of Jesus Christ.

7. Let the peace of God, *Agape* love, and unity be released into my family and other interrelationships, in the name of Jesus Christ.

8. I hold the blood of Jesus against all the powers that want to thwart or meddle with God's plans for my life, in the name of Jesus.

9. I bind every devouring spirit that wants to devour my peace, joy, and strength, in the name of Jesus Christ.

10. Heavenly Father, I say, "Yes" to You and "No" to the devil. Have your way in my life and relationships, in the name of Jesus Christ.

11. I speak peace to every storm in my life and relationships, in the mighty name of Jesus.

12. Apply the blood of Jesus on yourself and thank God for the breakthrough.

CHAPTER 3

Divine Relationships: A Spiritual Warfare

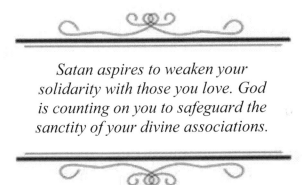

*Satan aspires to weaken your
solidarity with those you love. God
is counting on you to safeguard the
sanctity of your divine associations.*

pparently, the devil is envious of our familial,
professional, platonic, and divine ties because they
personify the relationship between God, His Son, Jesus,
and the Holy Spirit. He established earthly ties to embody His
standard for healthy interpersonal relations.

The devil is diametrically conflicted and opposed to harmony
hence he tries to discredit our connections. He is insanely jealous
when we have wholesome alliances because he understands the
power of a cohesive team. He fights relentlessly to disintegrate
our solidarity to vex God. Sometimes, the enemy will send
parasites to drain our focus, *"Jazebels"* to exploit our
vulnerabilities, *"Absaloms"* to topple our divine positions,
"Labans" to sabotage our efforts, *"Sambalats"* to taunt our
dreams, *"Achans"* to defile our souls with sin, and *"Tobias"* to
disparage us so we will abandon building our "interpersonal
relationship walls" for his malevolent agenda. We must be
likeminded and stand shoulder to shoulder because we are
stronger when united and weaker when divided. Recognizing the

following three biblical truths will help us avoid or combat conflict.

(1) The Need to Identify Satan as the Enemy

Until we identify Satan as the adversary in every relationship, we shall continue to fight one another. Also, we will envisage those in our inner and outer circle as the enemy when they are not dancing to our melody or satisfying our expectations. Until we see him as the intruder, we will not boot him out but accommodate and empower him to exploit us.

Satan is a thief! He aspires to steal your joy, distort your focus, wane your peace, abort your dreams, and interject the pulsation of your relationships. He yearns to weaken the bond between you and those you love, damage mutual trust, and accentuate your differences to incite strife. He wants to implant conflict in your alliances, and when you are at loggerheads, he will creep in to incapacitate your solidarity. There is a coalition of demonic forces that are fighting relentlessly against our relationships. We are in a spiritual warfare to nullify their attack and discomfit their consociation. *(See Ephesians 6:12-13).*

If you believe that some of the afflictions, warfare, trails, temptations or bizarre things in your life or relationships are normal, sit back and think again! Your adversary, Satan, and his confederacy of demons are fighting tooth and nail to destroy your valuable relationships. (See Ephesians 6: 10-18.) The devil does not want you to believe that he exists. He wants you to envisage him as a harmless illusive force, carved out of human imagination. Although he is an incorporeal being, his malevolence and abhorrence for humanity are quite palpable. He aims to harass, impair, and rescind humanity. He achieves these ambitions through demonic entities, depraved human agents, and evil personalities with scorched consciences. He assigns them to relationships, families, marriages, people, businesses, churches, governments, territories, and nations – with a motive to badger, debilitate, terrorize, and eventually obliterate. Beware of the devil! He exists exclusively to exhibit his demonic personae. He was crazy enough to rebel against God and will stop at nothing to exhibit his demented motives.

This is not the time to play games with our faith. Be spiritually alert, prayerful, and steadfast. You will have to patrol the boundaries of your close alliances to avert satanic invasion.

Why do I need to be vigilant?

Often, when the devil comes on the scene, parents that have lived righteously to raise their children, married couples that have withstood the test of knotty trials, friends that have bonded with each other in dire times, Pastors who have faithfully shepherded their congregants with truth, mentors and protégées that have remained divinely connected, and siblings with deep emotional and spiritual bonds suddenly seem disenchanted. They develop an irresistible compulsion to pick fights with each other and set their solidarity ablaze. Unless they are discerning, they may not even know how, why or when the enemy accessed their lives.

The devil comes from nowhere unannounced and inserts himself into relationships. His motive is to discombobulate and throw folks off balance. This is why we must refute his insinuations, cultivate reconciliation skills to ward him off, and sharpen our gift of discernment to guard against his craftiness. Rather than fight each other, we must eschew his bait.

The devil can utilize people to impair a relationship. Even when others are cantankerous, we must not attack them personally because they are not the real enemy. We must attack only issues, not people.

2) The Need to Yield Our Affections to God

We have despondent interrelationships because the enemy has embezzled our commitment, faith, integrity, and love for God. How can we even love others unconditionally if we do not love the Lord wholeheartedly? We must repent and reclaim our stolen affections and give them back to our Creator.

We cannot yield our affections to God and the devil simultaneously or pledge devotion to the Lord and yet dine with the enemy by our iniquitous mode of existence. It is absurd to think that we can romance and bind the devil at the same time, and he will comply – even when we are authorizing him to express his monstrous character through us in our formal and informal relations.

The devil does not leave when we cooperate with him to aggravate God. He lodges in relationships that utilize his goods – anger, bitterness, fear, pride, deception, and the like. Only when we surrender to God will he submit to us, obey our command, and flee. *"Submit yourselves therefore to God. Resist the devil, and he will flee from you. Draw nigh to God, and he will draw nigh to you. Cleanse your hands, ye sinners; and purify your hearts, ye double minded" (James 4:7-8).* Often, we fall into the morass of conflict because we concede to the prescriptions of the flesh. Because we are in incessant strife with the Spirit, it spurs us to act soulishly. However, we can overcome interrelationship challenges when we yield to Him.

As Christians, it is incumbent on us to subdue the flesh to avoid strife, not placate our soulish cravings. We must do God's will, not execute our selfish ambitions. The only way to avert a conflict quagmire is when we surrender our affections, vulnerabilities, and will to Him. Conceding implies loving Him. Loving Him is the prerequisite to loving others.

3) The Need to Protect the Sanctity of the Family

While the family is fragmented, Satan and his demons are a cohesive force. They are warring to subvert and disjoint families. We should be nauseated by the present state of the family and be willing to play a pivotal role to restore uprightness and dignity. We must get down on our knees and fight for our kids, submit to God, and resist sin and Satan, not roll out the red carpet for him to put us through the wringer and hang us up to dry! We can hang him in the nearest gallows for all his atrocious acts by getting back on track and epitomizing the fruit of the Spirit as a lifestyle.

The society is trying to redefine the family and use her carnal ideologies to negate God's purpose. Social media, humanism, false religions, evil fraternities, and secularism are vying for our focus and faith. We must contend for our *"most holy faith,"* so the devil will not reduce the family to an infinitesimal entity in the world. He is maiming the family so she will have a minuscule influence on humankind and become invalid. For years, the family has danced to his tune and assumed a diminutive role instead of the steering role mandated by God.

While the family is the foundation of the society, the society mirrors the strengths and weaknesses of the family. Thus, bolstering the family with Truth will replicate godly values in the world at large. Conversely, destabilizing the family unit with disharmony or divisiveness will subvert those values.

Psalm eleven, verse three says, *"If the foundation be destroyed what can the righteous do?"* The walls of the family have been torn by abuse, juvenile delinquency, moral laxity, alcohol and drug abuse, divorce, sexual perversion, idolatry, and depravity. Only the blood of Jesus can cleanse our foundation from these pollutants and heal our bloodlines. Consequently, we must go by the book to protect the sanctity of the family. Buffering the family is a divine mandate. It is our obligation to conform to God's benchmarks, find common grounds to harmonize our dissimilarities and begin to rebuild the family.

Rebuilding the Broken Walls of the Family

How do we rebuild and strengthen the family? We must accept responsibility, atone for our egocentrism, and refocus on applying the will of God for the family. Also, we must hunger and thirst for holiness, exhibit the fruit of the Spirit, cultivate social skills, and extend an olive branch to those who have offended us so we can wave goodbye to family feuds. It is incumbent on us to raise the paradigm of truth, morality, and character, not shift the responsibility to secular institutions.

We have no right to challenge others to practice truths that we reject. We cannot take others beyond where we are. Until we allow God to transform us, we cannot genuinely rouse others to do the same. Only when we are whole, can we nudge others to move beyond their personal hang-ups to embrace wholeness.

When we embrace spiritual hunger, it will ignite spiritual awakening and rub off on our families. Self-renewal will not only stir the family toward transformation but will also fuel the zeal for communal regeneration. The fireworks of change will glow and become a catalyst for societal revival. However, repentance and conversion must commence with us to prompt others to follow suit.

- **Scriptural Confession: Psalm 18:2, Psalm 68:1-3, Isaiah 54:15; 59:19, Romans 8:28**
- **Praise and Worship**
- **Pray and Make These Scriptural Declarations.**

1. Almighty God, possessor of heaven and earth, I hide myself in you because You are my God, Tower of Refuge, Light, Rock, Fortress, Strength, Joy, Peace, Buckler, Defender, Redeemer, Mighty Deliverer, High Tower, and the Horn of my Salvation.
2. Father, I yield all my affections to you, in the name of Jesus.
3. Almighty Father, cleanse and heal my family, in the name of Jesus.
4. Father God, rebuild the broken walls of my family, in the name of Jesus.
5. I take authority over principalities and powers, and spiritual wickedness in higher and lower places assigned to frustrate, beguile, cripple and instigate conflict in my life and relationships, in the name of Jesus. I bind and cancel all their demonic activities and plans against my home and relationships, in the name of Jesus.
6. Based on Isaiah chapter 54:15, I decree that all household wickedness, evil networking, principalities and powers, and spiritual wickedness in higher and lower places gathered against my household and relationships shall fall for our sakes, in the name of Jesus Christ.

7. When the enemy shall come against us like a flood, "The Spirit of the Lord shall lift up a standard against him," in the name of Jesus Christ.

8. Let God arise in my life, marriage, and relationships and let His enemies be scattered; Let those also who hate Him flee before Him. As smoke is driven away, so drive them away; As wax melts before the fire, so let the wicked perish at the presence of God. But let those who love Him be glad and rejoice exceedingly before the Lord, in the name of Jesus.

9. Heavenly Father, by the power of the Holy Spirit, I declare that all things shall work together for the good of my household, friends, neighbors, colleagues, and other valuable relationships because we are called according to your plan and purpose, in the name of Jesus Christ.

10. Heaven Father, let renewal, deliverance, revival, and restoration begin with me, my family, and relationships in the name of Jesus.

11. Father God, I apply the blood of Jesus on myself, and I thank you for answering my prayers.

CHAPTER 4

Conflict – A Relationship House on Fire!

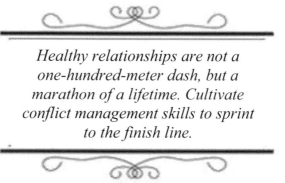

*Healthy relationships are not a
one-hundred-meter dash, but a
marathon of a lifetime. Cultivate
conflict management skills to sprint
to the finish line.*

C onflict is symbolic of a house on fire. While a house is illustrative of a relationship because it should be a safe harbor, fire is figurative of conflict. Relationships go up in flames when people do not defuse the conflict bombs they created with their hostilities.

When you think conflict, imagine a *house on fire.* Like a burning house, its combustibility should not be underestimated. If you visualize conflict as a blazing combustion, you will go to great lengths to avoid, manage, or dowse it when it surfaces. Relationships burn down when the people that should be accountable for them refuse to put out their unfriendly fires through reconciliation. They either rebuff repentance or assume that their squabbling will mystically disappear without any conscious effort on their part. Waiting for a hostile fire to peter out on its own is as ludicrous as anticipating that a house fire will extinguish on its own without lifting a finger. It is the duty of everyone in a relationship to douse conflict fire.

Conflict Arsonists

Are some of your relationships on conflict fire? Do you consider your relationships a safe harbor or war zone? Are you at peace or war with those whom God has placed in your life? Are you a Conflict arsonist!

Your response unveils the depth or shallowness of your commitment to your close or distant alliances. Furthermore, it reveals your temperament – whether you are a conflict fire starter or a conflict fire extinguisher.

Scores of people set their relationships ablaze with unbiblical reflections, conducts, and mindsets. Just as unscrupulous arsonists deviously set houses on fire so do some tetchy people consciously set their relationships on fire.

How do you set a relationship on conflict fire?

If you lose control when others disagree with you; bicker to get attention; squabble to manipulate others, and use insalubrious verbiage or retaliatory behavior to defy those in your inner or outer circle, you are gathering parched wood to start a conflict fire. When people shift responsibility to elude accountability or shelve reconciliation because they are unwilling to relinquish their rights for amity, eventually, their interrelationships will explode in conflict flames on account of their obstinacy and immaturity.

When we coerce others to dance to our drum beat, we are building a conflict bomb. When an introvert person repeatedly badgers a chatty friend, sibling or colleague to adopt her laconic trait, she is gathering parched coal to make a conflict fire. When a loquacious friend, brother, neighbor or family member pesters a taciturn person to become garrulous, he or she is building a conflict bomb that will eventually detonate. Since introverted people are bound to remain reticent; and extroverted people will remain affable, demanding that they reinvent themselves will certainly intensify hostilities in a relationship.

We set a relationship ablaze when we yield to fleshly desires or authorize fear to dictate how we give or receive love.

21

Conflict Has a Voice

Only those who are spiritually sensitive will heed the piercing voice of conflict. Those who are spiritually deaf and immature will not. We must heed conflict fire alarm blaring in a relationship or face the ramifications. What does conflict say with every clang? *"The relationship is on emergency alert and temporarily out of order; Pride and resentments are on display; fellowship is on hold; communion is frigid; trust is broken; the lines of communication are clogged; commitment is on intermission; friendship is brittle; empathy is on pause; understanding is out of alignment; friendship is incapacitated; and the hearts of the people invested in the relationship are bleeding profusely with hurt, and they urgently need healing and reconciliation."* The rumbling voice of conflict forewarns us to resolve our differences immediately so our relationships will not go up in flames. With each reverberation, the responsibility to conciliate falls on those involved in the dispute despite how incensed or malcontent they may be.

Regardless of whether you are in an informal or formal relationship, do you heed the voice of conflict, warning you to put out inharmonious flames?

Do you "hear" the hurt and frustrations that each other is communicating?

Do you often deal with discords or sweep them under the relationship rug; hoping they will miraculously disappear without resolution?

Despite hurt emotions, the burden to apply the healing balm of forgiveness to heal crushed feelings so we can renew fellowship again falls on us. If we do not tackle unresolved issues in a Christ-like manner, they will pile up as high as the Empire State building and eventually choke the relationship. What you blatantly refuse to confront may come back to haunt you. Avoid vulnerable situations where you are tempted to make your own conflict bombs, fan the flames of dissension or turn your relationships into a war zone.

May we not be like the obstinate prophet, Balaam, who was so spiritually blinded and undiscerning that God had to use his horse to confront his obduracy and rebellion (Numbers 22:1-35). Stubbornness, ignorance, and spiritual blindness will not be our portion, in the name of Jesus Christ. Amen. *"I will instruct you and teach you in the way you should go; I will guide you with My eye. Do not be like the horse or like the mule, Which have no understanding, Which must be harnessed with bit and bridle, Else they will not come near you" (Psalm 32:8-9).*

Cultivating Conflict Resolution Skills

Show me individuals that would eagerly yield their rights or sacrifice their needs to thwart conflict – and I will show you impeccable people. There are no flawless people. Instead, when we are offended by a colleague, neighbor, relative, believer or an acquaintance, we put on our boxing gloves and challenge the other person to a brawl. Our body language, behavior, and verbiage will be on high alert with, *"You want to fight? Common, let's trade punches!"* When we are slighted, the last thing we want to do is yield our rights, accept responsibility or say, *"I am sorry."* Instead, we want to win. People in a relationship are allies, not rivals who are competing in a wrestling match. The success of a relationship hinges on teamwork. We all lose or triumph together.

It is never whether we shall have altercations but how we will respond when we do. The Lord said, *"These things I have spoken to you, that in Me you may have peace. In the world you will have tribulation; but be of good cheer, I have overcome the world" (John 16:33b).*

The ability to avoid, manage or resolve conflict is not an intrinsic gift that kicks in naturally when warranted. Deconfliction happens only when we willfully trade our pride for humility, self-righteousness for accountability, and anger for understanding for the growth of a relationship. It takes patience to circumvent arguments and establish a good rapport with people. We must cultivate conflict management and reconciliation skills to help us deal with disputes until they become a pattern of life. God wants our divine relationships to be wholesome and long-lasting.

"No Sweat, No Gain"

We all desire hearty relationships within and outside our families. However, it will be only a figment of our imagination if we are unenthusiastic about making those aspirations a reality. We cannot build idyllic alliances if we are not willing to break a sweat or sow ourselves. Whether we succeed or fail in a relationship significantly depends on us. If we sow nothing, we will reap zilch. Those who have no trials to mature them will have nil testimonies to promote them.

We must foster the *"good,"* confront the *"bad,"* renounce *the "ugly"* in each of us, and dislodge our demons if there is any hope that others will expel theirs. Also, we need to boost our strengths, starve our weaknesses, and use our social skills to build a great rapport with people. *Do you desire blooming relationships? Roll up your sleeves and make every effort to sow good seeds in them.*

Building a Relationship Sacrificially

Throngs of interpersonal relationships crumble because many try to build autonomously from God. Those who disregard Him are doomed to fail before they even begin. It is unviable to build harmonious ties without co-laboring with the Lord. We must collaborate with Him or our efforts will be as futile as attempting to retain water in a basket. *"Unless the LORD builds the house, They labor in vain who build it" (Psalm 127:1a).*

Building wholesome relationships can be challenging and at the same time rewarding. Building not only necessitates commitment and sacrifice, but it demands that we *"break up the fallow ground"* in our hearts and rid ourselves of all the emotional debris that can suffocate our efforts. Likewise, we must lay a solid foundation on Christ the Rock and attach building blocks of

24

understanding, compassion, communication, and friendship to glue them together. We must exercise our "love muscles" so our relationships will not become flaccid.

We are called to do life with others and showcase the attributes of God so that those within and outside our inner circle will encounter Him through us. It is a tremendous blessing to relish in comradeship, accord mutual respect, sow love, serve and esteem one another in the liberty of Christ, not in the shackles of a physical penitentiary.

Do you feel trapped in any of your relationships?

What are you doing to count the cost of a robust relationship?

Are you willing to roll up your sleeves and do all it entails to solidify the footing you have with others?

More importantly, are you willing to let God change you first so He will utilize your obedience to effect the transformation you desire in others?

- **Scriptural Confession: John 10:27, Isaiah 54:17, Psalm 119:33-40, 2 Corinthians 12:9, Matthew 18:18, Galatians 5:19-21**
- **Praise and Worship**
- **Prayer Points**

1. Father God, give me the wisdom, grace, fortitude, forbearance, and anointing to avoid, manage, and resolve conflict in my relationships, in the name of Jesus.
2. By the blood of Jesus, I renounce spiritual blindness, deafness, dullness, and stubbornness, in the name of Jesus.
3. Almighty Father, I am your sheep and I hear only your voice. I yield myself to you. Give me the ears, eyes, and mind of the Holy Spirit so I may hear what you are saying, do what I see you doing, and discern the deep things of the Spirit, in the name of Jesus.
4. By the blood of Jesus, I silence and denounce every power instigating me against those within and outside my inner circle, in the name of Jesus.

5. Let every evil voice speaking lies or unpleasant things about my family and relationships be silenced, in the name of Jesus.

6. No weapon of evil formed against those whom I am divinely assigned to or those who are assigned to me shall prosper. I silence and condemn every negative, condemning, mocking, accusing, condescending, fearful, and conflicting voice that rises up against us in judgment, by the blood of Jesus Christ.

7. Let the blood of Jesus cause everyone in my divine relationships to be in one accord, in the mighty name of Jesus.

8. Lord Jesus, I renounce selfishness, hatred, obstinacy, ingratitude and all that Satan is using against my household and relationships, in the name of Jesus.

9. By the blood of Jesus, I renounce haughtiness, and "holier than thou" attitude, in the name of Jesus.

10. I put off pride and put on humility. I relinquish self-righteousness for accountability. I renounce anger and choose understanding, in the name of Jesus Christ.

11. I renounce all the works of the flesh, in the name of Jesus.

12. Father, I receive the grace, strength, wisdom, and anointing to count the cost and make a difference in my relationships, in the name of Jesus.

13. Abba Father, break and mold me according to your purpose and plans for my relationships. Help me to share unconditional love so that others will encounter You through me, in the name of Jesus.

14. Almighty Jehovah, help me to develop biblical skills to build my life and relationships to magnify your name, in the name of Jesus.

15. Apply the blood of Jesus Christ on yourself and thank God for answers to your prayers.

CHAPTER 5

Satan: The Author of Conflict

Beware...
Satan is the embodiment of discord,
division, confusion, and evil.

Who is Satan?

Satan is the prime source of discords. Remember, he came to steal, kill, and destroy (John 10:10). He instigated conflict between God and humankind from the very beginning. Adam and Eve were in perfect harmony with each other and with God until he arrived on the scene. Just as he created dissension between Adam and Eve, so will he try to whip up disagreements between you and your spouse, relatives, friends, colleagues, neighbors or fellow workers in God's vineyard. Why do you think hordes of family, friendship, business, and Church disputes are on the rise? Parishioners have unresolved issues with their Pastors, fellow members, and other Churches. Some Pastors do not encourage or allow their members to fellowship with other full gospel Churches. It makes sense if these *"forbidden"* Churches are occultic or if they preach false doctrine. But full gospel Churches? We must liaise with other believers, not let Satan bedevil and segregate us.

Why are families, Churches, Governments, and Communities divided?

We often seem to be at loggerheads with those we have close or distant ties with for no just cause. The devil is not only the instigator of mayhem and disintegration, but he is persistently weaving a web of friction to incapacitate the solidarity of flourishing relationships. Jesus identified Satan as the father of lies (John 8:44). He distorts truth and enlarges minute misunderstandings to his advantage. Thus, you must *"believe"* and *"do"* the opposite of whatever he insinuates about those whom the Lord has placed in your life.

The devil *"needs"* people to exploit. He hunts for human bodies to inhabit so he can evince his demonic aspirations through their thoughts and deeds. He stalks vulnerable families, businesses, neighborhoods, nations, Christian and secular institutions so he can manipulate them to do his depraved biddings. Like a roaring lion, he seeks rebellious folks who will yield to his evil overtones so he can wreck their godly ties.

Families, Churches, Governments, and Communities are feuding with each other because they are empowering Satan to replicate his monstrous character in and through them. He is the embodiment of the *"works of the flesh"* depicted in the book of Galatians 5:19-21a. When we engage in *adultery, fornication, uncleanness, lasciviousness, idolatry, witchcraft, hatred, variance, emulations, wrath, strife, seditions, heresies, envyings, murders, drunkenness, revellings,"* and other sinful acts that trigger interpersonal feuds, we are sanctioning him to reproduce his iniquitous personality in and through us.

We cannot achieve anything worthwhile in a relationship if we are not in one accord with those we are connected to. Two cannot work together unless they agree (Amos 3:3). Just as there is strength in unity, so is there weakness in division. When people lose consciousness of their vision, they begin to grow apart, pursue selfish aspirations, and thus dilute the strength of their coalition. Regardless of individual differences, we must endeavor to remain a glowing cohesive force with those we love. Amity in a relationship hinges on the solidarity of trust.

Blame Everything on the Devil?

Truly, the devil is the instigator of interpersonal feuds and cataclysms. However, we also have to bear some responsibilities. We cannot attribute self-sabotaging choices to him without taking liability for approbating and giving him access. He can influence our choices and lead us astray under duress only when we give him the thumbs up. We are as liable for sinful acts as he is because we invoke him, harbor his *"goods,"* and even let him use us as pawns to do his dirty job.

I am not suggesting, blame everything on the devil. What I am implying is mark who he is, what he does, and how he operates perfidiously. His middle name is conflict, and he will continue to utilize his evil machination to incite unsuspecting folks against each other. He is the epitome of wickedness and human depravity in relationships. He is like "parched coals" eagerly waiting to be ignited into a destructive conflict inferno. Often, he incites credulous people against each other to divert attention away from his devilry. While they are at each other's throats, he stands arms akimbo laughing and jeering at them.

The Devil's Pawn

Can the devil use us or others to instigate a quarrel? You bet! He used Isaac and his wife, Rebecca, to drive a wedge between two brothers, Esau and Jacob, which lasted for generations. He incited Aaron and Miriam against their brother, Moses, because of his Ethiopian wife. The devil instigated Absalom to overthrow his father, David. He stirred up Joseph's brothers against him, the Pharisees and Sadducees against Jesus, and Adam and Eve against the Almighty God. He is still striving to create a huge chasm between God and humanity today. The Lord warns against wickedness. *"The Wicked"* are not only those who commit heinous crimes but those who deliberately slander others or choose disobedience. *But to the wicked God says: "What right have you to declare My statutes, Or take My covenant in your mouth, Seeing you hate instruction And cast My words behind you? When you saw a thief, you consented with him, And have been a partaker with adulterers. You give your mouth to evil, And your tongue frames deceit. You sit and speak against your brother; You slander your own mother's son. These things you have done, and I kept silent; You thought that I was altogether like you; But I will rebuke you, And set them in order before your eyes. "Now consider this, you who forget God, Lest I tear you in pieces, And there be none to deliver: Whoever offers praise glorifies Me; And to him who orders his conduct aright I will show the salvation of God" (Psalm 50:16-23).*

Our egos can hamper a relationship as well as drag it down the drain. Just as we can be vessels used by God to create fruitful relationships, so can we also be instruments used by Satan to cultivate barren ones. Ungodly character, self-sabotaging habits, and unresolved issues can fling the door of a relationship wide open to him. He seeks those who will utilize his propositions to advance his fiendish agenda. You have the power to heal or fragment your valuable alliances. Why not let God use you to advance His cause rather than let Satan use you like a marionette to exhibit his ghoulish objectives?

In the next few chapters, we shall discuss the root of conflict, what Satan uses to instigate people against each other, conflict triggers, and Scriptural ways to avoid or deal with them. As we consider some of the factors that elicit conflict, you will discover that "living to please self" is the primary denominator.

- **Scriptural Confession: Psalm 33:10, Isaiah 46:10; 58:6**
- **Praise and Worship**
- **Prayer Points**

1. By the blood of Jesus Christ, I reverse every evil decree against my life and those I love, in the name of Jesus.
2. I decree that every counsel of the devil against my relationships shall come to naught, in the name of Jesus Christ.
3. By the blood of Jesus, I decree that only the purpose and counsel of God shall prevail in my life and relationships, in

the name of Jesus Christ. We belong to God. Therefore, let every power that wants to lay claim to our lives be paralyzed, in the name of Jesus.

4. By the blood of Jesus, Satan, you are a liar! You cannot touch or control my spouse, son, daughter, sibling or friend. (name those in the relationship you are praying for.) I nullify your influences over our lives, in the name of Jesus.

5. By the power in the blood of Jesus Christ, I loose the bands of wickedness in my life and relationships, in the name of Jesus.

6. I undo the heavy burdens in my life and relationships. I break every yoke of bondage in our lives, in the name of Jesus Christ.

7. Father, I seal my relationship with my daughter, son, and spouse with the blood of Jesus. Let the blood of Jesus Christ strengthen the emotional, spiritual, and physical bond between us, in the name of Jesus.

8. Let the fire of the Holy Ghost devour all the powers that want to devour my relationships, in the name of Jesus.

9. Father, bind my alliances with commitment, forgiveness, love, truth, faith, and friendship, in the name of Jesus.

10. I seal my relationships with the blood of Jesus and the fire of the Holy Spirit, in the name of Jesus.

11. By the blood of Jesus, I take divine insurance against household enemies, principalities and powers, and demonic spirits that are warring against my relationships, in the name of Jesus Christ.

12. Lord, thank you for your love, goodness, mercies, and for answering my prayers.

CHAPTER 6

Ignorance of God's Purpose of Relationships

(Conflict Fire Starter # i)

My people are destroyed for lack of knowledge (Hosea 4:6). Ignorance is a malady that can only be cured by knowledge of God's word.

Ignorance is a sickness that impairs relationships. It is sad to note that the devil is utilizing ignorance and strife to wreck throngs of relationships. *"My people are destroyed for lack of knowledge" (Hosea 4:6a).* Numerous interpersonal relationships are in hot water because they are clueless about why the Lord connected them. They wallow in pride, bitterness, and diverse forms of debauchery because they are unenlightened about how God wants them to relate to one another.

God linked us so we can learn how to relate to one another as well as form emotional and spiritual bond that replicates the union between Him and His Son, Jesus. Just as we have communion and fellowship with God our creator, so must we have with each other. In essence, our relationship with God embodies our relationship with others and vice versa. Jesus came to demonstrate how relationships should work or how we should relate to one another.

Why did God Connect You to Others?

Do you know why God positioned you in your family? Why did He link you with those supposedly weird folks? Why did He connect you with your Church, Pastor, and fellow parishioners? Why did He link you with those at your job or business? Do you understand why God assigned you to certain people?

Not discerning why you are in a relationship can generate strife, unfruitfulness or even estrangement. When people do not understand the divine purpose of their linkage, they will be emotionally and spiritually unfertile. Also, the devil will feel empowered to enervate their ties.

The primary goal of a relationship is not just to satisfy our needs or fuel our agenda. It is sinful to exploit and milk others simply because we have the power to do so. It is no wonder that we enjoy companionship and friendship with others but also remain angst-ridden, finicky, and acrimonious when they are not curtseying to our peremptory bids. Yes, we are connected by marital, spiritual, professional, familial, and platonic ties but also remain absentee siblings, associates, pals, nieces, parents, Pastors, nephews, in-laws, cousins, spouses, uncles, neighbors, aunties, brothers, and sisters within and outside the local Church. Why? We do not want to be bothered by others. Sometimes, although we are physically in these interpersonal relationships, we are spiritually and emotionally detached and miserable as well. *A man that hath friends must shew himself friendly: and there is a friend that sticketh closer than a brother (Proverbs 18:24).* We are stronger when we are like minded, not isolated. *Two are better than one; because they have a good reward for their labour. Again, if two lie together, then they have heat: but how can one be warm alone? And if one prevail against him, two shall withstand him; and a threefold cord is not quickly broken (Ecclesiastes 4:9, 11-12).*

Obliviousness Wanes Relationships

When people do not understand the objective of a relationship, they either emasculate, exploit or circumvent it altogether. If you do not cherish the value of a parent, friend, child, sibling, brethren, Pastor or those around you, you may be tempted to keep them at bay to avoid offenses, correction, confrontation or responsibility.

Adam and Eve did not understand why God created or desired their fellowship, obedience, and communion, or they would not have let the devil come between them and God. Just as the devil crafted a rift to distance them from God, so will he try to come between us and our loved ones if we do not recognize why He allied us in the first place.

If Cain had tapped into the blessings of siblinghood with Abel, he would not have murdered him. He never fathomed what real brotherhood meant or the importance of being his "brother's keeper."

Isaac and Rebekah abused their parental role and contributed to their familial woes. The enmity they incited between Esau and Jacob extended to generations. Parents who play favorites, enflame sibling rivalry or rebuff their parental responsibilities are toying with the destinies of future generations.

Laban did not value the role of a father in-law; hence he defrauded Jacob repetitively. He cared more about what he could possibly reap from Jacob than what he could plant in him as a son in-law. Joseph's brothers had no clue why God placed him in their lives as a sibling. They could have garnered wisdom from his dreams to become better, not bitter.

King Saul could have taken David under his tutelage. Instead of mentoring him to maximize his full potentials, he became a rival. He could have significantly benefited from David's anointing had he not yielded to jealousy.

Absalom ousted his father, David and defied his concubines in the *"eyes of all Israel"* because he did not recognize the responsibilities of a son or the value of a divine relationship.

Eli's sons, Hophni and Phinehas, trivialized their roles as Priests on account of their witlessness and wickedness. Had they

34

treasured the gravity of their Assignment; they would have served honorably, not abuse their priesthood privileges.

The Pharisees and Sadducees repeatedly strived with Jesus because their finite minds could not validate Him as a Redeemer.

Estranged families, friendships, and other valuable alliances are on the rise. It is vital to understand and appreciate why the Lord links you to others.

Identify the Purpose of Your Alliances

God connects us because He wants us to reproduce the harmony between Him and His Son, Jesus. Also, He desires that we embrace servanthood, build mutual trust, establish Scriptural boundaries for checks and balances, love, protect, inspire, and sharpen each other without any fear of backlash. Our conduct must meet biblical standards and glorify Him.

God does not link people randomly or purposelessly. There are reasons He links families, friendships, colleagues, neighbors, communities or nations together. When people in these relationships do not identify them, chaos and abuse become unavoidable. Ministers of the gospel, kindreds, neighbors, associates, and the body of Christ have to identify why God assigned them to various relationships. They must play their roles and liaise efficaciously.

When Abraham's nephew, Lot and his herdsmen, strived over the grass for their hordes of cattle, he settled the dispute because he understood the power of family ties. Instead of allowing the devil to cause strife in his bloodline, he allowed Lot to choose the more fertile field for his cows because their correlation was more treasured than material gain. In fact, he went beyond the call of duty to intercede for Lot when God wanted to destroy Sodom and Gomorrah.

David and Jonathan understood what was at stake if they did not meet the biblical standards for genuine friendships. They utilized their amity to honor the Lord despite many hurdles. Jesus knew that Peter would deny Him and Judas would betray Him. Yet He loved them and the other flawed disciples because He esteemed the purpose of their connection. Multitudinous families, Christian institutions, businesses, communities, and nations would have fewer feuds and live harmoniously if we all took the time to discern the mind of God regarding our interpersonal ties. The idea of pleasing oneself in a relationship is from the pits of hell! We are obligated to use our alliances to gratify God, not self.

Value of "Friends" and "Foes"

God establishes relationships based on His purpose. It is our duty to identify them and flow with His will. Whether we are connected to those that can advance or hinder us or those we need to keep at bay, God wants to use them to accomplish specific goals in our lives. We need cheerleaders because they inspire, sow into our dreams, and minister to us. However, if we value only relationships that are aligned with our reality, we will never broaden our capabilities. We also need haters, freeloaders, and demagogues to enlarge our capacity to love, forbear, empathize, and forgive. We may have to love them from a distance and establish healthy boundaries to protect our dreams. Nevertheless, we need them as much as our allies. We need faultfinders, gossipmongers, meddlers, nay-sayers, and all kinds of people in our outer circle to keep us humble, broken, and contrite on our knees.

God uses everyone around us to contribute their quota while en route to our Canaan. While our supporters will fluff our egos, accept our vulnerabilities, and *"shorten the distance to our goals,"* detractors will intensify our focus, expand our faith, provoke us to greatness, mature the giants in us, make the Lion of the tribe of Judah roar much louder in us, and drive us into the presence of God.

David needed King Saul to keep him on the straight and narrow path as much as he needed the prophet Samuel to keep him focused on ascending the throne of Israel. Joseph needed his father's love to maintain his sanity as much as he needed his brother's jealousy and greediness to validate his calling. If they did not sell him into slavery, he would not have become the governor of Egypt. More than anyone else, Jesus understood the importance of loving both those who love or abhor us. He knew that Peter's denial would help Him yield to the will of the Father, and also make Peter a better apostle. If Judas had not betrayed Him, He would not have gone through the cross; and without the cross, there would be no resurrection, redemption or all the victories and blessings we are enjoying as believers.

If we interrelate only with collaborators, we will become prayerless, unwary, reckless, and spiritually lethargic. Only adversaries can keep us vigilant, prayerful, and submissive to the will of the Father.

How do we deal with ignorance?
1). Repentance: Jacob was contrite about stealing his brother, Esau's, blessings (Genesis 33:1-11). Joseph's brothers repented for the atrocities they committed against him. (Genesis 50:15-21). Aaron felt penitence for speaking against the Ethiopian woman Moses married (Numbers 12:11-13). Peter wept bitterly when he was conscience-stricken for denying Christ (Matthew 26:75). We need to have godly sorrow for how we unconsciously corroborate with the enemy to exploit our relationships.

2). Apply truth to ignorance: *"Also it is not good for a soul to be without knowledge" (Proverbs 19:2a).* Ignorance is a malaise that can plague and incapacitate meaningful relationships. People perish or entangle themselves in bondage for lack of awareness of what God expects of them. The only remedy for ignorance is truth that sets us free (John 8:32). When you identify why God positioned you in diverse relationships, you will be able to determine what is expected of you and play your role proficiently. To avert obliviousness, we must study the ultimate interpersonal relationship manual – the Bible – and use it to build healthy ties that meet God's standard. Let us examine how we can achieve this in the next chapter.

- **Scriptural Confession: Galatians 5:19-21; Hosea 4:6a; Genesis 2:18; Genesis 1:28**

- **Praise and Worship**
- **Prayer Points**

1. Oh God, uproot all evil desires that battle within me, in the mighty name of Jesus.
2. Father, help me to do things your way, in the name of Jesus.
3. Lord, help me to bear fruits of repentance, humility, and the fruit of the Spirit, in the name of Jesus.
4. I renounce ignorance and embrace truth, in the name of Jesus.
5. Holy Spirit, help me to become an altruistic person to others, in the name of Jesus.
6. Father, empower me to rule over the works of the flesh in my life, not dominate or rule over others, in the name of Jesus.
7. Lord Jesus, I refuse to cooperate with the devil. He will not use my relationships to ennoble himself, fuel his personal ambitions, or belittle people in my life, in the name of Jesus.
8. Lord Jesus, help everyone within my circle to use our lives to worship you; fulfill your will; lift each other up; and sharpen each other like "iron sharpens iron," in the name of Jesus.
9. Holy Father, I choose to become a seed. I sow myself in others, in the name of Jesus.
10. Father, I thank you for my strength. Help me with my weaknesses, in the name of Jesus.
11. Father, I thank you for others' strength. Help them with their weaknesses, in the name of Jesus.
12. Almighty Jehovah, help me to build purpose-driven relationships, in the precious name of Jesus.
13. I seal your covenant relationship with me with the blood of Jesus, in the name of Jesus.
14. Let the thunder of God destroy all the powers that are assigned to tamper with your covenant with me, in the name of Jesus.
15. Let the fire of the Holy Spirit consume conflict and all that the devil is using against me, in the name of Jesus.
16. Thank the Lord for answers to your prayers.

CHAPTER 7

Abuse of Relationship Roles
(Conflict Fire Starter # ii)

When we do not know our roles in a relationship, chaos and abuse of power are inevitable. Relationships capsize when roles are obscure and abused.

Relationship Roles

Relationship roles are biblical responsibilities, tasks or assignments allotted to everyone in a relationship. They are in place to define expectations, avert abuse, and keep tabs on our behavior. God expects us to implement them so we can be in one accord and maintain our solidarity with Him and each other.

Ambiguity and negligence of these tasks are significant contributors to variance. When roles are vague, people are inclined to abuse their position, demand for the impossible, or even formulate self-serving rules. People maltreat and slander each other when they are unacquainted with their relational duties. Ignorance exacerbates power struggle, and when there is rivalry in a relationship, it becomes a combat zone, and everyone is caught in the crossfire. We must identify and execute these roles to avoid starting a civil war in a relationship.

God has a holy standard for relationships, and everyone has a divine role to play. We must use His criterion to gauge our conduct to see if we measure up. He wants us to utilize our relationships to emblaze His character, glory, and praise. Like Paul the apostle, we must be all things to people so we can win them to Christ. We must learn how to counsel in righteousness, correct in humility, and speak the truth in love.

It is your job to identify and implement your role as a friend, parent, neighbor, Pastor, brethren, protégée colleague, sibling, mentor, husband or wife. Will you esteem those whom God has placed in your life regardless of whether you think they merit it or not? Your response determines your level of brokenness and willingness to grow a relationship. Let us examine some interpersonal relationship roles:

1). Fellowship and communion: The perfect harmony between God, His Son, Jesus, and the Holy Spirit is archetypal of how earthly relationships should be. God established them so we can learn how to fellowship, converse, and relate to each other. Just as we have communion and fellowship with God, our creator, so must we have with each other. In essence, our relationship with Him epitomizes our relationship with others and vice versa. Jesus came to demonstrate how relationship should work, how we should relate to others.
But if we walk in the light, as he is in the light, we have fellowship one with another, and the blood of Jesus Christ his Son cleanseth us from all sin (1 John 1:7) "*Not forsaking the assembling of ourselves together, as the manner of some is; but exhorting one another: and so much the more, as ye see the day approaching*" *(Hebrews 10:25).*

2). Develop godly soul ties with one another: All relationships that model Christ must cultivate goodly soul ties. Through these salubrious interpersonal ties, we can form emotional and spiritual bond that replicates the bond between the Father, Son, and Holy Spirit that would benefit each other and exalt Him. He wants us to bond on a deeper level. "*That their hearts might be comforted,* *being knit together in love, and unto all riches of the full assurance of understanding, to the acknowledgement of the mystery of God, and of the Father, and of Christ..." (Colossians 2:2).* However, people develop bad soul ties when they are at loggerheads and blatantly rebuff repentance and reconciliation.

We should all learn from David and Jonathan's genuine friendship that evolved into a genial soul bond and prevailed over trials. *And it came to pass, when he had made an end of speaking unto Saul, that the soul of Jonathan was knit with the soul of David, and Jonathan loved him as his own soul (1 Samuel 18:1).*

3). Bear good fruits:*(Romans 7:4).* Jesus said; *"Ye have not chosen me, but I have chosen you, and ordained you, that ye should go and bring forth fruit, and that your fruit should remain... "(John 15:16a).* The fundamental objectives of a relationship should be to liaise with each other and bear good fruits that will enrich the kingdom of God and everyone involved. However, numerous interpersonal alliances are fruitless because we are obstinate, indifferent, and blind to the primary aim of our divine connections. We hardly *"die to self," "buffet"* or *"crucify the flesh"* or embrace penitence. We cling to a pseudo sense of reality even when in error. We must be willing to crucify selfishness and sow ourselves to bear good fruits. *What kind of fruits are you bearing in the relationships that you are identified with? Are you producing fruits of repentance, humility, forgiveness, selflessness, loyalty, and the fruit of the Spirit? Or are you manifesting the works of the flesh?*

4). Love one another: God's ultimate purpose is that we love and accept each other unconditionally just as He loves and endorses us. The following Scriptures speak volumes: *This is my commandment, that you love one another as I have loved you (John 15:12). And this commandment we have from Him: that he who loves God must love his brother also (1 John 4:21). He who does not love does not know God, for God is love (1 John 4:8). Beloved, let us love one another, for love is of God; and everyone who loves is born of God and knows God (1 John 4:7).* We cannot tie others in knots or suffocate their right to be who they are in the name of love, or it will create discord. We must respect our individuality and render others the freedom to grow at their pace.

5). **Exhibit Unity:** *(Ephesi6ans 4:3,13)*. God's relationship with His Son, Jesus and the Holy Spirit should be the prototype we emulate though imperfect people make up the Church. In order to achieve the goal of unity, we must consider the following factors:

a). **Fulfil Christ's prayer for unity:** It is abominable to sow discord among brethren (Proverbs 6:19b). When we engage in strife, we are aiding Satan to oppose Jesus' prayer for the Church and tear His Body apart. Our obligation is to fulfil, not undo His prayer by our choices. *"That they all may be one; as thou, Father, art in me, and I in thee, that they also may be one in us: that the world may believe that thou hast sent me.... I in them, and thou in me, that they may be made perfect in one; and that the world may know that thou hast sent me, and hast loved them, as thou hast loved me." (See John 17:21,23.)*

We are still worldly and immature if we let the devil use our insecurities and differences to tear us apart. *"For ye are yet carnal: for whereas there is among you envying, and strife, and divisions, are ye not carnal, and walk as men? For while one saith, I am of Paul; and another, I am of Apollos; are ye not carnal? Who then is Paul, and who is Apollos, but ministers by whom ye believed, even as the Lord gave to every man? I have planted, Apollos watered; but God gave the increase. So then neither is he that planteth any thing, neither he that watereth; but God that giveth the increase. Now he that planteth and he that watereth are one: and every man shall receive his own reward according to his own labour. For we are labourers together with God: ye are God's husbandry, ye are God's building"* (1 Corinthians 3:3-9). We must unite because we are interlinked by the name, blood, gospel, and authority of Jesus despite our denominational differences. Yes, we love our Churches, diverse denominations, and the Ministers who tend to us. Nevertheless, our allegiance must be to Jesus Christ before people.

b). We must be in one accord: Paul addressed the division in the Corinthian Church: *"Now I beseech you, brethren, by the name of our Lord Jesus Christ, that ye all speak the same thing, and that there be no divisions among you; but that ye be perfectly joined together in the same mind and in the same judgment. For it hath been declared unto me of you, my brethren, by them which are of the house of Chloe, that there are contentions among you. Now this I say, that every one of you saith, I am of Paul; and I of Apollos; and I of Cephas; and I of Christ. Is Christ divided? was Paul crucified for you? or were ye baptized in the name of Paul?"* (See 1 Corinthians 1:10-13.)

"Fulfil ye my joy, that ye be likeminded, having the same love, being of one accord, of one mind" *(Philippians 2:2).*

c). We need each other despite our deficiencies: *"Two are better than one; because they have a good reward for their labour. For if they fall, the one will lift up his fellow: but woe to him that is alone when he falleth; for he hath not another to help him up. Again, if two lie together, then they have heat: but how can one be warm alone? And if one prevail against him, two shall withstand him; and a threefold cord is not quickly broken"* *(Ecclesiastics 4:9-12).*

Despite Paul and Barnabas' sharp disagreement about John Mark, they understood the value of divine connection and set aside their differences for the sake of the gospel. (See Acts 15:37-39.) Later, John Mark – the bone of contention became an asset to Paul. *"Only Luke is with me. Take Mark, and bring him with thee: for he is profitable to me for the ministry"* *(2 Timothy 4:11).*

Once, I was very frustrated with working with certain Ministers because they gave me a hard time. Internally, I vowed never to make the mistake of teaming with them again after we finished the project we were working on. The Lord asked me, *"Do these Ministers also love me?"* *"Yes,"* I replied. *"Are they also my children?"* I answered, *"Yes, they are."* *"Are you all working for me, your Lord and Master?"* *"Yes, we are,"* I

43

retorted. *"Are they imperfect like you are?"* *"Yes, Lord."* Then, I got the message! I knew where He was heading. *"Daughter, I understand your frustrations. But can you name the perfect Ministers you would like to work with since you don't want to team up with these flawed ones? Don't divide My body."* Of course, I couldn't name anyone! My own defects convicted me! I sobbed in godly sorrow and repented for my ignorance.

Often, we fear folks we do not understand, avoid those that will challenge our mediocrity, and castigate those that will not succumb to our control because we view them as threats. Our differences should enhance us, not heighten our insecurities. We are stronger when united and weaker when divided. We must bond as one body of Christ despite our diversity.

d). We can disagree on issues but must also agree to reconcile our differences and work together: We cannot be in one accord if we feud with one another or refuse to reconcile our disparities. *"Can two walk together, except they be agreed"* (Amos 3:3). Churches or Ministries who exist autonomously for themselves because they feel that they do not need others are in direct opposition to Scriptures. *"Behold, how good and how pleasant it is for brethren to dwell together in unity!"* (See Psalm 133:1.)

Whenever there was a misunderstanding among the apostles, they settled it amicably to the glory of God. Paul confronted Peter and Barnabas when they stopped eating with the Gentile Christians for fear of what the legalistic Jews who thought that circumcision was a prerequisite for salvation would say. *"For before that certain came from James, he did eat with the Gentiles: but when they were come, he withdrew and separated himself, fearing them which were of the circumcision. And the other Jews dissembled likewise with him; insomuch that Barnabas also was carried away with their dissimulation. But when I saw that they walked not uprightly according to the truth of the gospel, I said unto Peter before them all, If thou, being a Jew, livest after the manner of Gentiles, and not as do the Jews, why compellest thou the Gentiles to live as do the Jews?"* (See Galatians 2:12-14). Peter did not get offended or quit the Church or ministry. Today, this same situation would split some churches or make some believers very upset because we easily get affronted. We should welcome confrontation or correction.

e). We are the body of Christ! *Now ye are the body of Christ, and members in particular" (1 Corinthians 12:27).* **We fall or rise together.** *"That there should be no schism in the body; but that the members should have the same care one for another. And whether one member suffer, all the members suffer with it; or one member be honoured, all the members rejoice with it" (1 Corinthians 12:25-26).*

We must endeavor to *"keep the unity of the Spirit in the bond of peace." "There is one body and one Spirit... One Lord, one faith, one baptism, One God and Father of all, who is above all.... and in you all" (Ephesians 4:3-6).* Through Christ, we have divine blood ties that can never be severed. We are bonded by His eternal covenant and sealed by the Holy Spirit (Hebrews 13:20, Ephesians 4:30). No demon in hell can detach us unless we give them the authority.

f). We must remain loyal to one common Master, Jesus Christ and combat one common enemy, Satan: The devil is a common enemy, not our brethren, elders, deacons, Pastors or other members of the leadership clergy. Enough of the schisms, lies, hatred, and deception that Satan is using to divide us! We must stick together. *"And the servant of the Lord must not strive; but be gentle unto all men, apt to teach, patient" (2 Timothy 2:24).*

g). We must aggressively attack the spirit of strife and division and detach from those who want to segregate us: *"Now I beseech you, brethren, mark them which cause divisions and offences contrary to the doctrine which ye have learned; and avoid them" (Romans 16:17).* **Why disconnect from them?** *"For they that are such serve not our Lord Jesus Christ, but their own belly; and by good words and fair speeches deceive the hearts of the simple" (Romans 16:18).*

We must avoid dissension and *"Reject a divisive man after the first and second admonition, knowing that such a person is warped and sinning, being self-condemned (Titus 3:10-11).* Like Nehemiah, we have to build our relationships with our brethren, protégées, friends, family, mentors, and colleagues with one hand and combat the devil and his division with the other.

6). Bear your own burden: *"For every man shall bear his own burden"* *(Galatians 6:5).* This is a divine duty everyone must fulfill. Bear your burden as a father, mother, protégée or mentor. Be accountable as a businessperson, an employer or employee. Carry out your obligations as a colleague, teacher or student. Perform your duty as a Christian, relative or neighbor. Fulfill your call as a leader, Minister of the gospel or whatever vocation you are in. Endorse your role as a husband, parishioner, wife, friend or whatever duty God has assigned to you.

Sometimes, others volunteer to assuage our burdens. Still, we are the primary burden bearers. We need to ask the Lord for help when others desert us or the burden of life becomes agonizing.

7). By love serve one another: We need to develop people skills, model Christ, and exude servanthood. *"For, brethren, ye have been called unto liberty; only use not liberty for an occasion to the flesh, but by love serve one another"* *(Galatians 5:13).*

8). Bear each other's burdens: *"Brethren, if a man be overtaken in a fault, ye which are spiritual, restore such an one in the spirit of meekness; considering thyself, lest thou also be tempted. Bear ye one another's burdens, and so fulfil the law of Christ"* *(Galatians 6:1- 2').* We are obligated to do whatever is within our ability to care for others. *"Rejoice with them that do rejoice, and weep with them that weep"* *(Romans 12:15). "We then that are strong ought to bear the infirmities of the weak, and not to please ourselves"* *(Romans 15:1).*

9). Forgive each other: *"Forbearing one another, and forgiving one another, if any man have a quarrel against any: even as*

Christ forgave you, so also do ye" (Colossians 3:13). "Grudge not one against another, brethren, lest ye be condemned: behold, the judge standeth before the door" (James 5:9).

10). Have dominion: Because all godly relationships are authored by God, He must be positioned at the pinnacle of our formal and informal ties. However, many are diametrically opposed to Scriptural protocol. While some want to play God and dominate others, others are forced to assume the position of a doormat. They toss God at the bottom of the relationship's hierarchy or drive Him out completely.

"God said to them, ... fill the earth and subdue it; have dominion over the fish of the sea, over the birds of the air, and over every living thing that moves on the earth" (Genesis 1:28). God commanded us to subdue the earth, not each other, and rule over the creatures, not topple one another. However, ignorance goads us to dominate and control each other instead of ruling over the creation and the *"works of the flesh."* We must learn to subdue the flesh, not people to avoid disputes. We are called to minister to people, not rule them with an iron fist like a *Pharaoh.*

11). Respect and celebrate differences: We must be fine-tuning our distinctive talents and anointings to better ourselves, not striving to outdo each other. There is nothing more antithetical to our Christian faith than allowing jealousy and rivalry to tear us apart. We cannot let Satan pit us against each other. *"Iron sharpeneth iron; so a man sharpeneth the countenance of his friend" (Proverbs 27:17).*

We are idiosyncratically sculpted in God's image, lavishly endowed with multifaceted talents, and interdependent on each other. *"For as the body is one, and hath many members, and all the members of that one body, being many, are one body: so also is Christ. For by one Spirit are we all baptized into one body, whether we be Jews or Gentiles, whether we be bond or free; and have been all made to drink into one Spirit. For the body is not one member, but many. If the foot shall say, Because I am not the hand, I am not of the body; is it therefore not of the body?*

And if the ear shall say, Because I am not the eye, I am not of the body; is it therefore not of the body? If the whole body were an eye, where were the hearing? If the whole were hearing, where were the smelling? But now hath God set the members every one of them in the body, as it hath pleased him. And if they were all one member, where were the body? But now are they many members, yet but one body.

And the eye cannot say unto the hand, I have no need of thee: nor again the head to the feet, I have no need of you. Nay, much more those members of the body, which seem to be more feeble, are necessary: And those members of the body, which we think to be less honourable, upon these we bestow more abundant honour; and our uncomely parts have more abundant comeliness. For our comely parts have no need: but God hath tempered the body together, having given more abundant honour to that part which lacked.

That there should be no schism in the body; but that the members should have the same care one for another. And whether one member suffer, all the members suffer with it; or one member be honoured, all the members rejoice with it. Now ye are the body of Christ, and members in particular" 1 Corinthians 12 :12-27).

12). Forbear with one another and be a safe harbor: *"He that covereth a transgression seeketh love; but he that repeateth a matter separateth very friends" (Proverbs 17:9). "With all lowliness and meekness, with longsuffering, forbearing one another in love…" (Ephesians 4:2). "And, ye masters, do the same things unto them, forbearing threatening: knowing that your Master also is in heaven; neither is there respect of persons with him" (Ephesians 6:9).*

13). Pray for one another: *"Confess your faults one to another, and pray one for another, that ye may be healed. The effectual fervent prayer of a righteous man availeth much" (James 5:16).*

14). Establish healthy boundaries to protect relationships: The oceans, mountains, vegetation, galaxies, and all of creation exist within their boundaries except human beings. *"Where there is no revelation, the people cast off restraint" (Proverbs 29:18). (See Proverbs 25:28.)* Godly boundaries will shield and steer your associations in the right direction.

15). Submit to God and to each other: *"Submitting yourselves one to another in the fear of God" (Ephesians5:21).* Satan was driven from heaven because of his pride. He rebuffed submission because he wanted to be like God. Just as he rebelled, he wants us to rebel against God and each other so he will not have to flee or submit to us when we bind him. He understands that he does not have to obey our command if we are rebellious. Therefore, he incites us to be disobedient so he will continue to topple our authority over him.

Sow Submission First

Lack of submission has ruined many meaningful relationships. We demand that the devil obey our command but seldom obey God. It is insane to think that he will cave in without our obedience to the Lord, Jesus. We have no right to impose submission when we oppose submission.

Husbands resist God's word but pressure their wives into submission. Wives crave their husbands' love but remain insubordinate. Children desire parental blessings and long life but balk at parental authority. Communal and national leaders desperately want control but kick against God, who is the Ultimate Boss. Congregants expect their Pastors to walk on water but will barely apply their faith. Conversely, Ministers insist on spiritual maturity without realizing that the growth of a people is largely dependent on the growth of a leader. Their receptibility and teachability depend on how much a leader is willing to learn from the wisest Teacher and Mentor – The Holy Spirit.

Until a leader fully surrenders to God, his parishioners will struggle with complying with appropriate authority. Till you are yieldable, teachable, and quick to repent, their hearts will remain hardened. Until the zeal to know, love, seek, trust or obey God consumes your heart, they will wrestle with whatever you are grappling with because everything flows from you, the head to them. Your level of faith, commitment or brokenness significantly influences theirs.

Submit to the body of Christ: *"That ye submit yourselves unto such, and to every one that helpeth with us, and laboureth" (1 Corinthians 16:16).*

Submit to elders: *"Likewise, ye younger, submit yourselves unto the elder. Yea, all of you be subject one to another, and be clothed with humility: for God resisteth the proud, and giveth grace to the humble" (*1 Peter 5:5).

Children obey your parents: *"Children, obey your parents in the Lord: for this is right. Honour thy father and mother; which is the first commandment with promise; That it may be well with thee, and thou mayest live long on the earth" (Ephesians 6:2-3).*

Parents submit to God's word: *"And, ye fathers, provoke not your children to wrath: but bring them up in the nurture and admonition of the Lord"* (Ephesians 6:4).

Husbands comply with God's word: *"Husbands, love your wives, even as Christ also loved the church, and gave himself for it; ...... So ought men to love their wives as their own bodies. He that loveth his wife loveth himself" (Ephesians 5:25,28). "Husbands, love your wives, and be not bitter against them" (Colossians 3:19). "Likewise, ye husbands, dwell with them according to knowledge, giving honour unto the wife, as unto the weaker vessel, and as being heirs together of the grace of life; that your prayers be not hindered" (1 Peter 3:7).*

Wives submit to your husbands: (See Colossians 3:18.) *"Wives, submit yourselves unto your own husbands, as unto the Lord. For the husband is the head of the wife, even as Christ is*

the head of the church: and he is the saviour of the body. Therefore as the church is subject unto Christ, so let the wives be to their own husbands in every thing" (Ephesians 5:22-24).
Husbands and wives must yield to each other. (Ephesians 5:21.)

Submit to authority: *"Submit yourselves to every ordinance of man for the Lord's sake: whether it be to the king, as supreme;" (1 Peter 2:13). "Obey them that have the rule over you, and submit yourselves: for they watch for your souls, as they that must give account, that they may do it with joy, and not with grief: for that is unprofitable for you" (Hebrews 13:17; Colossians 3:22).*

Why should I submit to people that do not deserve it?
While submission empowers relationships, resistance weakens them. Saul short changed his kingship because he did not defer to Samuel's counsel. *(See 1 Samuel 15:1-28.)* Gehazi thought he could outsmart Prophet Elisha by being disingenuous. He deceptively took Naaman's gifts and plagued his future generations with leprosy. He robbed their destinies to pay for his rapacious desires. *(See 2 Kings 5:27.)* Had Moses not interceded for Miriam, she would have wrecked her destiny. She had to learn submission through leprosy. *(See Numbers 12:1-15.)* Korah, Dathan, and Abiram were swallowed up by the earth because they revolted against Moses. *(See Numbers 16:1-35.)*

Hagar did not feel that her Mistress, Sarah, merited her compliance. Yet she humbled herself. Onesimus did not use his new found liberty in Christ to defy his Master, Philemon. Noncompliance generates friction. To avert dissension, we must submit to the Lord and each other. We cannot claim to love Him and not submit to Him and each other. Yielding to one another substantiates our surrender to Him. Counterattacking each other connotes we are willfully resisting Him.

Why should we obey God?
We should because we love Him and He expects our obedience. We want to take our rightful place to avoid or resolve interpersonal feuds. Likewise, we want to avert confusion and

ward off rebellion so history will not repeat itself. We do not want to replicate the mistakes of our foreparents in the Garden of Eden. We sow the seeds of submission because it is the right thing to do regardless of whether we feel that others deserve it or not.

What should we submit to?
We must yield to truth, righteousness, peace, and authority, not sin, abuse, evil or bondage.

What motivates us to submit?
Love for God and reverence for Him. (See Ephesians 5:21.)

Stay in Your Lane

The success of a relationship hinges on our eagerness to function in our specific roles in obedience to God. We must execute our respective roles to obviate discord and stay in our lanes to preclude rivalry and distrust. It is selfish to take over the driver seat of a relationship if it is not our place. As believers, we must act with proper decorum, not overstep others for our gain.

Sarah was subject to Abraham and called him, "Lord." Haggai ran away, but God told her to go back and surrender to her mistress. *"And the angel of the Lord said unto her, Return to thy mistress, and submit thyself under her hands" (Genesis 16:9).*

Moses heeded his father-in-law, Jethro's counsel. Joshua was answerable to Moses. When Samuel was a young man, he was liable to Eli. Ruth consented to her mother-in-law, Naomi's advice. Esther succumbed to her uncle, Mordecai's counsel and her obedience saved the Israelites. David collaborated with Samuel and was accountable to him. Abigail complied with her wicked husband, Nabal because it was the right thing to do. Elisha cooperated with Elijah to get the double portion anointing. The disciples were in one accord with Jesus and surrendered to His authority. Timothy yielded to Paul. Jesus submitted to the Father. *Whom are you called to submit to?*

- **Scriptural Confession: Psalm 144:7, 2 Timothy 4:18, Ephesians 5:22-33**
- **Praise and Worship**
- **Prayer Points**

1. Holy Spirit give me the grace, strength, patience, tolerance, wisdom, humility, brokenness, and the anointing to love those whom you have placed in life, in the name of Jesus.
2. Oh God teach us how to understand, appreciate, respect our differences, and celebrate each other, in the name of Jesus.
3. By the blood of Jesus Christ, I release myself from every yoke of rejection, fear, failure, conflict, unfruitfulness, and bondage, in the name of Jesus.
4. By the power of the Holy Spirit, Satan will not find anger, unforgiveness, resentment, pride, self-righteousness or anything that belong to him in me, in the name of Jesus.
5. By the power in the blood of Jesus, the devil will not use me against my blood ties, casual, close acquaintances or the kingdom of God, in the name of Jesus.
6. Abba Father, plant seeds of the Holy Spirit in my life so I can bear fruits of righteousness, tenderness, forgiveness and fruit of the Spirit, in the name of Jesus.
7. I choose to love and accept others as they are, in the precious name of Jesus.
8. Father, I thank you for what I understand about others and trust you with what I do not understand about them, in the precious name of Jesus.
9. By the blood of Jesus Christ, let the fire of the Holy Spirit locate and destroy every evil gathering warring against my home and associations, in the name of Jesus.
10. Oh God, let the devil and his demons turn their weapons against themselves, not those around me, in the name of Jesus.
11. Father, thank you for answering my prayers.

CHAPTER 8

The Selfish Desires That War Within Us
(Conflict Fire Starter # iii)

*Where is Satan making you to
itch or scratch? He makes us
"itch" in areas of weaknesses.*

When we allow manifestations of the flesh and ungodly desires to become deep rooted strongholds, Satan can utilize them to generate dissention.

The Real Source of Arguments

"Where do wars and fights come from among you? Do they not come from your desires for pleasure that war in your members? You lust and do not have. You murder and covet and cannot obtain. You fight and war. Yet you do not have because you do not ask. You ask and do not receive, because you ask amiss, that you may spend it on your pleasures" (James 4:1-3).

The flesh is a breeding ground for emulations, disputes, "adultery, fornication, uncleanness, lasciviousness, idolatry, witchcraft, hatred, variance, emulations, wrath, strife, seditions, heresies, envyings, murders, drunkenness, and revellings"

54

(Galatians 5:19-21).We lock horns with each other because of ignorance, unrealistic expectations, lies, self-aggrandizement, idols of the heart, intolerance, sanctimoniousness, unmet needs, misconceptions, illusions, blind spots, distorted focus, fear, insecurities, incompatibility issues, covetousness, irreconcilable differences, self-centeredness, pride, unbelief, stubbornness, manipulation, greediness, contempt, impatience, self-idolatry, sexual perversion, unforgiveness, infidelity, mistrust, emotional walls, discontentment, ingratitude, unresolved disappointments, false-reality, lack of healthy boundaries, indolence, unhealed wounds, incontinence, poor judgement, rivalry, insubordination, baseless accusations, misunderstanding, hardness of heart, foolishness, addictions, self- defeating habits, and hordes of ungodly desires that battle within us. We clash with others because of the selfish desires that battle within us.

We squabble when we deviate from God's purpose of a relationship. Often, we are drawn away by our selfish desires and enticed by the desperation to appease our cravings. *"But each one is tempted when he is drawn away by his own desires and enticed. Then, when desire has conceived, it gives birth to sin; and sin, when it is full-grown, brings forth death" (James 1:14-15).*

When people in a relationship have outrageously high expectations for each other and are not keen on lowering them, it becomes a battle of the wills. Often, we yearn to control others, cling to our rights, give tit for tat, shift blame to avoid accountability or have the last word.

Areas We Itch for Conflict or Sin

Where is Satan making you to itch or scratch? He makes us *"itch"* in areas of weaknesses. Itching is symbolic of who or what he uses to entice us. He knows precisely how and where to make us itch so we can *"scratch"* and have physical and emotional blisters in our lives and relationships. He tickles us with carnality to trip us over, caresses our blind spots to seduce us to stray, and preys on our vulnerabilities to trap us in bondage. He uses what is unhealed, out of control or out of order in our lives to stage booby traps to tangle us in relationships. Let's examine some of the areas we must confront with truth.

Where we lack character

When you are deficient in character, you have no conscience. When you have no moral compass, you are bound to act like the devil since he has no character. You will lie, steal, cheat, sin or do anything to appease yourself in order to exploit or control others in your interrelations because your conscience has been desensitized by sin. Those who brush God aside have no conscience to regulate their conducts. Godly character facilitates harmony. *Which area of your life do you lack character?*

Where we have raw emotional wounds

What is unhealed in your life or relationships? Where in your life are you still bleeding profusely because you refused to apply the healing balm of Jesus to induce healing? Some hurting people have conflicted emotions. Consciously or unconsciously, they are touchy, easily offended, and can transfer their anguish to their relationships. When you have emotional hurts, you tend to see everything around you, including your relationships through the lens of your pain. Until you reach for healing, mere words, reflections or situations will continue to enflame them, take you back to that desolate place of agony, and cause you to relive the trauma over and over again until you trust Jesus to heal you. People with raw emotional wounds are hypersensitive about words, thoughts, or deeds that seem to strike a chord with past unpleasant experiences. They are sensitive about situations that seemingly pick at old wounds or dig up skeletons from the past.

Where we lack control or healthy boundaries

What is out of control in your life? We are bound to be lawless when we have no righteous standard to judge our conscience. Also, we lose control or become reckless when there are no healthy boundaries to restrain us. We are inclined to do things that are detrimental to the body, soul, Spirit, and dealings with others just because they sound, look, and feel good to the flesh. Why? We are out of touch with reality! Whatever is out of order in your life and relationships will generate conflict.

Where we have blind spots

Do you have blind spots? Open your heart and be receptive to what the Holy Spirit is revealing about your life and relationships. Be mindful of the many options He is presenting to help deal with the difficulties in your life and relationships.

Where we evade commitment or shift responsibility

Do you resist accountability, commitment, and other relevant ingredients that grow relationships? If you do, it will be no wonder why your alliances may be gasping for spiritual oxygen to survive. When you shift accountability, you will barely admit that you are wrong or say, *"I'm sorry. Please, forgive me."* You will always perceive yourself as logical and others illogical because your judgment is deeply flawed. Eventually, your evasiveness will find you out.

If you are a non-committed person, you cannot and should not be trusted at all until you repent. Until you change, you will continue to be an absentee sibling, wife, friend, neighbor, mentor, coworker, husband, in-law, protégée, brother or sister in Christ who hang around others only to consume, not produce.

Where we have hang-ups

Do you have emotional, social or relational hang-ups? Our hang-ups reveal areas we have wrong or unscriptural belief systems. They expose where we are ignorant and out of touch with truth or reality. We have arguments because of the unbiblical mentality we display in relationships. Anxieties about appreciating individual differences, cultivating mutual trust, treating others with proper decorum, implementing relationship roles, embracing lasting change, sharing and receiving love can inhibit the growth of valuable ties.

Slam the Door!

Until you identify and close the access you gave to Satan via your inadequacies, he will try to use them to wring and destabilize your associations. Watch out! The devil is out to sell someone a bill of goods. Your weaknesses, hang-ups, emotional wounds, blind spots, noncommitment, unrepentant heart, and lack of character and healthy boundaries are his *favorite things.* They start the ball rolling for the devil to come to play and score points because your relationships have become his playground.

Are Satan's unresolved issues of rejection, resentment, anger, hurt, fear, and other works of the flesh deeply embedded within you? If you have his goods, he will come after them vigorously and hound you until you repudiate him. He could not exploit Jesus because there was nothing in Him that he could use to his advantage (John 14:30). Lack of contrition and refusal to renounce transgressions only provide him a good cover. He exhibits his decadent personae through unrepentant folks that have his goods entrenched in their hearts.

"Is there hope? How do I overcome these obstacles to build healthy relationships?"

It's easy! Be honest and confront yourself. Accept responsibility for any sin in your life and genuinely repent. *It is foolish to lie or cover up our blemishes* when God already knows about it. Jesus *understands our infirmities because He was tempted in every area but without sin. (*See Hebrews 4:15.)

Ask the Holy Spirit to help you and simply yield your addictions, blind-spots, hang-ups, deep emotional hurt, lack of character, and control to Him. Nail your resistance to accountability, truth, commitment, humility, and healing to the cross and the devil will have nothing in you to exploit anymore. If you make a mistake, get right back on track and repent again. Be willing to use truth to confront your limitations, mind unrealistic expectations, harmonize your differences, and relinquish misconceptions to harness your solidarity. Sow unconditional love and understanding irrespective of whether each person in the relationship merits it or not. Now, you know the truth, and it will set you free if you apply it to your life and relationships.

- **Scriptural Confession: Psalm 144:7, 2 Timothy 4:18, Ephesians 5:22-33**
- **Praise and Worship**
- **Prayer Points**

1. Oh God, stretch out Your hand from above; rescue and deliver us out of great waters, in the name of Jesus.
2. The Lord shall deliver those I love out of every evil work, every storm, trails, temptation, persecution, and preserve us unto His heavenly kingdom, in the name of Jesus.
3. Let the fire of the Holy Spirit burn in our hearts and consume the seed of ungodliness and sin, in the name of Jesus.
4. Father God, deliver me from my hang-ups, blind-spots, and idols of the heart, in the name of Jesus.
5. Let the healing anointing heal my emotional wounds in the name of Jesus.
6. Father, I yield myself to you. I nail my flesh, anger, unforgiveness, resentment, and pride to the cross, in the name of Jesus.
7. Almighty God, bring me to a place of brokenness and contriteness, in the name of Jesus.
8. Father God, have your way in my life and relationships, in the name of Jesus.
9. Lord, breathe upon me and my alliances, in the name of Jesus.
10. Oh God, enlarge my faith in You, in the name of Jesus.
11. Holy Spirit, help me to overcome my problems, in the name of Jesus.
12. Deliver me and everyone in my circle from any form of addictive or destructive behavior or sin, in the name of Jesus.
13. Thank you, Lord, for your unconditional love and power.

CHAPTER 9

Badgering Others to Change
(Conflict Fire Starter # iv)

*Only God can change those that are
need-driven to become purpose-driven;
self-centered to become selfless, and
flesh-driven to become Holy Spirit-driven.*

I n every relationship, we are forced to confront our idiosyncrasies, incompatibility, and seemingly aggravating issues when in conflict. Repeatedly, they not only generate disillusionment and pandemonium but can turn a relationship into a combat zone. Unless all the parties involved have a reverential fear of God, they may ruffle each other's feathers or turn it into a vicious vendetta.

"Yes days" ... "No days"

We are experts at nudging others to change their ways while we cling to ours. We barely give others enough room to make mistakes or grow. Often, we have what I call the "Yes days" and the "No days" regarding how we relate to others. On the *yes days,* our approach to others is: *"I will try to accommodate you as much as I can and purposely turn a blind eye to your inadequacies today."* On such days, even if we have misgivings about their shortcomings, we brush them aside. Somehow, we are able to garner some courage from within to be tolerant and close one eye to their weaknesses but open the other eye to their strengths.

On the *no days,* our cynical attitude towards others is: *"I can't stand you today! Don't get on my last nerve because you don't even stand a chance!"* We walk around jumbled, paranoid, and cantankerous, waiting for a *victim* to flip our lid with the slightest offense. Those around us are compelled to walk on eggshells because our *"demons"* are activated and on high alert, ready to pounce on whomever breaks our rules. We ought to learn how to forbear with one another daily, just like Christ forbears with us.

"What can You do for Me?"

Often, when God opens a door for a relationship, one of the first questions we explore or ask internally is, *"What can this person do for Me?" "How can I exploit his or her gifts, talents, and personality and use them to my advantage*? It is always about what we can get, not give to others. Our unverbalized thoughts are:

"How can I benefit from you?" Rather than, "How can you benefit from me?"

"How can you make my life better? "Rather than, "How can I improve your life?" "

"How can I change you to fit my mental portrait of an idealistic trait?" Rather than, "How can I change myself to accommodate you or initiate change to induce whatever God wants to work out in us?"

"I need to identify where you are vulnerable so I can exploit those areas." Rather than, "I need to identify your vulnerabilities so I can understand how to minister hope and healing to you."

People should enter relationships for love, friendship, companionship, goodwill, fellowship, communion, networking and for other noble reasons that will benefit everyone connected. However, our problem is we form alliances only for personal gain. We gravitate more to people that will chant our chorus or row our boat. We yearn for those we can dominate but abscond from those that disconcert our reality. We are drawn to toxic relationships because of our addictions, blind-spots, and vulnerabilities. Often, our character flaws cause us to shift the burden of responsibility to others, so we do not have to worry about change. Then, when accountability is off our shoulders, anything goes!

Connected by Hook or Crook

We are not only drawn to imperfect people like us but also excuse their toxicity for a guileful motive because they can meet our needs. We aspire to be connected to those we desperately need either by hook or by crook. Often, this desperation outweighs any obvious reservation we may have about forming ties with toxic people. It supersedes all cautionary signals to be wary of those whom the enemy may want to use to disrupt our destiny. Sometimes, we lie to ourself to justify the rationale for an unwholesome relationship that may benefit us.

"I need Danny though he is too reserved and passive to be my type. But he'll change after I work on him!"

"Sandy is too garrulous for my liking. I can't stand her! But I need to accommodate her for now because I need her help!"

Often, we frantically crave identity, love, significance, affection, acceptance, companionship, affluence, and friendship like we crave illegal drugs or sin. We placate others' inadequacies only when they can offer us the impossible or make us walk on water. Only to such ones do we let down our guard and dismiss any concerns to justify their erratic behaviors. We defend their complacency; marginalize their inconsistencies; excuse their eccentricity; rationalize with their jealousy; overlook their rage; absorb their abuse; disregard their lies; and pacify their edginess. We applaud their hyperbolic expressions; undermine their lack of character; cuddle their demons; pray that their unresolved issues will magically disappear by faith; and confess their deliverance without having to walk through the process of contriteness and transformation themselves. Why? We have an ace up our sleeves to discreetly and progressively milk them to the lowest minimum.

We know that their flaws would pose a potential threat to our well-being but snub the red flags anyhow. We circumspectly craft a ploy in place and connect for our gains anyway. Lo and behold, when their hang-ups do not magically dissipate, or they do not voluntarily change to meet our immense expectations, we step in with duplicitous schemes and superimpose our will on theirs.

Often, we team up with fallible people like ourselves because we have a clandestine motive to metamorphosize them into a marionette whose string can be pulled without any resistance. If they do not voluntary take the initiative to appease us, we resort to a surreptitious plan and try to sculpt them to fit our idealism. However, we seem to forget that only God can make a saint out of a sinner. By nature, we are fixers. We want to amend others but resist change. We counsel others but reject guidance and control others but would barely yield to authority. We demand excellence but exhibit mediocrity. We excuse ourself but put others through the wringer. We seem to live in a La-La land and are sometimes as devious as unbelievers. We need to be more empathetic and less parochial in our dealings. If we accommodate people the way we did at the onset of a relationship, we would have fewer broken ties.

"Majority of my relationships are bad."

Relationships do not turn sour by themselves. But people in relationships do because they are the driving force that steer them to the right or wrong direction. Relationships should not change people negatively or cause them to become spiteful. Often, people have vendetta against others because they idolize their idealism more than Truth. People elect to esteem or undermine the importance of a union. A relationship is a litmus test that exposes who and what people really are. Your relationships will expose the depth of your heart and will either bring out the best or worse in you.

We personify what we really are. Exasperating people will always be grouchy, and critical people will be faultfinding unless they repent. Unappeasable folks will remain discontented regardless of what others do to pacify them. Introvert folks will exhibit the same personae, and extrovert ones will remain gregarious, regardless of disapproval from others. People that are passive, selfish, belittling, abusive or controlling will maintain the same temperament. Conniving people will remain domineering and manipulate unless they allow God to transform their illusive mentality. No amount of pressure or badgering will coax them to compromise their individuality. Sometimes, we try to modify our behavior when under duress or pestered by others. However, this is only temporary because we often revert to our own personality when we can no longer put on a charade.

When people change their attitude for the better, so will their relationships. Conversely, when they change for the worse, their unions will take a hit! We need to stop blaming our hang-ups on relationships and realize that how we relate to each other is what defines the depth or longevity of our alliances.

"Take the Plank Out of Your Own Eye"

Over the years, have you found yourself asking, *"Lord, why is it taking so long to change my mother, Doran?" "When will you transform Mike, my brother?" "Why won't you change Tom, my Pastor?"*

Over time, you may have been praying: *"Oh God, please recreate James, my spouse." "Remake Sister Sue, the head usher." "Amend Hicks, my neighbor." "Metamorphosize my sister, Miriam." "Modify my friend, Cynthia." "Alter my father, Jacob."* However, the Lord is saying, "No, you must change first." Ouch!

Perhaps you have it all wrong! *"Judge not, that you be not judged. For with what judgment you judge, you will be judged; and with the measure you use, it will be measured back to you. And why do you look at the speck in your brother's eye, but do not consider the plank in your own eye? Or how can you say to your brother, 'Let me remove the speck from your eye'; and look, a plank is in your own eye? Hypocrite! First remove the plank from your own eye, and then you will see clearly to remove the speck from your brother's eye" (Matthew 7:1-5).*

"What? Are you insisting that I initiate change?"

Yes. If you resist change, then you are sabotaging the healing and renewal that transformation will produce in your relationship. Likewise, you are inferring that penitence depends on your stipulations, not God's; and obeying Him is contingent on others' behavior, not on your brokenness, humility, and love for Him. No one should ever endorse that mindset.

The Scriptures admonish us to confront our flaws before we demand that others follow suit. We cannot insist that others embrace repentance while we wallow in error. Rebuffing change suggests that we are still carnally minded and only existing to ennoble ourselves – not God (Romans 8:5-8).

Start the ball rolling. Cultivate good seeds that will nurture your relationship and your efforts will dilute the other person's defenses. Also, the Lord will reward your faithfulness and count it as righteousness. There is nothing more rewarding than God's approval of those who love, trust, and obey Him.

"I will change only if Sister Edith initiates change!"
"I will honor Mike only if he shares unconditional love first."

Your attitude is sculpted by how others react, not by your obligation to obey God – and that is dangerous. Like a thermostat, they regulate your emotions, moods, and approach to life. Consequently, you feel that you will embrace change only when others take the lead. Only when they show love will you gladly reciprocate accordingly to reward them. However, when they withhold love, you will equally hoard love to penalize their deplorable behavior. Reacting to others' obstinacy, evasiveness or lack of accountability expose yours.

What demarcates us from the heathens if we love only those who cherish us, forgive only those who absolve us, and punish those who penalize us?

"I will not change until George mends his ways!"
"I will share love with Trish only if she submits to me first."

If you are waiting for her behavior to rouse your obedience, the devil will haul the relationship into the pits before she does. Her conduct should not be the deciding factor for your forgiveness. Your love for God should motivate you to do the right thing and initiate change. Erratic and retaliatory behavior fuel conflict in relationships.

We need to stop appeasing the flesh and live righteously by faith. The nucleus of our faith hinges on God's perfection and faithfulness, not on human fallibility and unpredicted conducts. We live virtuously and share unconditional love, not because others deserve it or meet our expectations, but because we love God wholeheartedly and are willing to please Him.

If we are waiting for others to repent, change, extend love or forgiveness before we reciprocate, then we are as selfish, immature, and malicious as they are. We are implying that our obedience to God is at the mercy of how others respond or react to us. That is perilous! The rationale for obedience must be our love and devotion to Christ. We must yield to Him regardless of whether others walk in truth or error.

Manipulation is Witchcraft!

"Why should I not try to change others?" You are not the ultimate prosecutor, judge, teacher, juror or counselor to your friends, neighbors, brethren, co-workers, Pastor, colleagues, parents, siblings or those assigned to you. Stop playing these roles in your relationships. Stop trying to do the Holy Spirit's job! Cajoling others evoke arguments. You might as well turn your relationships over to the devil if you persist that others adapts to your taste or that they motivate you to obey God. You may be diametrically opposed to responding biblically. However, when you are adamant about your ways, it only leads to more chaos. By the way, has your past propaganda for behavioral adjustment been effective? Have you noticed that your past "memorandum of change" has only created far-flung frigid people in your life? Then why continue to sound like a broken record when your message is falling on deaf ears? Your devious actions will only add more fuel to the conflict fire in your relationships. Embrace the harsh reality of individual differences and learn to accept and celebrate others.

Badgering others to reconstruct themselves to comply with one's reality is witchcraft. Employing insidious ways to revamp others connotes you are influenced by the spirit of Jezebel. People that are seduced by a "Jezebelic" or witchcraft spirit not only inflict their will, expectations, and ill affections on others; but use guileful schemes to brainwash them into succumbing to their biddings. Those who use malice, abuse, intimidation, and other vicious machinations to extort others breach righteous principles. Craftily bewitching or beguiling others infringes on their rights.

Hordes of believers practice witchcraft in their relationships without even realizing it. Often, those that operate with witchcraft spirit obtusely think that their malicious behavior is not as ghastly as those who use diabolical powers to fuel evil. However, it is! If the Almighty God does not encroach on human will, it should scare us to impose ours on others. We must let God use us as vessels to heal our relationships rather than let the devil use us as guinea pigs to achieve his diabolic aspirations.

No one is a Whipping Post or Dumping Ground

As believers, we have no biblical basis to insist that others revamp their character while we cling to our demerits. We can neither use others as doormats nor badger them to be sacrificial lambs to bear our pain. Further, we cannot rule over them with an iron fist and expect harmony in our relationships. Whatever we sow will be reproduced in a relationship.

We cannot alter what we do not like about people on our terms. Terrorizing them into submission will last for only a season. We can only control them for as long as they allow us. We may have them eating out of our hand and before long, our spell over them will ebb, and they will catch up with our ploys and probably turn the tables on us. It grieves God when we use others as a whipping post or dumping ground. We are the body of Christ; called to serve one another, not trash one another. Epitomizing unconditional love like Christ will undoubtedly help us earn each other's trust and submission.

Trying to transform others is a worthless battle. Even if we succeed in metamorphosing them to meet our standard, it will only be momentary. Gradually, they will not only revert to their original temperament but will lose our respect. We cannot expect others to renovate themselves without taking the lead to reshape our attitude. Nagging reinforces people's fears and incites them to gravitate towards those who will appreciate, celebrate or validate them. Niggling, harassing, and squeezing sanity out of people only substantiate why they should not change or trust us.

Wear Your Own Hat!

Each one of us is accountable for his or her contrition and internal makeover. We must focus on fixing ourself, not others. When you try to recreate others or superimpose your will on them, a conflict bomb will erupt. You will ignite a conflict fire when you pressurize others to idolize your expectations, fret about their weaknesses, and use intimidation to get your way. Equally, withholding acts of endearment to punish them for not meeting your extremely high standards will detonate a conflict bomb. Your ungodly conduct will drench your relationships with conflict gasoline and energize Satan to set them ablaze. Halt your unchristian behavior in the name of Jesus! Get on your knees and ask God to deliver you.

It is delusional and hypocritical to demand that others repent or change when we need contrition and transformation ourselves. It is folly to revile others for what we are culpable of ourselves. When you are living a lie, you cannot change others even if you pray all day and night until the sky falls; fast until all the galaxies are inhabited by humans; "bind and loose" until the cows come home; try to inculcate the need to change others or guilefully bully them to dance to the rhythm of your own reality. Even if you succeed, it will not last. What a waste of valuable time and resources that should have be invested in cultivating a healthy relationship – God's way.

Often, we erroneously compare people with the *heroes* we esteem because we want them to replicate what we admire in them. But we also forget that regardless of how impeccable these so-called *heroes* may look visibly; they are just as flawed as the loved ones we are disparaging and badgering to change. *"Why can't you behave like Joan?" "I wish you were as generous as Nick."* Well, neither Joan nor Nick is perfect despite your approbation. The folks you are in relationship with are just as significant and should earn your respect. Making comparisons will only drive them farther away. You cannot coerce others to harmonize your tone or energize your hopes. It is one thing to define people and juxtapose their distinct traits but another to expect them to blend these dissimilarities on your terms.

We must focus more on changing ourselves than others. Also, we must try to renovate ourselves to conform to the biblical paradigm of a godly relationship, not embark on reconditioning each other. We cannot sacrifice each other on the altar of our frustrations in the name of change or self-interest. No one person can bear all our burdens, pacify all our fears or meet all our needs. Only Jesus can! We need to learn to be grateful for what others are eagerly doing to express endearment and trust God in areas they have challenges.

Who are you to people?

You are a model of Jesus Christ, a servant leader, an empathetic believer, a tolerant individual, not a drill sergeant. You are a replica of the church, an emissary of Christ, a facilitator for the kingdom, not a nitpicker or dripping faucet.

Who should teach those within or outside your circle?

The Holy Spirit! He is the Spirit of truth, the greatest Teacher, Mentor, Counselor, and most powerful Catalyst of change. If you yield, He will do a better job. Become a teachable student of the

Holy Spirit and focus on yourself, not invest in a worthless campaign of trying to amend others.

Who needs to change first?

Each one of us – the *"perfect geniuses"* that seemingly know how to define the mysteries of life, analyze people, and solve all human problems. We think we know everything but know nothing. Enough of our superciliousness, sanctimoniousness, and folly! We must amend our ways. Whether a saint or sinner, we must take the lead to repent. Often, people who nag or complain more need the most change. Often, the truth hurts. Like a bitter pill, it is hard to swallow. However, it heals and liberates. Pride and resistance to truth trap people in bondage.

If you feel that others are driving you insane, perhaps God is utilizing their supposedly peevish conduct to unmask where you have unresolved issues of anger, resentments, disappointments, rejection, real or imagined emotional hurt, and other unsettled issues. The question is will you allow Him to use seemingly exasperating things about others to enlarge your capacity for tolerance and forgiveness? Be more empathic and forbearing, and you will reap the rewards.

Who changes people?

God! Only He can transform need-conscious folks to become purpose-driven, egocentric ones to become selfless, flesh-motivated people to become Holy Spirit-driven, and carnally minded people to become spiritually minded. Only when we are zealously propelled by His love will we have relatively lax expectations of each other.

What changes people?

Truth – the word of God (John 17:17). It not only aligns us with His will, but refines, heals, sanctifies, convicts, and unshackles us from unbiblical mindsets. *"And ye shall know the truth, and the truth shall make you free" (John 8:32).* It is one thing to know the Truth and another to put it into practice. We have toxic relationships because we know the truths in God's word, but do not apply them. We recognize enough truths that can liberate us but do not model them. We understand that it is sinful to bear false witness, claim self-righteousness, harbor resentments, impose personal preferences, exploit others' weaknesses or breach their free-will. However, these are just a few of our favorite things. Often, we saddle people with unrealistic expectations that would cause them to stumble.

Many relationships are spiritually barren because people are not willing to practice truth or sow themselves. For truth to emancipate us, we must live by it. Acknowledging and practicalizing truth produce fruits of lasting change. Jesus said, *"Most assuredly, I say to you, unless a grain of wheat falls into the ground and dies, it remains alone; but if it dies, it produces much grain" (John 12:24).* Faith-driven believers must circumcise their hearts to reproduce the character of Christ and buffet the flesh to harness the fruit of the Spirit. It is incumbent on us to cultivate fruit-bearing relationships. Until we are willing to die to self, our relationships will barely yield good fruits. Instead, they will be on the threshold of "asphyxiation," grasping for spiritual oxygen. However, when we crucify the flesh, the Lord will use our submission to breathe healing into our alliances.

Do I need to repent?

Yes – if you want God to heal your relationships. Jacob lived a deceptive mode of life until the day he wrestled with an angel. When he was honest about living in conformity with the connotation of his name, God changed his name from "Jacob the supplanter" to "Israel, the Father of many nations." Shifting blame in a relationship is an attestation of immaturity. It proves that we love the shackles of sin more than redemption, or we would not resist repentance or genuine change.

You can't make an omelet without breaking a few eggs. Examine, confront yourself, and accept liability for your faults. Stop criticizing others. They will never measure up to your illusive model. Instead, boldly identify your issues, areas you lack healthy boundaries, self-control or have blind spots – where you are willfully or intuitively gullible. Identify and repent of the lies you feed yourself, renounce the malicious imaginations of your heart, relinquish selfish attitudes, and sow yourself in your relationships. When you close all the access doors that you opened through anger, resentment, rejection, and the like, the devil will not find anything in you to use against your associations.

Do you want others to change?

Start with yourself! You can neither change others by your power nor bicker your way through their hearts. Squabbling not only coarsens the soul but escalates the tension in a relationship. The more you nag others, the further you shove them away. They will become elusive, far-flung, and resistive to change. When you are frustrated with others, be patient, and release them to God rather than bicker and exacerbate your anger. If you let Him intervene in His time, things will perk up, and you and your loved ones can sing from the same hymn sheet. People are more receptive to change when they have enough leeway to do so.

One of the most proven ways to transform a relationship is, to begin with oneself regardless of the price it entails. Submitting to God will give it a face-lift and actuate the transformation that you desire in others. Roll up your sleeves and get ready to work your love, forbearance, forgiveness, and commitment muscles in subsequent chapters.

Now, pray these prayers soberly with a contrite heart.
- **Scriptural Confession: Matthew 7:1-5; John 12:24; Psalm 141:3-4; John 14:26;**
- **Praise and Worship**
- **Prayer Points**

1. Merciful God, I repent for trying to take your place in others' life. Only You can approve or disapprove of them. Forgive me for nagging and shifting blame. Wash me clean with the blood of your Son Jesus Christ.
2. Set a guard, O LORD, over my mouth; Keep watch over the door of my lips. Do not incline my heart to any evil thing, to

practice wicked works with men who work iniquity; And do not let me eat of their delicacies, in the name of Jesus (Psalm 141:3-4).

Holy Spirit:

3. Help me to tolerate and minister to those that I am assigned to, in the name of Jesus.
4. Teach me how to submit to others, in the name of Jesus.
5. Help me to understand and relate to others, in the name of Jesus.
6. Help me to minister to others where they are continuously resistant, in the name of Jesus.
7. Counsel me on how to meet others' needs, in the name of Jesus.
8. Minister to those I love in ways I cannot minister to them, in the name of Jesus.
9. Teach me how to love and accept others unconditionally just as you love and accept me, in the name of Jesus.
10. Holy Spirit, greatest Teacher, Mentor, and Counselor; teach me what others cannot teach me. Teach others what I cannot teach them, in the name of Jesus.
11. Teach us truths we cannot receive from each other due to our weaknesses and imperfections, in the name of Jesus.
12. Heavenly Father, transform, heal, strengthen, and restore my relationships beginning with me, in the name of Jesus.
13. Thank you, heavenly Father, for pouring out your grace and love on my family, friends, neighbors, colleagues, brethren, and other alliances.
14. Father, thank you for the breakthroughs and testimonies.

CHAPTER 10

"Hardness of Heart"
(Conflict Fire Starter # v)

*Whether you succeed or fail in a
relationship will depend on
whether you have a moist or
frigid heart-soil.*

" *A*nd because iniquity shall abound, the love of many
shall wax cold" (Matthew 24:12). The devil is using
"hardness of heart" to incite strife between friends,
neighbors, employers and employees, mentors and protégées, and
the like. Sibling rivalry, contention between parents and their
progenies, and kinsmen and kinswomen are escalating. *"For son
dishonors father, Daughter rises against her mother, Daughter-
in-law against her mother-in-law; A man's enemies are the men
of his own household" (Micah 7:6).* Relatives are contending for
lands, properties, money, birthright, seniority, and other
worthless causes. Husbands and wives no longer view marriage
as a sacred institution, but as a mundane contract that can be
entered into on human terms and violated at will – when it no
longer fuels their agenda. The divorce rate in Christendom is
outrageously alarming and appalling.

Nations are not excluded from the morass. They are stuck in
the quagmire of conflict as well. Rumors of wars are on the rise.

74

It is so sad that the body of Christ that should be the standard-bearer is not exempted from this cesspool of strife and division. Satan is utilizing doctrinal disagreements, dissimilar denominational ideologies, and mortal insecurities to incite division. These meaningful interpersonal ties that God intended for good are used for individual gain. Relationship ills can be attributed to cold, conceited, and impenitent, hearts. Only repentance can get us off board this train wreck.

God, the Sower

"Then He spoke many things to them in parables, saying: "Behold, a sower went out to sow. And as he sowed, some seed fell by the wayside; and the birds came and devoured them. Some fell on stony places, where they did not have much earth; and they immediately sprang up because they had no depth of earth. But when the sun was up they were scorched, and because they had no root they withered away. And some fell among thorns, and the thorns sprang up and choked them. But others fell on good ground and yielded a crop: some a hundredfold, some sixty, some thirty" (Matthew 13:3-8).

Jesus used the Parable of the Sower to illustrate the distinct hearts that humans have. The different soils are symbolic of the variations of the human heart. A Sower planted similar seeds on diverse soils – the wayside, stony, thorny, and the good ground soils. Only the seeds that fell on the good ground produced good fruits. (See Matthew 13:3-8; 18-23.)

God is constantly sowing seeds in our hearts in various ways. The problem is that our parched heart is rejecting them and making us unfruitful. Yet we wonder why we are disillusioned and unstable in our relationships. Whether we succeed or fail in a relationship will depend on the spiritual condition of our hearts. Remember, the problem in the above biblical narrative was not the seed but the aridity of the distinct soils. The seed sown was capable of bearing fruits. However, aside from the good ground soil, others were not harmonious with it.

The Parable of the Sower depicts how the heart influences our behavior. Daily, God sows His word in our heart soils through sermons, Holy Spirit-driven Christian media, anointed books, personal Bible study, or through other means by which He can get our attention. Indeed, He is using this book to plant biblical seeds in your heart as well as express His nature to you. However, your response will reveal if you have a wayside, stony, thorny, or good ground heart-soil.

The following Scriptures are seeds: *"A new commandment I give to you, that you love one another; as I have loved you, that you also love one another. By this all will know that you are My disciples, if you have love for one another"* (John 13:34-35). *"Therefore let us not judge one another anymore, but rather resolve this, not to put a stumbling block or a cause to fall in our brother's way"* (Romans 14:13). *"And be kind to one another, tenderhearted, forgiving one another, even as God in Christ forgave you* "*(Ephesians 4:32)*. *"Behold, how good and how pleasant it is For brethren to dwell together in unity!" (See Psalm 133:1.)*

In summary, The Lord is saying, *"Do not judge others, love one another; be kind to one another, tenderhearted, forgiving one another, even as God in Christ forgave you. Dwell together in unity."* If He were to sow these Scriptural seeds in your heart, let us examine how you would react or respond based on the diverse heart-soils represented in the parable.

The "Wayside" Heart-Soil (Matthew 13: 4; 19)

Do you have a "wayside" heart-soil? *"When anyone hears the word of the kingdom, and does not understand it, then the wicked one comes and snatches away what was sown in his heart. This is he who received seed by the wayside"* (Matthew 13: 19). Based on the word of God, the wayside soil personifies those who hear the word, and do not understand it. When trials come, lack of understanding chokes up the seed that was sown in their hearts, and it results in unfruitfulness.

If you have a wayside heart and you hear God's word; *"Do not judge others, love one another; be kind to one another, tenderhearted, forgiving one another, even as God in Christ forgave you. Dwell together in unity,"* you will neither understand nor apply the above truths because of ignorance. The truth we know and apply liberates us based on John 8:32. If you are a conceited, cruel, and hypercritical person, you may wrestle with exhibiting love, kindness or empathy to others. If you have an unteachable heart, you will have misgivings about forgiving others because you will feel that those who slight you deserve to suffer. Because you have no perception of truth, you have no conviction or commitment to truth. Therefore, the enemy comes and steals the seed that was sown, and you become unfruitful. Obliviousness to truth grants the devil access to embezzle what was planted – and unfruitfulness comes to play.

Why would you become unfruitful?

Your fallow and shallow heart-soil would choke the seed. Though the seed is in fine fettle, your untilled heart-soil will be incongruous with it. The word cannot grow in an incompatible heart-soil.

The "Stony" Heart-Soil (Matthew. 13:5-6, 20- 21)

Do you have a "stony" heart-soil? *"But he who received the seed on stony places, this is he who hears the word and immediately receives it with joy; yet he has no root in himself, but endures only for a while. For when tribulation or persecution arises because of the word, immediately he stumbles"* (Matthew 13:20-21). Based on the Parable of the Sower, the stony soil embodies those who hear the word with joy. It endures for a while until temptation and tribulation come as a result of the word that was sown. Lack of depth and "hardness of heart" choke up the seed and they become unfruitful.

If you possess this type of heart and you hear the word of God, *"Do not judge others, love one another; be kind to one another, tenderhearted, forgiving one another, even as God in Christ forgave you. Dwell together in unity,"* you will probably receive it with joy. *"Oh! This is so great. Hallelujah! This message will greatly impact my life and relationships."* However, what happens? Because the seed was sown in a rigid heart, it endures only for a while. When the temptation to exhibit pride, harbor resentments or contend with others arise, you will have no spiritual stamina to hold on to truth… and boom…there you go… conflict explosion! The unresolved issues in your hardened heart may incite hostilities and make you unfruitful.

Why would you become unfruitful?

The unyielding state of your heart-soil would make you infertile. Remember, the hindrance is not the seed but your stern heart. The seed sown has no depth in your heart. The word is fertile, but the soil of your heart is too discordant to receive it (Matthew 13:20-21). Since you view temptations as obstacles instead of opportunities to grow, you will easily get discouraged, resentful, and even become unfruitful. Besides, you may overlook something very significant. Based on Scriptures, temptations came because of the seed that was sown (Mathew 13:21). In other words, the seed attracted your trials or challenges. If *"tribulation or persecution arises because of the word,"* it indicates that the devil is seeking to devour the truths that the Lord wants to establish in your life and relationships. He targets those who *"hear"* the word of God, uses interpersonal feuds to sabotage their faith, and leashes out infernal darts to upset their solidarity.

The devil is a sadistic demon that is twisted in all aspects. Hence, he tries to bedevil your alliances. He will have insomnia when you utilize conflict to become better, not bitter. Conflict hurdles can be stepping-stones to breakthroughs if we allow God to use them to mature and enlarge our capacity for tolerance. Temptations and persecutions are trials designed to kick us out of our comfort zone and appraise our readiness to go to the next level. Hence, we must pass the test so our relationships will soar to new heights.

The "Thorny" Heart Soil (Matthew. 13: 7, 22)

Do you have a "thorny" heart soil? *"Now he who received seed among the thorns is he who hears the word, and the cares of this world and the deceitfulness of riches choke the word, and he becomes unfruitful" (Matthew 13:22).* The thorny heart soil epitomizes those who hear the word but allow the cares of the world and the deceitfulness of riches to choke up the seed – and they become unfruitful.

If you exemplify this type of heart and you hear, *"Do not judge others, love one another; be kind to one another, tenderhearted, forgiving one another, even as God in Christ forgave you. Dwell together in unity,"* you will receive the word but consciously choose to flout it due to the *"cares of the world and the deceitfulness of riches."* Your noncompliance would throttle the word, and you would become unfruitful.

Why would you become unfruitful?

The coarseness of your heart-soil would make you fruitless. The obstacle to growth would not be the fertile seed but your thorny heart-soil. *"The cares of the world"* are indicative of anxieties about health, family, bills, friends, job, career, and other responsibilities. The deceitfulness of riches signifies *"the love of money which is the root of all evil" (1Timothy 6:10).* When money becomes a god, people can become greedy, competitive, or live a profligate lifestyle. The strain of materialism or keeping up with the Joneses can rend their unanimity.

Because *"the deceitfulness of riches"* stiffens the heart, you would have no fear of God or accountability to measure up to biblical standards in your relationships. Valuing money more than people may cause you to become an absentee friend, brother, sister, parent, neighbor, boss or the like. You may be physically in a relationship but emotionally unavailable. The *"cares of the world"* would consume you, and you would have little or no time for others or God. Because you have misplaced priorities, outside influences will blur your focus, and it will be no wonder if your relationships become a war zone. Those who idolize mammon or allow the anxieties of life to define their relationships are oblivious to satanic ruse. His nefarious ploy is to utilize their abrasive hearts to detonate a conflict bomb so they can barrage and obliterate relationships that matter.

The "Good Ground" Heart-Soil (Mathew 13: 8, 23)

Do you have a "good ground" heart-soil? *"But he who received seed on the good ground is he who hears the word and understands it, who indeed bears fruit and produces: some a hundredfold, some sixty, some thirty" (Matthew 13:23).* The good ground soil characterizes those who hear the word and obey it. They produce fruits regardless of various challenges.

If you have this type of heart and you hear, *"Do not judge others, love one another; be kind to one another, tenderhearted, forgiving one another, even as God in Christ forgave you. Dwell together in unity,"* you would embrace it with joy, practicalize it, and become fruitful. In spite of *"temptations," "persecutions," "the deceitfulness of riches,"* and *"the cares of the world,"* as you enthusiastically personify this truth; it would produce good fruits of love, patience, understanding, compassion, and genuine friendships in your relationships. Trials cannot sway those who have the seeds of truth deeply ingrained in their moist heart- soils. The depth of the seeds will not only empower them to withstand whatever life throws at them but will solidify the bond they have with others.

Why would you become fruitful?

The plowed and moist condition of your heart-soil would make you a prolific person. The soil of your heart is not only tender enough to grow the seed but is in harmony with it. The seed sown would yield fruits because your heart is one hundred percent focused on obeying God and maturing spiritually.

Of what use are we to the kingdom if we are not bearing good fruits and using our relationships to bolster the Lord's cause? He linked us so we can learn how to replicate the bond between Him, His Father, and the Holy Spirit. We have a choice to bond or clash with each other.

"Hardness of Heart" inflames Conflict

The heart is the soil on which we build our lives and relationships. Hardness of heart makes relationships unfruitful. People with hard-boiled hearts are egotistic, vindictive, paranoid, obstinate, and hoity-toity. They camouflage wrong, rebuff repentance, and run from accountability to placate their supercilious temperament.

Disputatious people with seared consciences barely accept responsibility or say, *"I am sorry... Please, forgive me. I admit that I made a mistake." Why?* Acknowledging insensitive behavior would expose their inadequacies and the need to change – and make them look vulnerable. One with a reprobate heart sees humility or contriteness as a disparagement of one's sense of self.

Those who will not allow God to tenderize their prideful hearts will continue to rant and rave about others' limitations. However, until they let the water of the word irrigate their parched souls, their relationships will remain unfruitful.

Frigid Heart-Soils Produce Frigid Folks

Only a loving and moist heart will produce a healthy relationship. Expecting commitment, gentleness, meekness, or forbearance to mature in a decadent heart will be like reversing the laws of nature. Without repentance, it would be a long stretch to expect righteousness to flourish in a crusty heart. The stiffness of the heart-soil will stifle the seed. Unconditional love, loyalty, and mutual trust cannot penetrate the rigidity of a scorched heart. A frigid heart will reject temperance and harmony. Forgiveness cannot germinate in a reprobate mind because there is no tenderness in there to sustain it. Because the soil of the heart is discordant with the seed, its rigidity will suffocate it.

A crooked heart will produce a distorted relationship – given the toughness of the heart-soil that is incongruous with love, forgiveness, and tolerance. Its aridity will ruin the seed, and the relationship will become unfruitful. Our heart-soil must be totally softened by repentance if we want our alliances to be prolific.

Many cold-hearted individuals are emotionally and physically remote because of deeply entrenched emotional wounds that have left them scared. They are clueless about how to give and receive love because of timidity, fear of vulnerability, rejection, failure, betrayal, and other deep-rooted psychological complexities. Only the Holy Spirit can pull them out of their shells or rescue them from demonic incarceration.

We need a Holy Ghost plunger to unclog the dirt, gunk, and sin build-up in our hearts so unconditional love can take deep roots. Our heart soils must be moist enough to accelerate our relationships from precept to precept, strength to strength, and faith to faith so we can soar to new dimensions.

Relationships: A Heart Issue...

Why do people turn to pride, abuse, hostility, and all the other dynamics that wreck relationships?

They do because of the cold, impenitent, and unteachable state of their hearts. The works of the flesh come straight from the heart! *"But those things which proceed out of the mouth come from the heart, and they defile the man. "For out of the heart proceed evil thoughts, murders, adulteries, fornication, thefts, false witnesses, and blasphemies" (Matthew 15:18-20). "For out of the abundance of the heart, the mouth speaks" (Matthew 12:34b).*

Whether a relationship flourishes or nose-dives depends on the spiritual status of one's heart – not on race, gender, economic or social status. You cannot attribute the pressures in your life or interrelations on those dynamics. The success or collapse of any relationship is not a cultural, financial ranking, male or female issue, but a heart issue (Proverbs 4:23). While tenderness of heart builds a relationship, the hardness of heart obliterates it. People that are spiritually minded rise and fall on humility, obedience, and Truth. On the contrary, those that are carnally minded rise and fall on pride, self-idolatry, and a false perception of truth. The solidity of a relationship hinges on the spiritual standing of our hearts, not the flimsy excuses we utilize as smokescreens to dissolve meaningful alliances. How we perceive relationships is a point of conflict between the Bible and our human sense of reality. We need to part company with our ignorance and confront our seared hearts with the help of the Holy Spirit.

What hardens the heart?

The deceitfulness of sin stiffens the heart (Hebrews 3:13). It causes us to resist the conviction of the Holy Spirit to be penitent when in disobedience. Yielding to Him not only induces godly sorrow but leads to repentance. However, the more a person repels His nudging, the more his or her heart becomes callused.

What moistens and plows scorched hearts?

Repentance. Applying the "water of the Word," confession or renunciation of sinful behavior breaks down hardness of heart. Accepting responsibility and acting in ways that please God soften the heart. *"For thus says the LORD to the men of Judah and Jerusalem: Break up your fallow ground, And do not sow among thorns. Circumcise yourselves to the LORD, And take away the foreskins of your hearts, You men of Judah and inhabitants of Jerusalem, Lest My fury come forth like fire, And burn so that no one can quench it, Because of the evil of your doings" (Jeremiah 4:3-4).* We need a spiritual heart transplant or heart circumcision to release our minds from soulish mentality.

Our daily cry to God must be:

Father Lord, sprinkle clean water on me and cleanse me from all my filthiness and idols. Give me a new heart and put a new spirit within me. Take away my stony heart and give me a heart of flesh. Put Your Spirit within me and cause me to walk in Your statutes, and keep Your judgments and do them, in the name of Jesus (Ezekiel 36:25-27).

- **Scriptures Confession: (Psalm 139:23-24) (Jeremiah 4:3-4) (Ezekiel 36:26, 2 Corinthians 10:5, John 17:17); (Matthew 15:13).**

- **Praise and Worship**
- **Pray These Prayers With a Contrite Heart.**

1. Search me, O God, and know my heart: try me, and know my thoughts: And see if there be any wicked way in me and lead me in the way everlasting.
2. Heavenly Father, break up the fallow ground in my heart. Circumcise the foreskin of my heart. Let the fire of the Holy Spirit melt every arrogance, stubbornness, selfishness, hardness, self -righteousness, wickedness, and pride in my heart, in the name of Jesus.
3. Almighty God, remove my wayside, thorny, and stony heart. Give me a new heart and a new Spirit, in the name of Jesus.
4. I lay the axe of the Holy Spirit to the root of ungodly seeds in my heart, spiritual barrenness, and unfruitfulness in my life and relationships, in the name of Jesus.
5. By the blood of Jesus, I cast down "wicked imaginations and every high thing that exalts itself against the knowledge of God and bring into captivity every thought to the obedience of Christ," in the name of Jesus Christ.
6. Let every plant that my heavenly Father has not planted in my life and relationships be uprooted, in the name of Jesus.
7. Let every root of anger, pride, bad-temper, restlessness, fear, bitterness, ungratefulness, intolerance, evasiveness, and self-righteousness in my life and relationships be uprooted, in the name of Jesus.
8. Father, sanctify me with your word. "For your word is truth."
9. Let the judgment of God fall upon the powers that will dare interfere with your will, purpose, and plans for my loved ones and interpersonal relationships, in the mighty name of Jesus.
10. Thank God for answers to your prayers.

CHAPTER 11

The Blame Game
(Conflict Fire Starter # vi)

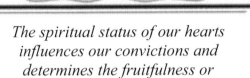

*The spiritual status of our hearts
influences our convictions and
determines the fruitfulness or
barrenness of a relationship.*

W hether you have healthy or anemic interpersonal
relationships will depend on the spiritual status of your
heart. What has a relationship got to do with the heart?
Everything! The heart is like a garden soil on which we build
our lives and relationships. The condition of your heart soil
reveals whether you will avoid or incite strife, embrace or reject
reconciliation or have wholesome or wishy-washy relationships.

Shifting Accountability

Why do we play the blame game? We shift accountability
because of the deviousness of our hearts. *"The heart is deceitful
above all things, And desperately wicked; Who can know it? I,
the LORD, search the heart, I test the mind, Even to give every
man according to his ways, According to the fruit of his doings"
(Jeremiah 17:9-10).* Consequently, we tend to claim self-

righteousness to avoid contrition; play victim to evade responsibility and defend our issues to elude change. When God confronted Adam and Eve about their transgression, they blamed each other and never atoned for it. Adam impugned Eve; *"The woman whom thou gavest to be with me, she gave me of the tree, and I did eat."* Eve pointed the finger at the serpent; *"The serpent beguiled me, and I did eat" (Genesis 3:12-13).* I am quite sure that the serpent impugned God for creating it. Only God accepted responsibility for creating them.

Often, we play "catch me if you can," and like a blasé cloud in motion, it is tough to pin us down to accept liability for wrongdoing. Shifting responsibility is a significant contributor to disputes. Accepting responsibility plays a pivotal role in cultivating a salubrious relationship with those we claim to love.

It is a paradoxical fact that we blame discords on everyone and everything else but grasp the nettle. Probably, you might blame conflict on racism, in-laws, culture, financial instability, stress at work, irreconcilable differences, incompatibility concerns or others' indolence or refusal to measure up to your prospects. However, these are your escape, coping or defense mechanisms. You are utilizing these rationales to evade and camouflage the real problem – the hardness of heart. Whatever you blame for disharmonies is not only a disguise of the multifarious issues you need to confront in your relationships, but also a distortion of truth designed to deviate you from dealing with the source of your dilemmas. These pretexts are the fruits of a toxic heart-soil that is contaminated by hurt, disappointment, bitterness, rejection, and the like, not the seemingly alleged reasons. Call a spade a spade rather than misconstrue the obvious. Truth emancipates us, not lies.

We can run from ourself and people but cannot hide from God. It is ludicrous to think that we can outsmart Him. Truth will always confront us everywhere we turn whether we like it or not. Until we examine our hearts, confront the lies we tell ourselves, renounce the idols of the heart or become accountable for the truths we know, change or healing will not ensue. Let's examine the various ways we dodge responsibility.

Escape, Coping and Defense Mechanisms

The following are typical comments and grievances people use to evade self-responsibility. Do they sound familiar?

"What is wrong with people? They can't do anything right! I can't stand 'em... They get on my nerves!"

Your scathing attitude is nothing to sing about either. It gets to others as well! A cold heart is easily irritable, unappeasable, and paranoid. When you have a hardnosed heart, others will find it hard to gratify you regardless of how much they invest in the relationship. You will always demand more than they can deliver. Even if they were to merit your validation, you would never be content enough to reciprocate their efforts. Instead, you will dig up other reasons to substantiate your posture. Even if they were to bend backward to satisfy you, you would still grapple with forgiveness, pout about the slightest fault, and remain ungrateful for their sacrifices because you want to chop logic.

It would have no bearing if others endorsed you. You would still treat them like garbage – even if they were to treat you like royalty. You would still castigate them even if they were to live up to your outrageous prospects because you have a faultfinding spirit. It would not row your boat even if your career were stress-free, your in-laws approved you, culture was in sync with your reality, race was not an issue, or others measured up to your appraisal – considering your grouchy heart. The rigidity and idols of your hypercritical heart will cause you to raise the bar continually because you want something else to mull about – regardless of others' efforts. Habitual nitpickers are overly sensitive, demanding, and unpleasant. A sibling, friend, spouse, parent, colleague, son, daughter, coworker, brethren, neighbor or anyone can hardly appease them.

"Yes, my mouth stinks, but blame the toothbrush!"

Often, when our mouth stinks with sin, we point the finger at the dentist or toothbrush rather than accept accountability for dysfunctional behavior. When we lash out in anger, we ascribe it to others' insensitivity and ability to aggravate us rather than confront our lack of self-control. We denunciate others when they abuse us without accepting responsibility for our vulnerability to their mistreatment. We never really deal with why they see us as punching bags or dumping grounds for their frustrations. We attribute complacency and garrulousness to genetic make–up rather than admit negligence or lack of self-control.

We stigmatize others for disparaging our worth instead of being accountable for our negative appraisal of self. When people misuse us, we brand them before we accept liability for our passivity, lack of identity or healthy boundaries. When we feel unlovable, we query God for creating us. When life overwhelms us, we upbraid Adam and Eve for making our lives such a mess because of their fall. We badger others to change but cling to our blemishes and infirmities. It is always others' fault, never ours. Oh, God, deliver us!

"It's not my fault but Bob's. He made me do it!"
This is just a smokescreen to cover up sin. Nobody can make you do what you totally resist. Are you utilizing the" blame game" to defend sinful behavior? Others may let it slide by to placate you. However, God will hold you liable! *"But I say unto you, That every idle word that men shall speak, they shall give account thereof in the day of judgment" (Matthew 12:36).*

"You have to understand. It is a male thing..."
"It is a female thing... you know..."
Often, people blame unacceptable behavior on gender dissimilarities. We must not utilize the emotional and physical distinctions between men and women to masquerade or defend sinful attitudes. The word of God supersedes gender divergences. We need to superimpose the word of God on our egotism regardless of femininity or masculinity. Whether male or female, we need to emulate Christ and learn how to identify with others.

Each gender must hold the other accountable. Unlike Adam and Eve, we must use our talents, anointings, and gender differences to inspire each other to obey God.

"Bridget, my folks are just too cranky and weird. You'd also give them a piece of your mind if you knew them."

The "crabbiness" of your blood relatives is pointless because you remain liable to the Lord regarding how you treat them. Just because you have a bone to pick with them does not give you the right to denigrate them or disobey God. Their supposedly irrational conducts do not excuse your impious reactions. Ask the Holy Spirit to wash your mouth with His word so you will relate and communicate wholesomely with them.

Joseph forgave his brothers and continued to shower love on them despite their ill-treatment of Him (Genesis 50:19-21). Moses interceded for his sister, Miriam when she became leprous as a result of her badmouthing him because of the Ethiopian woman he married (Numbers 12:13). Saul was a mad and jealous king who did not deserve David's loyalty. Nevertheless, David *"behaved himself wisely"* before him and never blew his cool because he was *"the Lord's anointed."* (See1 Samuel chapter 18 and 19.) Abigail interceded for her husband, Nabal when he did not merit it because she feared God (1 Samuel 25:1-38). Others may not deserve your love or respect, but you owe God your obedience. Love them regardless and leave the consequences of their actions to Him.

"I yell at Kayla because she makes me so mad!"

No, you fly into a rage because you hold all the aces. You want to control and penalize her for "unacceptable" behavior with your wrath since you feel that you can get away with it. Kayla may really make your blood boil. However, you have no right to maltreat or incarcerate her in your mental cell. You want to manage the consequences of her responses and punish her. Her behavior threatens your ego; hence, you are desperately utilizing your rage to chastise her to mend her ways or face your wrath. *What will you really gain by daunting her? Do you understand the trauma of having to walk on eggshells around you simply because she is terrified of blowing your fuse?* You have a choice to treat her decently like a human being or rule over her with an iron fist simply because you have the power. However, one day, you will stand before God and give an account of yourself.

You do not abuse people because they tick you off, but because you have a violent temper that is out of control. You are a barrage of explosives in human flesh! You go ballistic when you feel empty on the inside, need a quick fix, and when you can no longer restrain your compulsion to vent. You lash out because you utilize people as the dumping ground for your frustrations, the scapegoats to validate your self-worth, and the sacrificial lambs to bear the pain of disappointments and other unresolved issues in your life. Your lashing out is an escape mechanism used to circumvent self-accountability and validate a false perception of reality. You are terrified of rejection, accountability, betrayal, vulnerability, and being control. Your behavior is a cry for deliverance!

If you have an arid heart, you will use others as a whipping post to pump your ego – and worse, indict them for your impious conduct. When you blow a fuse or denounce others for your unethical conduct, you make more waves. Why not tag your rage and renounce the spirits of fear, anger, and hatred? Command them to leave your mind and body because you are the temple of the living God. Take back your authority and regain control of your heart. Vent at the devil, not people. Release holy anger at him for trespassing your life and relationships. One of the greatest gifts you can render to others is when you become a "Living Epistle of Christ" to them.

"I can't stand people that are so passive and indolent. To make matters worse, I have many of them around me. I have no choice but to step into their shoes and make things happen. Someone has to take charge!"

You do not control others because you have a strong personality or because they are passive. You are domineering because you have a Jezebel spirit that wants to manipulate and dominate everyone and everything that seems to pose a threat to you. It will be no surprise if you are frantically trying to utilize all the conflict ammunition available – malice, self-righteousness, resentment, frigidity, rejection, rebellion, and the like to coerce or manipulate them into meeting your needs. You are using their supposedly indifference as a smokescreen to camouflage your insecurities. You have a hardened heart and need deliverance.

I applaud your courage to take over and run things because others are not functioning in their roles. However, you can follow biblical protocol and treat them with dignity and still make things happen regardless of their seemingly nonchalant attitude. Despite their purported apathy, God still recognizes them as a significant part of your associations. Stay in your lane and function in your role as a true relative, friend, good Samaritan, colleague, confidante, Man or Woman of God and let Jesus steer the wheel of your relationships. As He takes over the driver seat, submit to each other anyway – irrespective of your differences because you love the Lord. You may not trust people. However, you must trust the Lord to work out His purpose for you and those within and outside your inner circle.

"I can't stand my friend, Stacy. I have no respect for her."

You need to repent of your lies before God and admit that the real reason you find your friend repulsive is that you have grudges against her. Withholding respect from her is your way of coping with your frustrations as well as punishing her for living below your expectations. The moment she begins to dance to your beat, "okey-dokey" … alright – you will soften your heart and restore her honor.

Like a faucet, you have deliberately shut off your love flow because you feel that she does not deserve it. Your behavior is proof that you are sharing carnal love with strings attached – based on your perception and her performance. Cut her some slack, renounce your wicked ways, and share unconditional love based on biblical mandate. Abide in Christ and genuine love will flow through you to her. If God were to love or define us based on our humanity or attractiveness, we would not stand a chance.

However, He not only loves and accepts us unconditionally but demands that we do the same for others.

"Mike, my cousin and I are incompatible and have hordes of irreconcilable differences. We can't agree on anything. We are as different as day and night!"

You are using unresolved incompatibility issues to masquerade the real source of your conflict. The main bone of contention in your relationship is rooted in your hardened, prideful, unteachable, and unrepentant hearts. Unsettled disputes are like ticking time bombs waiting for the right situation to set them off. They make us easy targets for the enemy as well.

You can learn a thing or two from God's creation. Day and night are poles apart. However, they never collide because they respect and celebrate their idiosyncratic configurations. We have more things that unite us than divide us. Embrace your similarities and respect your dissimilarities. Hardness of heart triggers inharmoniousness. Use the truths in God's word to check and balance your differences, and your relationship will bloom beyond your wildest dreams.

"I am distraught because others are too insensitive to meet my needs."

Before you *"cast the first stone,"* can you honestly say that you are meeting all the needs of those in your life? You are distressed because you are trying to get from others only what God can give you. People have become your god, joy, peace, fulfillment, faith, identity, significance, purpose of being, and the thermostat that regulates your life. Like a puppet, they manage your moods and determine which button to push to uplift or tear you down. You have roller-coaster emotions because your happiness, creativity, contentment, productivity, and sense of serenity are dependent on others, instead of God. Often, people that have yo-yo emotions use how others respond to their needs as a yardstick to measure their worth. They feel valuable only when others validate them but worthless when others are not serving their needs. Our contentment in life should rise or fall on God, not people.

It is a Scriptural obligation to meet each other's needs in a relationship. However, we should never use it as a burden to crush each other. We must handle "unmet needs" with wisdom, so they do not create a rift between us and those we love. Appreciate whatever others are contributing to your life – whether it is minute or immense, and they will be more inclined to do more. Be grateful for whatever "little" or "much" others can voluntarily contribute to your life and trust God to meet other needs.

If people can meet all your needs, then you do not need Jesus. However, you do! Take back your authority and stop depending on others to police your moods. You determine your highs and lows, not people. Rely more on God than others to meet your needs. *"And my God shall supply all your need according to His riches in glory by Christ Jesus" (Philippians 4:19).* The *"joy of the Lord"* vitalizes and fulfills you – not the joy of a mate, friend, parent, friend, sibling, neighbor, job, economic or social status (Nehemiah 8:10).

Let us garner some wisdom from an African aphorism that has sculpted me from childhood: Please, bear with me if it is not quoted verbatim. "The hen eats corn, drinks water, and swallows pebbles, yet complains of having no teeth. Let her ask the cow that has teeth yet eats grass." Humans have teeth but remain ungrateful and insatiable. We desire the ability to masticate steel or gold despite our limitations. Like the hen, even if we had everything at our disposal, we would find something else to whine about. We must learn how to be appreciative regardless of our situation. *"Let your conduct be without covetousness; be content with such things as you have. For He Himself has said, "I will never leave you nor forsake you" (Hebrews 13:5).*

"My friend, Debra and I are growing apart."
You are because either one or both of you are in transition or in a new season. Your needs may be changing hence you are pursuing different agendas and at loggerheads. *Why were you linked in the first place?* Among several things, perhaps, you were allied on

account of genuine love, great rapport, compatibility, and the eagerness to give mutual support. But when you deviate from them, pursue conflicting interests or allow your desires to override God's will for your friendship, you will be poles apart in your bearings. People grow apart when their needs change. Also, they lose focus or develop acrimonious hearts.

We labor in vain when we try to build relationships autonomously from the Lord (Psalm 127:1). Friends, families, colleagues, couples, congregants or neighbors can grow together in the same direction when they accept accountability for their roles and genuinely repent when they are wrong. Only repentance can melt our antithetical hearts, realign our desires to benefit each other, and gratify God.

"If only we had enough money, we would not be fighting so much in my family."

Really? Oh yeah, right! Since when did money become the criteria for living amicably with others? If it was not money, you would blame the conflict on something else! Fighting over money proves that it has become a god, not slave. Even if you were the wealthiest on earth, your relationship would still be bleeding profusely because you have a crusty heart. If "enough money" is what fortifies relationships, why are there many affluent dysfunctional families, business, friendship and marriage ties? Yes, poverty can exacerbate conflict. It should not. It does only because we are soulish minded. There are folks who live on easy street but are still troublemakers, and poverty-stricken ones who are peacemakers because they are content just to be alive. Some people are wealthy but poor in love and tolerance. Others are poor financially but rich in love and compassion.

If you were to be wealthier, your frigid heart would always look for other justifications to flush your alliances down the drain. Reverence for God is what softens our hearts, not one's socioeconomic status. It produces contriteness and prods us to respond to others biblically. Our obedience should revolve around God's faithfulness, not how others respond or react to us. Manage your finances! Do not let it wring your relationships.

"My boss nags and drives me nuts because he expects too much from me."

Sometimes, people complain about their employers because they are slothful and want to cut corners. Indeed, some bosses need to care more about the welfare of their workers than profits. However, whether your boss is considerate or overbearing, he should not expect less from you because he pays your salary. If the tables were turned, would you expect anything less from your employees?

"I am very frustrated! How do I handle dysfunctional folks that are so naïve and messed up?"

Actually, some relatives, friends, brethren, and other formal and informal associates can be selfish, discourteous, and make life a living hell for others. Someone may say, *"Bridget, you've got that right! I have them around me—work, Church, family, you name it!"* So was Joseph! We can learn a thing or two from him. He did not give his insanely jealous brothers tit for tat but forgave them. Also, King David continued to love his son, Absalom, after he toppled his kingship and sexually defiled his wives publicly in the sight of all Israel.

Generally, most people have a good heart despite their blemishes. No one, not even Satan, came into existence depraved. Satan was an archangel who worshipped God *"until iniquity was found in him."* Consciously, people elect to be nefarious based on their life experiences. When people around us willfully embrace sin, we must willfully embrace righteousness in the face of persecution. Like David, we must learn to *"behave ourself wisely"* when dealing with venomous folks.

"I wish people would learn how to meet my needs."

Perhaps, others are expecting the same thing from you. Often, we are guilty of what we blame others for. Their infuriating conducts genuinely mirror our own inadequacies. Are you learning how to meet the needs of those whom God has assigned to you? They matter to God just like you do.

"Bridget, I would be much happier if I were born into a different family."

I am yet to find a perfect family with no superfluous baggage, dirty laundry or ancestral skeletons in their closets. Even if the grass were greener on the other side, you would still have to tend and mow your lawn in a new family, friendship, Church, business, neighborhood or relationship. Relationships alone do not mature or disintegrate or become healthy or toxic autonomously. People in relationships do. I implore you in the name of our Lord Jesus Christ to let the fire of the Holy Spirit melt your acrimonious heart and learn how to be grateful and make ado with what you have. Weed your own garden and till the parched soil of your heart, and you will begin to enjoy a greener pasture.

"My mate ignored me, and I became attracted to this other person. Things sort of got out of hand."

It did because your body and soul craved relentlessly for the "forbidden waters." Dissatisfied with the waters in your cistern, you yearned for stolen waters because you felt that it tasted better despite the risks (Proverbs 5:15). You sacrificed the sanctity of your marriage and the future of your children on the dais of self-gratification. You strategically premeditated each sexual rendezvous with your clandestine partner because you had no respect for your spouse, children or God.

Unfaithful couples awaken in the arms of another man or woman only because they have a meticulous and calculated choice to do so. Your mate may have disregarded you but did not impose the sin of adultery on you. You willfully allowed the enemy to utilize your marital dilemma to push you to the edge and jumped from the frying pan into the fire. Instead of racing into God's arms for solutions, you knowingly dashed into the arms of a strange person for a phony solace.

Satan may have cajoled you to engage in an extramarital affair. However, he did not force you to defile your marriage bed at gunpoint either. While perambulating in your reality, he distorted your focus because you ignored the voice of the Holy Spirit, imploring you to repent. If the shoe fits, wear it and accept responsibility. Repent and slam the door against adultery and protect your future generations. Clinging to sexual sin not only grants the devil legal entrée, but it makes our bloodline vulnerable to sexual spirits and various kinds of demonic harassments. Somebody fasted, prayed, and jumped through hoops to protect our destiny. We must be willing to do the same for our kids, not trade their future for carnality or self-gratification.

"The brethren in my Church are in conflict because we hardly agree on anything!"
Or you meant to say, *"My Church is in conflict because we choose to disagree with the word of God because of our insecurities. We deliberately fight over everything because we each want to be right and prove God wrong."* We have the power to love or hate or be peaceful or hostile to one another. No more excuses!

"I'm sick of people! They make me edgy."
Perhaps others feel the same way about you too, yet they manage to accept you. Let love, tolerance, and other social skills come on stream. Emulate the Lord's compassion and forbearance.

Humans are Unappeasable!
We are flawed, yet pressure others to be flawless so we can utilize them to propel opportunistic ambitions. We are nitpickers, manipulators, users, spongers, and the know-it-all egotistical micromanagers. Often, we fire and wound one another when we should be bombarding the enemy with spiritual missiles. We denigrate ourselves when we should take great pleasure in lifting each other up.

During the winter months, we nag, *"It is too cold!"* When God blesses us with the summer season, we protest, *"It is too hot!"* During the wet season, when the flowers are blooming and the farmers can grow their crops, we grumble, *"It is raining too much!"* When we put on excess weight, we pout, *"I wish I was much skinnier!"*

We whine about who or what dares defines our reality. *"This is too small for me!" "I don't like the color of my car!" "I am tired of this country!" "My house is too small." "I can't stand my kids!" "I'm too tall!" "I'm too short!" "I wish I have a car."* Then, *"I wish I did not have to pay for this car!"* When it is humid, we whine, *"It is too stuffy!"* When God solves the problem, we complain: *"It is too windy!" "I have no job!"* Then, when God provides one, *"My job is too hard!"* Try this for its size. *"I am tired of being single!"* When God provides a marriage partner; *"My wife acts like a witch!" "My husband is egotistic. He is not romantic. He is like a brick wall!" "I am tired of my spouse. I want a divorce!"* Our myopic and soulish views are tantamount to unbelief and ingratitude.

Other sources of conflict – irreconcilable differences, incompatibility issues, unmet needs, growing apart, falling out of love, and the like are all rooted in our overheated hearts. We will not have to deal with voluminous distresses if our hearts were broken, contrite, and moist before each other and God.

"The Devil Made Me Do it!"

Oh really? Since when did the devil own the power of our will? We blame the devil for milking our relationships without identifying why and how he gained access so we can shut the door. Satan may hold some hostage to sin. However, how many are utilizing truth to free themselves? In actuality, many believe that they are at his mercy as if he is holding them at gunpoint in captivity and forcing them to sin or violate their will.

"You better dishonor your parents, or I will slap you!"
"Quarrel with your sister, Claire, or I'll chop you up."
"Yell at Vicky, manipulate her or else I'll shoot you."
"Lie to Gabriel, or I will make your life miserable."
"Stay in shackles. If not, I'll nip your head."
"Abuse your employees, or I'll skin you alive."
"Feud with people, or I will impair you!"

"Transgress against God, or you are a dead man!"

Often, we claim *"The devil made me do it"* defense when we are caught red-handed and forced to face the ramifications of our choices. Perhaps, Satan is standing before God with a puzzled expression, *"Lord, why do they blame me for everything? Didn't you give them a free will to say, 'yes or no' to me? I do only what they authorize and go only where they invite me."*

Run or Accept Responsibility

We have a parochial view of responsibility. Often, we lie to ourselves because we want to ease our conscience, buy more time to wallow in bondage, and postpone the need to repent or change. The following is self-deception:

"I will work on my anger problem after I deal with my relatives." That is a myopic and inaccurate view of the problem. Fixing your anger issues may well save your family ties.

"I will be a better person.... a loving husband after I divorce Stacy. "I will be a submissive wife after I deal with my mate." Obedience to God may well rescue your marriage.

"I will repent of my bitterness after I punish my cousin, Jane." Perhaps – only if the devil does not make you bite what you cannot chew or sabotage your associations first. Sometimes, we are deceived and soulish-minded like the world and do not even realize it. Remember, vengeance is God's, not ours. We must forsake our deceitful ways.

We must relinquish our *"let George do it"* conceited mindset if we are to be fruitful in our relationships. We need to cease pointing at others because we are as guilty as they are. Playing the blame game reveals our shortfalls. Faulting others for our wrong patterns of behavior will cause us to repeat circles of defeat and generate repeated warfare. We must confront, evict those *blame game* demons, and shut the door. Satan can use stubbornness as an access to gain entrance into one's heart and erect demonic strongholds. When we are in this desolate place, we characterize truth as lie and lie as truth; and never really accept responsibility or embrace repentance because we are deceived.

Those who insist on flip-flopping with Truth will face the music. *"Therefore you are inexcusable, O man, whoever you are who judge, for in whatever you judge another you condemn yourself; for you who judge practice the same things. But we know that the judgment of God is according to truth against those who practice such things. And do you think this, O man, you who judge those practicing such things, and doing the same, that you will escape the judgment of God? Or do you despise the riches of His goodness, forbearance, and longsuffering, not knowing that the goodness of God leads you to repentance? But in accordance with your hardness and your impenitent heart you are treasuring up for yourself wrath in the day of wrath and revelation of the righteous judgment of God, who "will render to each one according to his deeds": eternal life to those who by patient continuance in doing good seek for glory, honor, and immortality"(Romans 2:1-7).*

People who choose rebellion over obedience will eventually stew in their own juice on the day of reckoning unless they repent.

"Whose Job is it?"

Years ago, Anthony, my darling husband, read and shared an intriguing story with me titled "Whose Job is it?" It was about four people who played the blame game because they wanted to elude accountability. The hard facts in this tale echo immensely in many relationships today. May the Lord help us to examine our hearts and embrace repentance as we reflect on the narrative.

"Whose Job Is It?

This is a story about four people named, Everybody, Somebody, Anybody, and Nobody. There was an important job to be done and Everybody was asked to do it. Everybody was sure that Somebody would do it. Anybody could have done it, but Nobody did it. Somebody got angry about that, because it was Everybody's job. Everybody thought Anybody could do it but Nobody realized that Everybody wouldn't do it. It ended up that

Everybody blamed Somebody when Nobody did what Anybody could have done."

"Whose job is it" to define and implement interpersonal relationship roles? Every one of us! We must all accept responsibility as a Christian, Colleague, Father, Mother, Friend, Minister of the gospel, Niece, Uncle, Neighbor, Sibling, Aunty, Cousin, Mentor, Protégé, and our respective roles in our vocations.

Plow Your Heart-soil

Plowing the soil of your heart will significantly change how you relate to people and respond to dissension. Whether you succeed or fail in relationships will depend on either the hardness or softness of your heart-soil. The spiritual status of our hearts influences our convictions and how we handle fracas. It determines emotional, physical, and spiritual fruitfulness or barrenness in a relationship. Hence, we must allow the Holy Spirit to do a spiritual heart transplant in us, break up the fallow ground, and circumcise the foreskin of the heart. *"Sow for yourselves righteousness; Reap in mercy; Break up your fallow ground, For it is time to seek the LORD, Till He comes and rains righteousness on you" (Hosea 10:12).*

- **Scriptural Confession: Pray Psalm 51, Philippians 4:8-9**
- **Praise and Worship**
- **Prayer Points**

1. By the blood of Jesus and the help of the Holy Spirit, I renounce self-deception, shifting blame, unfounded justifications, malicious imaginations, sinful attitudes, and all "coping and escape" mechanisms that I have been using to avoid accountability, in the name of Jesus.
2. I renounce all ungodly influences and behaviors that I have yielded to, speculative defenses, baseless excuses, fallacies

that I use as cover-ups; lies I tell myself and lies I allow the devil to whisper in my ears, in the name of Jesus. I nail them to the cross, in the name of Jesus.

3. I repent of ungodliness, worldliness, carnality, and selfishness, in the name of Jesus.
4. I bring the blood of Jesus against every lying spirit inciting me to shift blame and responsibility. I bind your influence and control over my life, and I command you to loose your hold on me and my relationships, in the name of Jesus Christ.
5. I strip off every mask that I have utilized to camouflage my faults, in the name of Jesus.
6. Father, I can of my own self do nothing. I ask that You deliver me from sin and empower me to live a godly life, in the name of Jesus.
7. Almighty God, cover me with your glory, righteousness, presence, and the blood of Jesus.
8. I put on and adopt the mind of Christ.
9. The devil cannot make me do what I don't want to do. I have the power of choice! I have the power to say, "Yes," to God and "No," to the devil. Therefore, I accept responsibilities for my choices and deficiencies, in the name of Jesus.
10. Father, I ask for divine wisdom, patience, and the power to conform to your character, in the name of Jesus Christ.
11. I meditate on "whatever things are true, whatever things are noble, whatever things are just, whatever things are pure, whatever things are lovely, whatever things are of good report, things that are virtuous and praiseworthy," in the name of Jesus
12. Almighty God, thank you for manifesting your power in my relationships and answering my prayers.

CHAPTER 12

"Let's Split the Relationship in Half"

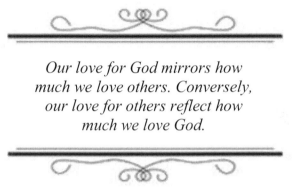

Our love for God mirrors how much we love others. Conversely, our love for others reflect how much we love God.

Relationships disintegrate when we do not want to make sacrifices that gratify God. We want to reap what we have not sown, withdraw what we have not deposited, and have everything for nothing. We desire a relationship trophy without breaking a sweat. Withholding and hawking love are devious ways we exhibit egocentricity, stinginess, and depravity. The biblical account of two mothers who disputed over a living and dead baby depicts how "hardness of heart" can manifest in some relationships.

"Let's Split the Baby!"

"Now two women who were harlots came to the king, and stood before him. And one woman said, "O my lord, this woman and I dwell in the same house; and I gave birth while she was in the house. Then it happened, the third day after I had given birth, that this woman also gave birth. And we were together; no one was

with us in the house, except the two of us in the house. And this woman's son died in the night, because she lay on him. So she arose in the middle of the night and took my son from my side, while your maidservant slept, and laid him in her bosom, and laid her dead child in my bosom. And when I rose in the morning to nurse my son, there he was, dead. But when I had examined him in the morning, indeed, he was not my son whom I had borne."

Then the other woman said, "No! But the living one is my son, and the dead one is your son."

And the first woman said, "No! But the dead one is your son, and the living one is my son."

Thus they spoke before the king. And the king said, "The one says, 'This is my son, who lives, and your son is the dead one'; and the other says, 'No! But your son is the dead one, and my son is the living one.'" Then the king said, "Bring me a sword." So they brought a sword before the king. And the king said, "Divide the living child in two, and give half to one, and half to the other." Then the woman whose son was living spoke to the king, for she yearned with compassion for her son; and she said, "O my lord, give her the living child, and by no means kill him!" But the other said, "Let him be neither mine nor yours, but divide him." So the king answered and said, "Give the first woman the living child, and by no means kill him; she is his mother." And all Israel heard of the judgment which the king had rendered; and they feared the king, for they saw that the wisdom of God was in him to administer justice" (1 Kings 3:16-28).

You may wonder what this biblical narrative has to do with a relationship. Everything! King Solomon is symbolic of the Lord; the two women are figurative of people, and the baby in question is emblematic of a relationship. The counterfeit mother argues, *"Let's split the baby into half." "Let him be neither mine nor yours, but divide him."* Why? The baby is not really hers. Therefore, she has no emotional, physical or spiritual bond with him and does not care whether he lives or dies. Who protects the baby? His real mother! She protested, *"No!" "O my lord, give her the living child, and by no means kill him!"* She pleaded for the baby's life and yearned for him because he was an integral part of her. She was willing to give up her rights for his life because their souls were knitted spiritually and emotionally.

Are you an altruistic or egocentric person?

How would you respond to your children, Church members, protégé, kinsfolks, friends, mentors, colleagues or neighbors in situations when you cannot have your way? Would you shield the relationship or throw it under the bus because it no longer meets your lofty paradigm? Are you the empathetic nurturer who lays his or her life down to protect others or the unsympathetic person who wants revenge?

The Altruistic and Unassuming Person

Just like the real mother of the child in the biblical account, the one who genuinely loves the Lord cares deeply about others and honors his or her divine associations. He or she eagerly assumes responsibility for the strength and limitations of a relationship and will pay the price to protect it – regardless of who is right or wrong. Often, this person is purpose-driven, Holy Spirit-motivated, and the one that relinquishes his or her rights to nurture the relationship so that God gets the glory.

This unassuming believer is ready to roll with the punches and make bricks without straw when the relationship is in distress. Primarily, he is eager to sow peace, shield the vision of the relationship, and align it on the right path. He is the one that will roar in holy anger against the kingdom of darkness, fight the devil on his knees, and cast his *"bread upon the waters"* until the glory of God glows in the lives of those he is called to. When it comes to the crunch, this idiosyncratic person will continue to reach out in love even when others are evasive, unaccountable or nonchalant about doing the right thing.

Often, altruistic people exude tenderness. Their warmth is like a healing balm; their selflessness a wholesome encounter; their voice a soothing melody; and their gentle temperament an archetype of Christ. They are the vessels of love, ambassadors of reconciliation, and the oasis of serenity that are always radiating the quietude in their souls. They are willing to yield their rights or sometimes even take the blame for others' insensitive behavior.

They are *"slow to anger,"* quick to forgive, and will bend over backwards to sow themselves as seeds to heal their relationships. Rather than badger others to change, they take the lead to initiate change so others can follow suit. Nevertheless, they are not punching bags or sponges that absolve abuse. They know how to put up healthy boundaries so they can still reach out to those they love without compromising their convictions.

The Egocentric Person

The conceited person has a big head with his nose in the air. He is full of himself and feels that he is "god junior." He always wants to pull strings because micromanaging others is a way of compensating for his negative self-concept. He is a holier-than-thou braggart on an ego trip. He is soulish, need-driven, evasive, insecure, resentful, and often shifts responsibilities to others.

Just like the fraudulent mother in the Scriptural account wanted to split an innocent baby to satisfy her demonic cravings, so do carnally-minded believers want to split Churches, families, and other valuable relationships to satisfy their flesh. They are flighty, cantankerous, moody, noncommitted, and illusive. They roam from one Church or relationship to another and always find a reason to disconnect when they are confronted with accountability. When they feel that a relationship is no longer addressing their needs, they find excuse to leave for a new one. We need to renounce the following self-centered mindset.

"Let's terminate the relationship because it no longer fulfils my needs."

"I don't care whether my conduct pleases God or not. Either I call the shots or I want out!"

"If I can't have my way, then no one in my family can!"

"If I can't benefit from this friendship, neither can you!"

"If you don't share love, don't expect anything from me!"
"Let's tear down the business if I can't have the promotion!"
"If I can't be the head usher, let's split the Church!"
"Let's malign the boss if she won't let us cut corners."

Time and again, such a callous outlook can enflame conflict inferno. People with a carnal and competitive spirit are engulfed with an intense desire to win at all costs. They break the rules and hardly play fair to the detriment of their relationships. They are easily slighted, emotionally detached, and will rarely stoop to conciliate because they relish discord. They may be physically in a relationship but are emotionally unavailable. They are absentee friends, parents, neighbors, bosses, colleagues, protégées, children, mentors, siblings or brethren. They are not there when you need them. Often, they are always in a hurry to leave or throw the *"baby"* out with the bathwater altogether when they cannot manipulate you. If you are an embittered person, repent and toe the mark so you will not sacrifice your divine relationships upon the altar of your egocentricity.

Releasing or Withholding Love is a Choice

As long as we are connected to Jesus, the True Vine, love will flow through us to others. However, when we rebelliously detach, we become like a disoriented wretched fish that flaps its fins aimlessly outside its aquatic habitat. Not only that, sharing *Agape* love becomes grueling because we are sharing a heathenistic form of love, living autonomously from Him, and huffing and puffing foolishly outside His will – and unbeknown to us, in desperate need of spiritual oxygen.

We can deliberately sever our love flow to make others suffer, taste our tears, feel our pain, come crawling, and begging for mercy when it is our prerogative to do so. Often, we deviously use our so-called *loving* to exploit others so they will feel obliged to sample our reality. Superfluities of emotional wounds incite us to share love with strings attached and mandate others to earn our love when we feel that they do not deserve it. Often, we raise the bar extremely high so we can chastise them for living beneath our expectations. We need to repent and reattach ourselves to the True Vine so we can become an overflow of God's love again.

Releasing or withholding love is a choice.

Sharing love is curative, fulfilling, and liberating.

Hoarding love is deleterious. It enslaves and bruises the soul.

"I Love God... but Hate Nick and his Wife, Kate."

Our relationship with the Lord characterizes our relationship with others. Equally, our relationship with others personifies our relationship with God. How much you love God is directly proportionate to how much love you extend to others. Conversely, how much you love others hinges on how much you love God. You cannot say, *"I love God... but can't stand brother Nick and his wife, Kate." "I love God but can't stand my Pastor, relatives, colleagues, neighbors, blacks, brown, or white people."* If you really love God, you cannot help but love others. You cannot truly embrace His love and not love your siblings, children, neighbors, colleagues, and those He commanded you to consider. Also, you cannot truly receive His forgiveness and not go easy on them either – that will be hypocrisy (1 John 4:20-21). The only proof that we love God is when we love and accept others unconditionally just as He loves and accepts us.

When we find ourselves wrestling with loving others, it is because we are wrestling internally with loving and obeying God. Often, I wrestle with loving and absolving others only when I camouflage my shortcomings. When I am not seeking God, the flesh kicks in and tries to take over, and I find myself wrestling with obedience. However, the more I seek Him, the easier it is to yield to Him. The more I am in love with Him, the more it becomes easier to love others despite their flaws. In those times, because I am so much in love with the Lord, they can do no wrong. They all seem perfect and enchanting to me until I yield back to the flesh. Loving the Lord tenderizes my heart toward them. The more I draw closer to God, the more I am aware of my blemishes. The more I seek and worship Him, the more He deepens my love for my husband, children, family, friends, associations, and all of humanity. *How do you know Bridget?* I live and breathe it moment by moment – by His grace. It is a spiritual phenomenon that often mesmerizes me.

We all agree that the more we yearn for God, the more our hearts are tender toward people and the more we recognize our own weaknesses, the more we can accommodate others' limitations. It is only when we disremember our own fallibility that we castigate others – Oh, boy! We easily forget! Each time you catch yourself playing prosecution, judge, and jury against those around you, remember to tally your own shortcomings. If you are candid with yourself, they will keep you sober and penitent – on your knees, not on their case.

How Much Do You Love God?

How much we love God is the yardstick that measures how much we love others and vice versa. Until you dip a tea bag in hot water, you will not really know its true color or taste. Our response to conflict reveals how much our love for God weighs. How much we love Him influences how we resolve disputes. Like a litmus test, it unveils the depth or shallowness of your love, the level of your commitment, and how much you are willing to invest or withhold emotionally, financially, physically, and spiritually in others. Furthermore, it exposes how much you appraise a relationship and how far you are willing to go to cultivate it. Your attitude toward forgiveness or reconciliation is directly proportionate to how much you love God and His word.

Will you choose to patch things up with those you are feuding with because you love God genuinely, or will you resist reconciliation and asphyxiate your relationships? Those who eschew peace are like the wicked counterfeit mother. This is what they are really advocating: *"Let's split the baby in two halves so we would both lose." "Let's tear the relationship apart so none will benefit from it."*

When we are equally yoked with God, He breaks and tenderizes our hearts toward others. Wanting to split a divine relationship on our own terms is only an attestation of our spiritual detachment from Jesus, the True Vine. If not, our hearts would be overflowing with love to others. When those we love are not exuding love or tenderness, it is probably because they have a plethora of unresolved issues of anger, rejection, disappointment, bitterness, and the like embedded within.

Until you resolve to stay dyed-in-the-wool and walk in love, you will cling to other adverse alternatives and become imperceptive of other solutions that God is making available to heal your relationships. *How much do you care about your relationships?* The degree to which you are willing to defer your rights and respond virtuously determines the weight of your commitment to God and those you love. Your character is a true depiction of either a cocky or a contrite heart. The condition of your heart determines if you will nurture *"your baby"* with reconciliation or shred it with bitterness.

Do Not Split the Children!

Ex-spouses who are utilizing their children as bargaining chips to score points need to be mindful of playing like the world. If you are divorced or in a new relationship, do not try to rip the children's souls to penalize your ex-spouse. Divorced couples that withhold their children from each other out of egoism or vindictiveness will explain to God why they feel that they are smarter than He is. You do not own the children alone. The blood that flows in your children's veins belongs to you and your ex-spouse. If two of you elect to split the marriage union, do not try to "split" the children's hearts by trying to keep them from each other unless there is evidence of abuse. You need to stop finding umbrages with an ex-spouse because your resentments against him or her will cloud your judgment and willingness to respect his or her parental rights.

A child needs the love, support, and nurturing of both a father and mother. Neither partner can play both roles efficaciously. You are tempting God when you hamper the other person from fulfilling his paternal or her maternal role. Moreover, you are robbing a child of the affection that he or she deserves on account of your egocentricity.

- **Scriptural Confession: Mathew 19: 5-6, Philippians 4: 13 and19**
- **Praise and Worship**
- **Pray These Prayers Sincerely**

1. Father, I repent for considering anger, bitterness, and malice as options instead of embracing the other alternatives that You are presenting to me, in the name of Jesus.
2. Oh Lord, open my eyes, ears, and understanding to discern the solutions that you are providing to reconcile my relationships, in the name of Jesus
3. Lord, help me to view problems in my relationships as opportunities to trust you and grow with others, in the name of Jesus.
4. Father, let me begin to see obstacles as stepping-stones to my breakthroughs, in the name of Jesus.
5. Psalm 133:1 says, "Behold, how good and how pleasant it is for brethren to dwell together in unity!" I bring the blood of Jesus against the power that wants to put my divine relationships asunder. I bind your power and cancel all your plans against us, in the name of Jesus.
6. I decree by the blood of Jesus that no demon, principalities or powers can destroy my divine relationships, in the name of Jesus
7. I decree that all the devil's plans against us shall not stand, in the name of Jesus.
8. I can do all things through Christ who strengthens me. My God shall supply all my needs in my relationships according to His riches in glory by Christ Jesus.
9. Oh God, strengthen all those that are divinely connected to me with your power. Let the blood of Jesus bind our love, friendship, commitment, faith, and all that concerns us, in His precious name.

10. Almighty Father, let the zeal to know, love, and obey You consume me more than my own needs, in the name of Jesus.
11. Father, I desire to do your will and finish strong, in the name of Jesus.
12. Almighty Jehovah, let your will become my will, your purpose, my purpose, and your counsel, my counsel, in the name of Jesus.
13. Almighty God, help me to become purpose-driven, not need-driven and Holy Spirit-driven, not flesh-driven, in the name of Jesus.
14. Father, realign my life and relationships with your purpose and plans, in the name of Jesus Christ.
15. Thank God for answers to your prayers.

CHAPTER 13

Seven Lethal Mistakes That Delay Reconciliation

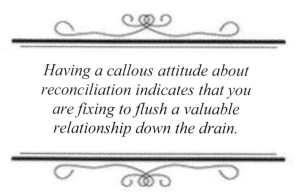

Having a callous attitude about reconciliation indicates that you are fixing to flush a valuable relationship down the drain.

I f we are not mindful of how we conduct ourselves when in conflict, there will be no difference between us and unbelievers who have no spiritual boundaries to referee their choices. Let us examine the following barriers to resolving conflict.

1). Pride: Satan fell from grace because of pride. He uses one of his most prominent traits to block reconciliation. Does this sound familiar? ***"I will not stoop down to their level or reason with them."***

Pitfall: *"Pride goes before destruction, a haughty spirit before a fall" (Proverbs 16: 18). What is the danger of pride? When you raise the bar of expectations for others, you also increase the* *prospect of them falling short of them. Also, the higher the bar, the more defiant others may become. Stubbornness sabotages a relationship. "By pride comes nothing but strife, But with the well-advised is wisdom" (Proverbs 13:10). "Do you see a man wise in his own eyes? There is more hope for a fool than for him" (Proverbs 26:12). "When pride comes, then comes shame; But with the humble is wisdom" (Proverbs 11:2).*

2). Shifting responsibility:

2). Shifting responsibility: As I denoted earlier, we claim self-righteousness to avoid repentance, play victim to elude responsibility, and defend our issues to circumvent change. Shifting blame started with Adam and Eve. While Adam impugned Eve for his rebellion, she faulted the serpent for hers. Only God took responsibility for creating man and sent the Savior. We have adopted the Adam and Eve's syndrome to camouflage truth.

Pose Ken a question, "Who started the conflict?" Probably, he'll retort, *"Don't ask me... ask Andrea, my sister. She made me angry!"* Question Andrea and she'll probably snap back in defense; *"Oh no, don't blame me... Ken started it. It's all his fault!"*

The following evasive patterns of behavior are very familiar:

"It's Patrick's fault! I reacted only because he made a mountain out of a molehill and made me mad."

"I got upset only because Jenny blew it out of proportion."

"I overreacted to Allen's rumor and his irrationality caused me to go over the top."

It takes two to tango. *"A person may think their own ways are right, but the LORD weighs the heart" (See Proverbs 21:2).*

Pitfall: Shifting responsibility impedes reconciliation and divine intervention. When a relationship is sweating bullets and others associated with it are caught in the crossfire, until someone steps in and accepts responsibility, there will be no cease-fire or lasting peace.

3). Indifferent attitude due to fear and weariness: Often, we are apathetic about settling our differences because we feel that things will never change or get better.
"I am sick of this relationship. Things will never get better."

Pitfall: When you resist reconciliation, you are okaying the dissolution of your relationship. The devil will "Amen" your misgivings and nonchalant attitude. *"For as he thinks in his heart, so is he" (Proverbs 23:7a). ".... According to your faith be it unto you" (Matthew 9:29). "For by your words you will be justified, and by your words you will be condemned" (Matthew 12:37).*

4). Waiting for the other person to initiate reconciliation: *"I will straighten things out only if Alex takes the initiative."* The question is, how long will you wait if the other person has the same mindset like you? Will you dump the relationship if he or she does not make the first move?

Pitfall: If the other person has a similar temperament, then both of you may have an elongated and grueling wait. Rebuffing reconciliation implies you have no fear of God. It denotes that you would rather throw caution to the wind than obey Him because you do not conceptualize the relationship as the Lord sees it. The danger is that while you are playing Russian roulette with the devil, the conflict flames will get even more intense and exacerbate the situation. How much longer do you want to dodge bullets in the crossfire of your hostilities? Rather than let the relationship swelter while waiting for the other person to take the bull by the horns, why not salvage it with forgiveness?

If we sow the seeds of peace, we will be able to salvage numerous relationships that would have been flushed down the drain. "A stitch in time saves nine."

5). Waiting for feelings, emotions or motivation to prompt reconciliation: *"I will resolve this only when I feel like it."* Your relationship is sizzling with conflict and you are relying on feelings to inspire you to bite the bullet? Lay it on the line and admit that you are livid – and you want the other person to suffer as much as you did. Those who shilly-shally with obedience will face the music if they are unwilling to defuse the conflict bombs ticking precariously in their relationships.

Pitfall: The devil delights in wrath, rancor, and erratic emotions. Feelings fluctuate like the weather. Your emotions will never sway you to negotiate with others or find the middle ground. Depending on feelings to trigger reconciliation is a devious way to wallow in pride and bitterness. When you keep dilly-dallying with peacemaking, eventually the devil will tow your relationship to his rubbish dump. We live by faith, not by emotions and by truth, not by feelings. God did not admonish us to resolve our differences only when our feelings warrant it. *"They that are in the flesh cannot please God" (Romans. 8:8). "For if you live according to the flesh you will die; but if by the Spirit you put to death the deeds of the body, you will live" (Romans. 8:13).* Depending on feelings indicates we are yielding to the flesh instead of the Spirit. Relying on emotions will accelerate the hostilities on both sides. *"But if you bite and devour one another, beware lest you be consumed by one another!" (See Galatians 5:15.)* The cessation of hostilities can only be achieved through reconciliation.

6). Hoping and praying that things will magically work themselves out without any effort: Often, we sweep unresolved issues, ill feelings or bruised emotions under the rug of a relationship until they pile up as high as the Empire State building – and hope that they will voluntarily disappear without tackling them. We pray and hope that all the scattered pieces of a relationship puzzle will miraculously fit impeccably without doing our part. To avoid confrontation, we caution ourselves,

"Let sleeping dogs lie." What we are ignorant of is that one day, those dogs will awaken and not only defile our dreams but take a bite out of the relationship.

Remember, unresolved issues will "sleep" just for as long as we can calm them. When we have exhausted all our mental resources trying to cuddle them, they will arise and bite off the relationship. *"Don't let the cat out of the bag,"* we tell ourselves. Of course, it will when we can no longer pacify it. In due course, it will leap out... and oops...there the relationship is – in the devil's junkyard!

Pitfall: What people do not resolve in a relationship will come back and deal with them. We must be willing to humble ourselves and crucify the flesh so we can tackle unresolved issues in our relationships biblically. Confront what needs to be dealt with at the right time – with prayer, gentleness, and love.

7). Unforgiveness and the overwhelming need to retaliate: *"I want Joe to suffer as much as I did. Let him taste my tears and pain and come crawling, begging for mercy."*
Giving Joe a taste of your tears may backfire. Instead, release your anger and resentment to God. It is not worth the trouble. Remember the adage: "Do not cut off your nose to spite your face.

Pitfall: The more you want to pay Joe back in his coin or make him suffer, the more you delay resolving the issues. Moreover, waiting for him to taste your hurt will harden both of your hearts toward each other and God. *"Vengeance is mine,"* not yours. *"I will repay says the Lord" (Hebrews 10:30). "Let all bitterness, and wrath, and anger, and clamour, and evil speaking, be put away from you, with all malice: And be ye kind one to another, tenderhearted, forgiving one another, even as God for Christ's sake hath forgiven you (Ephesians: 4:31-32).*

Also, learn to distinguish the voice of the Holy Spirit from hordes of conflicting views that may mean well but are sincerely wrong. Hordes of clashing voices can be very confusing. Some may be reverberating, *"Restore harmony. Do it God's way. Trust*

Him with the relationship." Others may be echoing, *"Don't conciliate Joe! He does not deserve it. Make him sweat!" "You are better off without him. Don't give him another chance. You can do better without him."* You need to turn off all pessimistic voices, obey God, and enjoy the rewards.

A Word of Caution – Exercise Wisdom

We need to be precautious when counseling folks that are going through turmoil in their relationships. Often, people are focused primarily on their anguish, offenses, and the overwhelming need to retaliate when they clash with others. It is our job to bring their focus back to pleasing God, not pacifying the flesh. We need to prayerfully help them realign their responses to gratify God, not add more fuel to the blazing conflict fire.

When you do counsel, give them hope because there is always a light at the end of the tunnel. Do not play favoritism or take sides, or others will reject your counsel. Be on God's side and throw them a lifeline; not because they are perfect or deserve it, but because you are your brother's keeper. You are fallible yourself, and you would appreciate empathy when you find yourself between a rock and a hard place too.

Do not advise parents to break up with their children or vice-versa. The Scripture urges us to honor our parents and refrain from provoking our children to anger. If you want to live long to enjoy the fruit of your labors, honor your parents regardless of their imperfections.

Also, we must be careful not to split-up families, friends, neighbors, colleagues or brethren in Churches for selfish reasons, so the curse of disobedience will not be upon our relationships. The ripple effect of disobedience is astronomical.

It is a grievous sin against God to advise others to divorce their parents, children, friends, co-workers or siblings while you clutch tightly to yours. *"Well, my relationship with my family is much better than the Logan's."* Indeed! If you are flawless in your relationships, then you can claim sanctimoniousness and "cast the first stone" at seemingly culpable people. However, before you recommend that others annul their formal or informal ties, pause and ask yourself; Have you resolved all your personal and relational issues or challenges? Are you and those whom you have close or distant ties with flawless? If you are not, how come you are clinging to your imperfect relationships, tolerating and forgiving those connected to you, and yet you are inciting others to dissolve theirs? Isn't it a double standard to cleave to your fallible associates but instigate others to detach from theirs due to their inadequacies? If you were in their shoes, would you want to be thrown under the bus? Don't you fear God? We have no authority to sever any ties by our own standards. *"Fear ye not me? saith the LORD: will ye not tremble at my presence, which have placed the sand for the bound of the sea by a perpetual decree, that it cannot pass it: and though the waves thereof toss themselves, yet can they not prevail; though they roar, yet can they not pass over it? But this people hath a revolting and a rebellious heart......" (Jeremiah 5:22-23b).*

Often, we hop in and out of relationships leisurely without considering the ramifications. Only God can detach a divine relationship biblically. We should not play judge and jury or bring the curse of disobedience upon ourselves, children, and future generation by trying to disjoin priceless alliances. Yes, we must use Truth to confront people in strife. Nevertheless, we must also allow the same Truth to reconcile and realign them with righteousness.

What about situations where there is abuse or dysfunction? (We shall deal with this issue later.) Meanwhile, prayerfully ask the individuals to seek counsel from their Pastor, a biblical counselor or involve anyone that can help, intervene or make a difference. Fast and pray for them until you see the power of God manifested in their relationship. Take them out to dinner or sow whatever you can in their lives to illustrate God's love. There are so many other practical things you can do that will make a tremendous difference. Please, do not announce your efforts or their challenges on the News. Respect their privacy and dignity. Sow prayer, tolerance, encouragement or whatever you can, and reap acts of kindness when you need them the most.

- **Scriptural Confession: Matthew 6:33, Mark 12:30**
- **Praise and Worship**
- **Prayer Points**

1. By the blood of Jesus, I repent of pride, indifferent attitude, and playing the blame game, in the name of Jesus.
2. I accept responsibility for my shortcomings and choose to change, in the name of Jesus.
3. I choose to be led by the Holy Spirit and walk by faith, in the name of Jesus.
4. I choose to allow the Word of God to change my life and relationships, in the name of Jesus.
5. I bring the blood of Jesus against the powers that are inciting me to delay reconciliation, in the name of Jesus.
6. By the power of the Holy Spirit, I will not walk contrarily against those I love, nor will they work contrarily against me, in the name of Jesus.
7. The devil will not use me against those I love, and those I love will not be used against me, in the name of Jesus.
8. All my close ties are in one accord. We shall not work against each other or against the will and counsel of God for our lives, in the name of Jesus.
9. Let the fire of the Holy Spirit destroy the powers that are opposing my relationships, in the name of Jesus.
10. Oh God, change me by your power, in the name of Jesus.
11. Almighty God, melt me, break me, mold me, and use me for Your glory, in the name of Jesus.
12. Oh God, help me to seek first your kingdom and righteousness above everything else, in your precious name.
13. Lord Jesus, I thank you for answering my prayers.

CHAPTER 14

Hampering Reconciliation is Sin

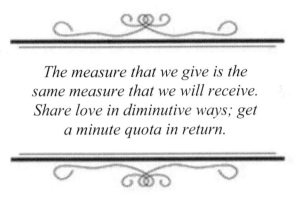

*The measure that we give is the
same measure that we will receive.
Share love in diminutive ways; get
a minute quota in return.*

The truths in Scripture reveal the implications of delaying reconciliation. When we cling to hostilities, we are wrestling with God, taking His long-suffering for granted, and trying to minimize the consequences of our stance. Stubbornness impairs the growth of relationships.

What inhibiting Reconciliation implies

Hampering reconciliation grieves God and opposes who He is. Let us examine what it means to obstruct peace.

1). An impediment to the purpose and plan of God

When we deter conciliation, we are not only diametrically opposed to God's will, but we are standing in His way. We are deliberately defying Him with our anger, stubbornness, and resentments because our egocentric mentality makes us feel that we can resist Him without grievous ramifications. We are not only obstructing love, joy, and peace in our lives and relationships but are collaborating with the devil to crush those we claim to love.

2). Inflaming conflict

Impeding reconciliation connotes that you are adding more gasoline to your conflict fire and fanning it to keep it ablaze. Also, you are firing more conflict ammunition with your hash words and cynical attitude. Often, this will emasculate solidarity and trust. It is not right for others to be caught up in the crossfire of your anger or fair for them to be dodging bullets or running for cover because of your resistance to peace. It is selfish to threaten the welfare of others on account of self-aggrandizement.

3). Overextending God's grace and mercy

Hampering reconciliation signifies that you are stretching God's grace and mercies. Those who obstruct peacemaking overstretch His grace to defend their impious behavior. They presuppose that His mercy will always be available when He can repossess it and impose judgment without their acquiescence –just as the Master of the wicked servant did (Matthew 18:21-35). It is precarious to take His grace and mercies for granted. The more we defer settling our disparities, the more our hearts become callused against each other and against God. The need to proffer leniency begins to depreciate as we develop a parched conscience. Today, as the Holy Ghost says, *"... If you hear His voice, harden not your heart..." (Hebrews 3:7-8).*

You may protest, *"Bridget, you don't understand how much my family hurt me. I have a right to be terribly angry and resentful."* Of course, you do! However, handle the right to be irate with circumspection so it does not cause you to stray. You can be angry, but not for long (Ephesians 4:26-27). Based on Scriptures, we have no right to remain aggravated for too long or the devil will utilize it to his advantage. Remember, God will use the same measure that is utilized to critic others to judge us

(Mathew 7:2). It should scare us to go to bed incensed with a brother, sister, parent, son, daughter, brethren or anyone because firstly, nobody is guaranteed tomorrow. Secondly, what happens if Jesus comes in the middle of our exasperation? That will not be our portion in the name of Jesus. Despite justifiable feelings of rage, we must resolve anger quickly so it will not set off a conflict bomb!

Often, I hear this all the time: *"Bridget, I really want to forgive, but I don't know how to deal with my anger."* Yes, it is human nature to cleave to fury when we are affronted. Sometimes, we want to hang the other person's pride, self-righteousness or indifference on the nearest gallows when our efforts are not reciprocated. Nevertheless, we have no choice but to make peace because God demands it of us. Start by confessing your sin of anger and resentments, and they will begin to dissipate as you release them to Him. Forgive and ask the Lord to heal your traumatizing emotions and painful memories so that the enemy can no longer utilize them to trigger pain or bitterness. Then, trust Him to create beauty out of your ashes.

4). Living to please self

Inhibiting peace indicates that we are selfish, egoistic, and self-centered. It signifies that we are living to please ourselves, not God; we are focusing only on our gain, not on the welfare of a relationship. *"Me first," "Only I matter"* or *"Only my way"* outlook is opposed to Scriptures. God commands us to adore Him, not self, esteem others as better than ourselves, not elevate ourselves, and deny, not indulge ourselves (Philippians 2:3b; 3:3b). We must only live to please Christ. *"For none of us lives to himself, and no one dies to himself. For if we live, we live to the Lord; and if we die, we die to the Lord. Therefore, whether we live or die, we are the Lord's" (Romans 14: 7-8).* This connotes that true ambassadors of Christ do not live for themselves but for the Lord. *"And He died for all, that those who live should live no longer for themselves, but for Him who died for them and rose again" (2 Corinthians 5:15).*

Why did Christ die? He died so we would not live to please ourselves but Him. Life does not revolve around us but around God. We must endeavor to fulfill God's will in a relationship, not fuel our own agenda. Therefore, remove the focus from pleasing yourself to pleasing God.

5). A display of parsimoniousness

Obstructing reconciliation shows that we are stingy with the love and forgiveness that God has given us to share. We resist patching up things because we are still bleeding from the emotional wounds incurred from conflict fire and want those who hurt us to taste our pain and sweat as well. Obviously, we realize that absolving them implies that we must reach out to commune, love, trust, and demolish our emotional and physical walls despite the risk of becoming vulnerable again. Consequently, because we are upset, we are neither in a hurry to embark on that volatile venture nor embrace them swiftly just yet. We want their heart, body, mind, and soul to ache like ours. We want them to desperately miss our smile; grieve for our affection, do penance for the alleged hurtful behavior, atone for not meeting our needs, and hope that they would learn the hard way. Furthermore, we utilize "silent treatment" to keep them at bay. Like a faucet, we intentionally shut off our love, compassion, and tolerance until they pacify our wrath. We would rather revenge than extend mercy; hence we hold off reconciliation as much as possible until we feel that they have atoned enough to merit it. Go ahead; demand for a "Pound of flesh" and settle the score – however, remember the catch: *"Nothing more, nothing less."*

The Parable of the wicked servant is an ideal case study that depicts egotism and stinginess. (See Matthew 18:21-35.) Thwarting reconciliation is equally as horrible. We cannot harbor grudges and yet have the nerve to ask God for His forgiveness. We cannot expect His benevolence but withhold kindness from others. Deterring reconciliation implies we do not want to reciprocate the gift of forgiveness we have received from God or want others to benefit from what we are enjoying. We must absolve others if we want God to absolve us or face the consequences.

The Perils of Stinginess

1). Stinginess with love or forgiveness decreases our capacity to love and extend mercy.

"There is one who scatters, yet increases more; And there is one who withholds more than is right, But it leads to poverty. The generous soul will be made rich, And he who waters will also be watered himself" (Proverbs 11: 24-25). This means that the more we communicate love, the more we enlarge our aptitude to love and accommodate others. Conversely, the less we exhibit love; the propensity to share love and extend forgiveness becomes inhibited. Remember, the measure we give is the same measure that we will receive. *"Give, and it will be given to you: good measure, pressed down, shaken together, and running over will be put into your bosom. For with the same measure that you use, it will be measured back to you" (Luke 6:38).* Sow nothing and reap zilch; share love in diminutive ways and get infinitesimal blessings in return. However, when you lavish love on others, you will reap abundance and become an overflow of divine benefits.

Do not sow love merely because you want reciprocation. Sow because *"It is more blessed to give than to receive" (Acts 20: 35b).* Generally, givers have far less stressful lives than takers. Be more concerned about what you can sow, not reap, what you can release, not withhold, and what you can deposit, not withdraw in a relationship. How much you invest in a relationship will determine its strength and longevity.

2). When we are stingy with love or forgiveness, we are bragging about God's gratuitous gifts.

Often, when we are incensed or offended, we employ all the resources within our power to come down like a ton of bricks on others. We flaunt our value in braggadocious ways that relegate others and the relationship. Also, we not only hoard but lay claim to God's unmerited favors because we feel that others do not deserve them. If they are not pirouetting to our beat, we deny them the enjoyment of our warmth because it is within our power to do so.

Is love, peace, and forgiveness ours?
Do the following expressions sound familiar?

"I will not extend love to my Church folks because they do not deserve it."

"I will not extend forgiveness because I want Richard and Charlotte to taste my pain."

"I will not share compassion because Camelia deserves to suffer."

"I will not make peace with my relatives because I can't stand them!"

But… wait a minute! In truth, is it really your love, forgiveness, mercy or peace? These gratuitous gifts are God's, not yours! It is not our love, mercy or peace in the first place – but *"the love of God that is shed abroad in our hearts by the Holy Spirit," "the LORD's mercies,"* and *"the supernatural peace of God"* that He wants us to extend to others (Romans 5:5; Lamentations 3: 22; Philippians 4: 7).

Hawking Unmerited Blessings is Sin!
Both *"I will"* or *"I will not"* give us a sense of power and authority regardless of whether we use them in positive or negative ways. The power of choice should be used to revere the Lord who gave it to us.

The following Scripture should keep our pomposity in check. *"For who makes you differ from another? And what do you have that you did not receive? Now if you did indeed receive it, why do you boast as if you had not received it?" (See 1 Corinthians 4:7.)* Although it is within our power to share love, extend forgiveness or make peace, did we not receive them as unmerited gifts from God?

He wants us to share, not peddle or suppress them. Yet we demand that others merit what we did not earn from Him; deserve the love that we did not earn from Him; acquire forgiveness that we did not merit from Him, and labor for compassion that has been freely granted us.

Did you deserve God's love? Has He ever told you to merit His forgiveness? Do you earn His daily mercies and blessings? He gives them at no cost and lavishes His love on you. If you did not merit His love, why do you want your coworker, friend, Church members, neighbors or kinsfolks to merit yours? If you did not earn His forgiveness, why do you want others to earn yours? If you did not labor for His peace, why would you want others to pay for peace that has been bestowed on you free of charge?

Now, we understand why sabotaging reconciliation is an act of wickedness or selfishness. We cannot live a double standard and expect God to be merciful to us while we are cruel to others. It is reprehensible to hoard or merchandise God's benefits. We exhibit ingratitude when we demand that others toil for our love or tolerance. When we make others sweat for what we ought to share wholeheartedly, we are bragging in a self-aggrandizing way and boastful about God's undeserved blessings that are not ours in the first place.

We demand that others labor intensely for divine benefits because our concept of love is worldly. Furthermore, we have no "milk of human kindness" and have not genuinely encountered God, or we would reciprocate and share His love irrespective of their inadequacies.

When others Have to Merit Love

It is impious to make others merit love that we did not merit from God. If a son, daughter, brethren, friend, neighbor, sibling, colleague or anyone has to deserve your love and forgiveness, you might as well tell him or her to chase the wind or clasp the cloud. Trying to merit your love would force the other person to live on the edge, walk on eggshells, and still live below your extreme expectations.

When people have to earn our love and forgiveness, then we are not sharing them as complimentary gifts from God. Instead, we are hoarding or hawking what He has liberally given us to share. The danger is that those who hoard, hawk or peddle God's blessings will answer to Him.

Love is a free gift from God that must be shared freely with others. Our reflections, responses, and words must communicate unconditional love regardless of whether others deserve it or not. Demonstrating love is not based on how people respond to us but obedience to God. *"By this, we know love, because He laid down His life for us. And we also ought to lay down our lives for the brethren. My little children, let us not love in word or in tongue, but in deed and in truth" (1 John 3:16, 18).*

It is impious to insist that those we are supposed to love earn God's blessings that have been freely given to us. We dare not share love in supercilious ways that will exalt Satan. If we do, then we are unappreciative and ruthless braggarts given that we are disguising our callousness with braggadocious conduct. We must share unconditional love in unassuming and bountiful ways that venerate God.

Freely, we receive from Him; freely, we must give.

He will not applaud a ninety-nine percent sharing of love and compassion when we can give a hundred percent.

We must give all of ourselves or give nothing at all!

- **Scriptural Confession: Luke 6:38; Acts 20: 35b; Romans 5:5;1 Corinthians 4:7**
- **Praise and Worship**
- **Pray These Prayers With a Heart of Repentance.**

1. Father, I repent for stretching your grace and taking your mercies for granted, in the name of Jesus.
2. I repent for using my behavior to control and manipulate others into meeting my needs, in the name of Jesus.

3. I repent of selfishness, wickedness, and everything that is unlike Christ in my life and relationships in the name of Jesus.

4. By the blood of Jesus Christ, I bind all witchcraft, Jezebel, and other exploitative spirits in my life and relationships, in the name of Jesus. I nullify their influences and control over my life and relationships, in the name of Jesus.

5. By the blood of Jesus, Satan, you will not use me against those I love, in the name of Jesus.

6. Let the spirit that is assigned to influence me to delay reconciliation be bound, in the name of Jesus

7. Let the powers that have vowed to destroy my divine relationships self-destruct, in the name of Jesus Christ.

8. I command every greedy and stingy spirit to get out of my life and relationships, in the name of Jesus.

9. Father God, thank you for all your manifold blessings, in the name of Jesus.

10. Almighty God, it is within my power to share your gratuitous gifts. Therefore, I choose to demonstrate love, extend forgiveness, and share peace freely. Freely I have received from you, and freely I give, in the name of Jesus.

11. Thank you, Lord, for your delivering power and answers to my prayers.

CHAPTER 15

A Call to Extinguish Conflict fires!

*We cannot swap our future
for a fleeting gratification of
carnality or fan the flames of past
generational bondage.*

"*Better a dry crust with peace and quiet than a house full of feasting, with strife*" (Proverbs 17: 1).
Dissension not only defeats God's motive for a relationship but also corrupts and weakens its strength. It hardens people's hearts against each other and God. Discord destroys mutual trust, dulls one's sensitivity, blocks the flow of communication, and hauls relationships to the dumps. We need to relinquish bitterness, yield to God, and embrace reconciliation. The need to manage or resolve conflict cannot be overstated.

Why Manage, Resolve or Extinguish Conflict Fires?
1). Extinguish conflict fire for God's sake.
You may have a lot of axe to grind with those that have offended you. We are ministers of reconciliation. *And all things are of God, who hath reconciled us to himself by Jesus Christ, and hath given*

to us the ministry of reconciliation *(2 Corinthians 5:18)*. It is your responsibility to handle fracas God's way because it is His will. Utilize Truth and your social skills to negotiate. Come to a compromise to please Him or you will have to pay the piper.

2). Defuse conflict bombs because too many lives are at stake.

Vendetta against others implies that your wellbeing and that of those around you are in the line of fire. Own up to your actions because your insubordination aggrieves God and threatens your relationships. Those attached to you may be dodging bullets in your crossfire, and their welfare is at stake. Remember, *"If the two big ox fight then the rubble gets the brunt."* Cessation of hostilities on all sides will do some good. Face the facts and be careful not to crush the hearts of those that are relying on you for strength and hope.

3). Quench conflict fire for love sake.

Reconciliation is the only proof that you love God and others. *"Love suffers long and is kind; love does not envy; love does not parade itself, is not puffed up; does not behave rudely, does not seek its own, is not provoked, thinks no evil; does not rejoice in iniquity, but rejoices in the truth; bears all things, believes all things, hopes all things, endures all things. Love never fails… And now abide faith, hope, love, these three; but the greatest of these is love"* (1 Corinthians 13:4-8; 13).

"And let us consider one another in order to stir up love and good works" (Hebrews 10:24).

"Let love be without hypocrisy. Abhor what is evil. Cling to what is good. Be kindly affectionate to one another with brotherly love, in honor giving preference to one another" (Romans 12:9-10).

"For all the law is fulfilled in one word, even in this; Thou shalt love thy neighbour as thyself" (Galatians 5:14).

We cannot really love God and not love others.

4). Find the middle ground for peace sake.

Don't make waves or rock the boat. Start the ball rolling and opt for peace. We are called to be peace makers. But *"Pursue peace with all people, and holiness, without which no one will see the Lord: looking carefully lest anyone fall short of the grace of God; lest any root of bitterness springing up cause trouble, and by this many become defiled" (Hebrews 12:14-15). "Therefore let us pursue the things which make for peace and the things by which one may edify another" (Romans 14:19).*

"If it is possible, as much as depends on you, live peaceably with all men" (Romans 12:18). "But the wisdom that is from above is first pure, then peaceable, gentle, willing to yield, full of mercy and good fruits, without partiality and without hypocrisy. Now the fruit of righteousness is sown in peace by those who make peace" (James 3:17-18). "…… Become complete. Be of good comfort, be of one mind, live in peace; and the God of love and peace will be with you" (2 Corinthians 13:11).

5). Settle arguments for your emotional, physical, and spiritual well- being.

Swallow the Truth pill to maintain your sanity and garner wisdom from the popular axiom: *"Bitterness is like drinking poison and expecting the other person to die."* We cannot imbibe the venom of wrath, antipathy, and pride, yet anticipate that an offender will be penalized by our foolish actions. We need to release resentment and free our souls from demonic enslavement. Conflict is unhealthy for the body, mind, soul, and spirit.

6). Resolve conflict for the sake of the children

I am amazed at some Christian counselors who use secular ideologies to contradict Scriptures when counseling couples or parents. Some erroneously counsel couples to dump their marriages if they are unhappy without considering the welfare of their children. They advocate that couples should not remain in a marriage simply because of their children; indicating that their needs or personal fulfillment should come first.

Marriage is not primarily about meeting only your needs or your mate's. Children are a significant part of a marriage covenant. Superimposing your desires on God's will for the kids is wickedness. By the same token, undermining their welfare to meet selfish needs is brutal.

Annulling a marriage union rebelliously is like jumping from the frying pan to fire because the children will pay dearly for your defiance. Immolating their welfare on the altar of your egocentricity will make them become the casualties of divorce. Thank God for audacious parents who see their children as an integral part of their marriage. They make sacrifices and stick it out amidst tumultuous times because they understand the perpetual damages that divorce could do to a child. Instead of filing for divorce to evade accountability, they continually set their needs aside and buffet their flesh to reconcile their differences for the welfare of the kids. I am very thankful that my courageous and forbearing mother, Comfort Aihebhoria, (God rest her soul) never gave up on her marriage, husband, and children. Her indomitable faith in God emboldened her to fight assiduously for her family amid turbulent times and propelled her to victory.

Often, we use the kids as justifications to dissolve a disintegrating relationship and affirm that, *"We are doing what is best for the children."* Often, we are not! We are only doing it to advance a selfish cause and dodge accountability. How about tossing disdain for meekness; vanity for contrition; and selfishness for altruism to salvage marriages for the interest of our children? My prayer is that each nation will enact a law that will force parents to stay together, confront their issues in a biblical manner, and raise their kids within the security of a healthy relationship.

Children can thrive only in a loving, stable, and peaceful home, not a war zone. God gave them to us *"for signs and wonders,"* not as scapegoats to bear our insecurities. They should not be used as sacrificial lambs to bear the pain of disappointments or as escape mechanisms to avoid self-accountability. Parents have a right to divorce each other and live apart if they choose to. However, their children also have a right to enjoy their love and nurturing under the same roof because they are a substantial part of the marriage. Our children do not deserve to be shuttled back and forth between parents in divorce or separation situations.

I shudder at parents that consider their own interest above their children's. When you allow conflict fire to burn down your marriage house, you fling the door wide open for your children and future generation to become susceptible to divorce. Children of divorced parents are more predisposed to opt for divorce. Until someone steps in and stops the destructive circle, they remain vulnerable to dysfunctional relationships. Yes, building a fruitful relationship can be exhausting. However, we must live by a righteous standard for our children to emulate. Since the paradigm we live by will sculpt their choices, we must accept responsibility and confront friction in our homes, not pass the buck to the next generation.

Like Father, Like Son...

The old maxim, "Like father, like son" is true. Fathers, when you do not live righteously, you are sending the wrong message to your sons and daughters. When you demonstrate anger, hatred, and bitterness in your associations, you are mentoring them to emulate your behavior in theirs as well. You are coaching them to become absentee husbands, brothers, fathers, cousins, uncles, nephews, and brethren. Physically they may be in a relationship but emotionally far-flung. If you are verbally, emotionally or physically abusive, you are handing them a whip to lambaste those within and outside their circle. To make matters worse, you are aiding and abetting your daughters to be attracted to men or husbands that are bitter, aloof, and evasive like you.

If you are married and endorse divorce, it will be so much easier for the children to embrace divorce as well. Their mentality will be: *"If dad and mom could not resolve their differences, why should I with my mate?" "Since mom and dad divorced, certainly*

I can." Our sons and daughters are under our tutelage and they are watching closely like a hawk. Our conduct must accurately illustrate what we believe.

"Like Mother, Like Daughter..."

The popular axiom, "Like mother, like daughter" is spot-on. When you refuse to live like a godly woman regardless of your stance, you are training your daughters to follow your footsteps. If you are controlling, you are imparting the spirit of Jezebel into them, and it will manifest in their marriages and relationships. They will rebel rather than submit to their potential husbands because you taught them how. Your blatant resistance to God's word will expose them to passive, controlling, domineering or abusive men or they will do the lashing out themselves. They will either become passive or possessive depending on their individual trait. Moreover, they will learn how to be absentee wives, aunties, nieces, cousins, sisters, mothers – substantially in a relationship but emotionally distant.

"Monkey see, Monkey do."

Live righteously to preserve your family's integrity. By demanding that others merit your love, you are teaching your children how to hoard or hawk love instead of sharing freely with others. You are impairing your sons and daughters when you compromise truth. Issues you rebuffed will become unresolved issues in their lives and relationships. Evading responsibility will make it so much easier for them to cut corners to avoid theirs as well. Weaknesses you do not deal with will be the same hang-ups they snub.

Camouflage your shortcomings, and they will learn how to mask theirs to evade change. Withholding forgiveness will teach them how to eat the sour grapes of bitterness, and their teeth will be set on edge. Resist reconciliation, and they will combat

135

reconciliation and will never learn how to give and take or find the middle ground in their relationships.

Shift the responsibility of dealing with pride and acrimony, and they too will shift accountability to their children. *Why?* They learnt by observing and encountering you daily. They will be inclined to mimic what you imparted as a way of life. Remember the adage, *"Monkey see, monkey do."*

Learn from Biblical History

Again, remember the old adages: *"Like father, like son." "Like mother, like daughter."* When Abraham lied about his wife Sarah to king Pharaoh and then to king Abimelech, king of Gerar to protect his life, he made it so much easier for his son, Isaac, to replicate his behavior (Genesis 12:11-20; 20:2-14). Isaac buckled under pressure and misrepresented his wife, Rebecca, before the men of Gerar to save his skin as well (Genesis 26:6-11). Remember, our children are watching intently.

Isaac and Rebecca not only played favorites with their children, Esau and Jacob, but also sowed sour grapes of bitterness in them (Genesis 25:28). It made it so much easier for them to follow suit. Like his parents, Jacob also favored one of his sons, Joseph, above others, and it incited conflict among his children (Genesis 37:3- 4). Esau sowed the seeds of bitterness into his children and his descendants, the Edomites' teeth were set on edge (Numbers 20:14-21). Children can easily absorb holiness or sin like a sponge.

David dented his kingship when he committed adultery with Bath-Sheba and killed Uriah to conceal his transgression. (Look up 2 Samuel chapters 11 &12.) Although God forgave him, the aftermath of an ephemeral indulgence of carnality lingered on for generations. His son Absalom not only toppled his kingdom and tried to assassinate him, but sexually defiled his concubines in the *"sight of all Israel"* (2 Samuel 16:20-22).

Because of David's sins, Israel was divided into the Northern and Southern kingdom. *"Bridget, it's my life. I can do whatever I like."* Really? *No, it's not yours.* Your life belongs to God, and

He can retrieve it at any time. Regardless of your beliefs, you are liable to Him. What you do is His business, your children's, the community's, and even ours. Each choice affects all and sundry because we are all interrelated.

Reconcile With Your Children

I understand the frustrations and challenges that some parents and children may have. However, we cannot use them to defend any form of resentment toward one another. We are parents forever and have a divine mandate to love our offspring unconditionally, pray, and shield them with the blood of Jesus.

Spiritually, it is dangerous to be at loggerheads with our children. Unforgiveness hinders prayers and God's blessings. Parents who refuse to reconcile with their children are deliberately handing them over to the enemy. The devil wants our sons and daughters but can never have them in the name of Jesus Christ.

"Bridget, you don't know my children! They don't care about my welfare!"

It hurts when parents feel betrayed and rejected by their children. However, we must learn to respond, not react to their poor choices so we are not collaborating with Satan to mar them. Never stop being a parent. Go out of your way to love and pray for them.

"Mike, my son does not talk to me! I call and leave messages, and he does not return my calls."

Don't give up! When you call, bless him, prophesy on him, leave a prayer regardless of whether he reciprocates or not. Eventually, God will use your love and obedience to melt his hardened heart.

"My children cannot stand me!"

Great! Here is a wonderful opportunity for God to manifest His power. Stay on your knees until you see the salvation of the Lord in this matter. What is your testimony if you are at war with your children? Remember, once you were a prodigal and rebellious child as well until your heavenly Father redeemed you from destruction. Even now, you still need His mercies because of your imperfections.

The devil is a twisted cantankerous demagogue whose goal is to incite conflict between parents and their children because he is insanely jealous of them. Don't become a victim! When you are not on speaking terms with a child, it opens the door to generational feuds and bondages. Slam the malice door! Punish Satan by obeying God. Take biblical steps to reconcile with your children and humiliate the enemy.

What will you impart in your children?

What will you entrust to your progeny? Consciously or unconsciously, you will either transfer a righteous or a worldly standard to your offspring, depending on the spiritual condition of your heart. We have no right to live carnally or expose our bloodline to demonic harassments. We must live sacrificially and uprightly to break the circle of ancestral oppression. It is deplorable to abort the divine destinies of our children on the rostrum of narcissism. We cannot trade our spiritual convictions for a bowl of self-gratification. Often, such perilous and fleeting pleasures of the flesh are only designed by the enemy to distort our focus and sway us from the truth, so we can make reckless choices that would bolster familial bondages.

Our daily decisions will either empower or cripple our children or make them victims or victors. We can either transfer or accept responsibility and release the next generation from satanic thralldom. Someone paid the price for us to be where we are today. Consequently, we must reciprocate the sacrifice, not drop the ball because of distorted priorities.

For the sake of posterity, we must pass the mantle of truth, faith, obedience, forgiveness, holiness, and deliverance to the next generation, not reinforce unbelief, idolatry, disobedience, lukewarmness, error, bitterness, ancestral sins or curses in our bloodlines.

7). Disable conflict bomb for the sake of the present and next generation.

When we quit on each other, we quit on the current and succeeding generation. Equally, when we belittle and maltreat each other, the consequences of waging a vendetta on others will rub off on them. One reason the younger generation is distraught is that they have no role models to emulate. Those who should be shepherding them are not only lost but have dysfunctional relationships. When we shun settlement, we are setting off a conflict bomb to obliterate a relationship that God has designed to bear fruits. While stubbornness will hamper the manifestation of God's power, it will aid the devil to intensify evil patterns of ungodliness in our lineage. If we hold on to hatred, the emerging generation will *"eat the sour grapes of bitterness and their teeth will be set on edge."* Whatever we refuse to resolve or repent of will eventually come back and deal with them.

Until we superimpose penitence over self-righteousness, crave obedience above rebellion, embrace brokenness more than we display arrogance, and choose passion for God over indolence, the trend of generational wantonness will continue to hamper current and prospective lineages. God has called us to be watchmen, watchwomen, and gate-keepers of our ancestries. He expects us to be vigilant, patrol the boundaries of our families, and deflect satanic intruders. We cannot afford to be lackadaisical or aid satanic encroachment. We must interject and halt the barrage of devilish activities in our homes, workplaces, communities, and Churches if we are to unshackle our bloodlines from demonic incarceration. Tell the devil to go to hell where he belongs!

- **Scriptural Confession: Psalm 36:11; Isaiah 54:17; Isaiah 45:2**
- **Praise and Worship**
- **Pray These Prayers with a Heart of Repentance.**

1. Father God, I repent of vanity, animosity, and all other sins in my life, in the name of Jesus.

2. By the blood of Jesus, let every root of sin, every seed of pride in me wither and die, in the name of Jesus Christ.
3. Everyone in my relationships – friends, associates, brethren, and loved ones belong to God. We are created in God's image and likeness. We are God's property.
4. Therefore, let the judgment of God fall on the power that refuses to release us, in the name of Jesus.
5. Let the fire of the Holy Spirit roast to ashes any strongman that wants to hold my loved ones in bondage, in the name of Jesus.
6. I use the blood of Jesus Christ to draw a demarcation between my loved ones and demonic activities, in the name of Jesus.
7. Let the blood of Jesus break and remove every barrier in my relationships, in the name of Jesus.
8. I use the blood of Jesus to slam the door against conflict now, in the name of Jesus.
9. By the blood of Jesus, I break and renounce every curse, evil covenants, conscious and unconscious ungodly vows I have made concerning my life, relationships, and children, in the name of Jesus.
10. Almighty God, let not the foot of pride come against my family and I and let not the hand of the wicked remove us, in the name of Jesus
11. By the anointing of the Holy Spirit, I silence every demonic voice instigating me against my brethren, friends, children, neighbor, all my relationships, and the will of God for my life, in the name of Jesus.
12. Thank you, Almighty Father, for doing more than I have requested, in the name of Jesus.

Chapter 16

Convey an Impactful Message

*The message we convey
through our choices
matters a great deal.*

What Message are You Sending?

We are erroneously taught to dump relationships that are not supposedly fluffing our egos, pacifying our demons, or benefiting our interests. If we do, the question is, how can we enlarge our capacity to become tolerant and empathetic of others if we connect only with those that make us happy? We need both thoughtful and insensitive people in our lives to keep us humble on our knees.

We are sending the wrong message if we feel that God places us in relationships just to address our needs. That is not the foremost reason He attaches us to people or we would be parasitic like the devil. The enemy takes what belongs to others but never sows anything good in their lives. God places us in relationships primarily to bear good fruits for the kingdom and cater to others' needs. As we relate to them biblically, our needs will be met as well. Nevertheless, we insist on accommodating only our needs because a controlling or an obsessive spirit is influencing us. When we place our interests above others, we are immolating their wellbeing on the altar of our egocentricity and creating casualties that will mar destinies. No one should take the fall for our narcissistic attitude and lack of self-accountability.

Spreading a Detrimental Message

We are tarnishing the name of Christ and propagating an atrocious message of hate when we are resentful of our family. It is typical for families to quarrel but abnormal and demonic not to resolve it. People have a chance to choose their friends, neighbors, colleagues or acquaintances, not relatives, God put kinsfolks together because He wants them to learn how to love and accommodate each other. Families that feud over lands, properties, money and other earthly things do not understand the value of divine relationships.

"I hate Tom, my brother!" I will never forgive him as long as I live!"

Well, you cannot claim to be a Christian and lock horns with your siblings or relatives. You have to extend an olive branch. If you insist on idolizing your hatred, you better not sin against God because He will not forgive you. Furthermore, do not waste your time giving offerings because He will not accept it until you forgive. (See Matthew 5:23-24.)

" I will never talk to my parents again!"

It is amazing how people consciously disobey Scriptures, disrespect, and harbor resentments against their parents, yet pray to live long. We profess to be believers, but willfully disobey God, dress up and go to church every Sunday, lift up filthy abominable hands before Him, and expect Him to do our bidding. *"Honor your father and mother so that you may live long on earth"* is a mandate, not a suggestion. Respect them whether you feel that they deserve it or not. If not, you will pollute your offspring with hatred and continue the sinful trend. The devil will ensure that he reinforces the bitterness in subsequent generations. Close that door with repentance and watch how God would reward your obedience. I pray that you will reconcile with your parents and send the right message.

"I will never reconcile with my sister, Lucy – if I could get away with it."

No one can escape the ramifications of unforgiveness or disobedience. When you sever family ties on your terms, you fling the door wide open for future generations attached to such relationships to become susceptible to conflict as well. We must reconcile our differences to avoid the perpetual damages that the enemy could do to sabotage our divine relationships. Regardless of how grueling it is to build healthy relationships; we must live by example and establish a righteous standard for others to emulate. The paradigm we live by will sculpt our homes, market places, neighborhoods, and Churches. We must accept responsibility and confront friction in our interrelations.

"I love my children and will never do anything purposely to hurt them! How are my choices affecting them?"

When you lie, gossip, backslide, commit adultery, divorce, dabble in the occult or persistently engage in any ungodly conduct, you are opening the door of their lives to the enemy. Also, you are intensifying ancestral bondage and empowering him to exploit and weaken them naturally and spiritually.

Some children are distressed because they are reaping the repercussions of past parental disobedience. Many are struggling with diverse problems because we, the parents or somebody in the bloodline dropped the ball. Someone opened the door to addictions, immorality, idolatry, witchcraft, spirits of perversion, and a range of ancestral iniquities that may be afflicting them. Thus, they are replicating the generational sins from a polluted foundation. They will be emancipated to maximize their potentials only when we close that doorway through repentance.

Enough!

It is wrong to trample on our children's rights or deny them their generational blessings. They cannot continue to be in thrall to the oppressor because we are not raising a pious standard to buffer their destinies. Indeed, the blood of Jesus has liberated them. However, when we live soulishly, we are replicating the same deadly sinful pattern from the past, and liaising with the enemy to impair them. If we are not modeling Christ or cultivating a godly environment to "train them in righteousness," we are aiding and abetting the enemy to mar their potentials.

If we are not living holy and ardently mentoring our children to hunger and thirst for righteousness, we are a significant part of the problem. *"Oh Bridget, don't say that! I do more than enough for my children!"* The question is not how much we are splurging on them but how much of Christ we are imparting in them. That is the bottom line. We seem to be doing everything else except the most needed, which will never be taken away from them (Luke 10:38-42). It is a disservice to invest more in developing their natural knowledge than faith or personal relationship with God. Yes, we want them to excel in life. However, we cannot afford to rob their divine destinies to pay for sublunary exploits just because we want them to attain a higher socioeconomic status. We should be just as passionate about equipping them to live biblically as we are about cheering them to acquire material gains.

Parents have more work to do than their children. Like unbelievers, we are caught up in the rat race and hardly have time to fast, pray fervently, study the word or volunteer to help others as we ought. We yearn for the mundane rather than the supernatural because we are earthly minded. We prefer mediocrity to excellence; hence, we hideout in our comfort zone. We are complacent, spiritually lethargic, and want everything for nothing. We would rather have what God has in His hands than His heart and desperately hanker for His miracles than His ways. We want to reap the fruits of the kingdom without sowing obedience. Often, we excuse disobedience on the merits of God's grace, mercy, and love because we have no reverential fear of

Him. We forget that *"It is a fearful thing to fall into the hands of the living God.* Although He is a loving God, *He is also "a consuming fire" (Hebrews 10:31; 12:29).*

We are sending the wrong message because our marriages, Churches, interpersonal relationships, and mode of life are nothing to sing about. Our children watch us squabble, cheat on our taxes, lie without a flinch, flirt with adultery, engage in abuse, gossip about folks, dabble in the occult, toy with divorce, belittle each other, act fraudulently, settle for a Pharisaical standard, use alcohol, illegal drugs, pornography, and various perversions to dissimulate and assuage our hang-ups. Enough of the jiggery-pokery in Christendom! We must atone for our sins, close the revolving door that the enemy is using to access our offspring's lives, and denounce ungodliness to unshackle them. We need to buckle down to practice the tenets of our faith, rid ourselves of what is in us that magnetizes the devil, pursue God zealously, and be the standard-bearer for the cause of the kingdom.

Our homes should be an oasis of holiness amidst the mayhem of a dissolute world. We ought to be marshaling and training our children to be kingdom warriors, not spiritual whips. We need to shepherd them with Truth, so they too can forge ahead and chaperon their own offspring with the same Truth. We should be generation builders and strengtheners that pioneer repentance and change. We need to be familial restorers, societal transformers, and environmental influencers that push the envelope with faith, break new grounds for the kingdom, steer the wheel of righteousness, fan the flame of revival, and shine the light of the gospel. We and our sons and daughters are the conquering generations that must seek the face of God and live radically to execute His purpose.

Rahab Intercepted Ancestral Bondage

Interpersonal relationships that are plagued by hordes of unresolved issues are more predisposed to demonic exploitations. Until someone steps in and interrupts the destructive circle, they remain vulnerable to satanic intrusion.

How do you interrupt bondage in a family, business, Church or community?

We do by praying fervently and living virtuously for Christ. Firstly, take authority over strongholds and break their power over your life, family or divine associations, in the name of Jesus. Utilize the blood and name of Jesus to reverse curses and demolish yokes that Satan is utilizing to bind them.

Secondly, break the evil or sinful pattern by living uprightly. *Do you have a vendetta against your children? Are you at loggerheads with a sibling, colleague, brother or sister in Christ? Is there a misunderstanding between you and your parents? Are you feuding with a friend?* Interrupt the flow of resentments with forgiveness, misunderstandings with tolerance, and other feuds with reconciliation. Forgive or risk the sour grapes of bitterness spreading like a cankerworm in your alliances. Establish a new pattern of righteousness, raise a new standard of character, and walk in the newness of God.

It is never too late to repent, renounce sin, break generational shackles and intercept the evil patterns that plagued your alliances. Like Rahab, someone has to say, *"Enough of the conflict, sexual perversion, drug addiction, malice, idolatry, curses, alcoholism, oppression, diseases, failures, abuse, late marriage, jealousy, divorce, stagnancy, hatred, polluted foundation, poverty, lies, and demonic captivity in my lineage, neighborhood, business, Church, and relationships!"* Somebody has to stand up for truth and break the yoke! The repulsiveness of satanic enslavement has to grieve us enough to crave and pursue repentance and deliverance.

Rahab came to a point in her life where the abhorrence of her carnal lifestyle drove her to God. She did not wake up one day to find the two spies mysteriously in her home without previously crying out to God for help. Remember, she said to the men: *"I know that the LORD has given you the land, that the terror of you has fallen on us, and that all the inhabitants of the land are fainthearted because of you. For we have heard how the LORD dried up the water of the Red Sea for you when you came out of Egypt, and what you did to the two kings of the Amorites who were on the other side of the Jordan, Sihon and Og, whom you utterly destroyed. And as soon as we heard these things, our hearts melted; neither did there remain any more courage in anyone because of you, for the LORD your God, He is God in heaven above and on earth beneath. Now therefore, I beg you, swear to me by the LORD, since I have shown you kindness, that you also will show kindness to my father's house, and give me a true token, and spare my father, my mother, my brothers, my sisters, and all that they have, and deliver our lives from death"* *(Joshua 2:9-13).*

Rahab's heart melted due to the providence and sovereignty of God. She was disgusted with her perverted lifestyle because she understood the repercussions of falling into the hands of a holy God. Consequently, she yearned for His deliverance, the divine protection of her ancestry, and a new mode of life. The danger of continuing her promiscuity and possibly infecting her future generations with sin drove her to halt the evil pattern she once fueled. She resolved to raise a holy standard. Therefore, when the spies showed up on her doorsteps, it was the answer to prayer. She was ready! She seized the moment and utilized her obedience to change the course of history.

Rahab repented of harlotry and assisted the Israelites in fulfilling God's will. *"Likewise, was not Rahab the harlot also justified by works when she received the messengers and sent them out another way?"* *(See James 2:25.)* The fear of God compelled her to risk her life to protect the spies. Thus, she became a woman of faith and the catalyst that rescued her lineage from annihilation. *"By faith the harlot Rahab did not perish with those who did not believe when she had received the spies with peace"* *(Hebrews 11:31).* Her compliance with God and the Israelis preserved her bloodline and placed her in the "hall of faith." (See Joshua 2:1-21; 6:17, 22-25.) It also positioned her in the lineage of the Lord Jesus. *"Salmon begot Boaz by Rahab, Boaz begot Obed by Ruth, Obed begot Jesse, and Jesse begot David the king... And Jacob begot Joseph the husband of Mary, of whom was born Jesus who is called Christ"* *(Matthew 1:5-16).*

What is your Assignment? What are you called to transform, redeem, heal, restore, or revive in your family, community, Church, workplace or generation?
You are assigned to say or do what no one is willing to say or do, go beyond where others have been, and confront what others dread to activate restoration. Identify what has been torn down in your place of worship, home, work or neighborhood and rebuild it. Discern what is lukewarm and revive it; what is polluted and cleanse it; and what is broken and fix it! Find the lost, heal the wounded, rescue the endangered, and set the captives free. Rather than shift responsibility, welcome the opportunity to become a trailblazer of hope, healing, and change. Life is not about how much we can get, but give. We must become aggressive about the healing and restoration of our Churches, families, communities and alliances more than ever before.

God Deserves Veneration, Not mockery

Our families, neighbors, coworkers, unbelievers, children, and even our adversaries are watching intently to see how we respond or react to difficult circumstances in life. Our responses will sculpt or influence their behavior. Those who insist on wallowing in skirmishes or splitting godly relationships only for personal gains are conveying an iniquitous message and living a dual standard. Their wrong mindset will rub off on others. Unless they repent, God will hold them accountable for the lives they negatively influenced by their actions.

The devil wants people to labor in vain and utilize their hands to demolish relationships that they have built over the years. It is deception, foolishness, and satanic sabotage in the highest order to put God's credibility on the line and destroy relationships we have invested in for years. When we trade meaningful ties for acrimony to mollify the flesh, we dissuade others from paying the price to obey God.

The sovereign God has given up so much for our welfare. We can no longer take His goodness, mercies, and forbearance for granted. He deserves our veneration, not mockery. We need to be mindful of the fact that although He is a caring Father, He is also *"a consuming fire." "It is a fearful thing to fall into the hands of the living God" (Hebrews 10:31).* The ramifications of tempting and deriding Him are awful.

A Fallacious and Horrendous Message

When we refuse to repent, extend benignity, share forgiveness or opt for reconciliation, these are some of the awful messages we are blatantly and allusively conveying to our children, families, neighbors, colleagues, unbelievers, Churches, and future generations:

"Children are worthless and have no rights. Therefore, we can sacrifice their well-being on the dais of our egotism. We can superimpose our selfish needs on them, bruise their souls with the trauma of conflict, and use them as bargaining chips to get our way. We can utilize them as dumping grounds to absolve our disappointments and sacrificial lambs to bear our sins."

"The word of God is a lie. It may work for others, but certainly not for us. We do not have to obey every word of God. We have a right to cherry-pick only Scriptures that validate our mentality. Bravo to pride, stubbornness, selfishness, and immaturity!"

"We loath self-responsibility and are only accountable to ourself, not to anyone or even God. We are living to please ourself, not God. We care more about our personal gratification and meeting our needs more than paying the price to lay a solid and godly foundation for the next generation. Sacrifice and obedience are archaic; it should not be a blueprint for life."

"It is okay to Band-Aid your issues and conceal them under a relationship rug. Be lazy and passive about resolving your issues because they are just too messy. Defend your blind spots, excuse your hang-ups, and utilize your gender, culture, status, and experiences to masquerade your faults."

"It is futile to live and die by your spiritual convictions. Consequently, true love is not worth risking our convictions for.

We ought to unconditionally love only those who conform to our sense of reality and loathe those who do not agree with us."

"You do not have to turn the other cheek or absolve others if it is not in your best interest. It is all right to retaliate because God is too merciful and slow to anger. He will let our 'enemies' go scot-free. So, vengeance is ours, not His."

"The marriage covenant is not sacred or worth fighting for. Commitment, endurance, forgiveness, compassion, tolerance, and faith are insignificant. Marital vows are meaningless. We can swap spouses as often as we trade our cars."

"You can walk away from godly relationships when you can't have your way. It is alright to corroborate with the devil to labor in vain and throw away years of love, blissful memories, and future possibilities because we are exhausted, exasperated, and can no longer trust God to work out our differences."

"Why should I care? After all, God cannot be trusted to heal interpersonal relationships, especially mine. Irreconcilable differences and incompatibility issues are too complex for Him to solve. I don't have to obey Him or consider His options."

"Let's continue the trend of abuse, unbelief, living a lie, carnality, disobedience, divorce, and chastise others for our own shortcomings. Let us shift the responsibility of obedience, repentance, transformation, and deliverance to the next generation."

"The Lord rebuke thee, O Satan...." (Zechariah 3:2, Jude 9). Satan, the blood of Jesus Christ is against you! God will empower us to proclaim and practice the redemptive and transformative message of the gospel, in the name of Jesus.

Why impart a message of redemption and change?
We should because others will be drawn to God and encounter Him through us. It is an effective way to lead by example and effectuate change. Besides, it is the right thing to do. If you genuinely love God more than your pride, bitterness, and anger, set your grudges aside, come to grips with your fallibility, and use the word of God to harmonize your differences. Why bother to live righteously if our faith does not hold water? Of what benefit

is our ambassadorship to the kingdom of God if we are not willing to truly represent Him?

Spiritual indolence, selfishness, lack of accountability, fear, stubbornness, unbelief, bitterness, wickedness or the works of the flesh is not our portion, in the mighty name of Jesus. We must shun disagreements and embrace peace. How we respond to discord is an ideological litmus test of faith. Convey the right message, pass the test, and proceed to the next level.

- **Scriptural Confession: Psalm 36:11; Isaiah 54:17; 45:2**
- **Praise and Worship**
- **Pray These Prayers with a Heart of Repentance.**

1. By the blood of Jesus, I repent of selfishness, unforgiveness, exposing my children and future generations to demonic harassment, in the name of Jesus.
2. Lord Jesus, I repent in ways that I have compromised my faith, dishonored you by my conduct, and disparaged others, in the name of Jesus.
3. I bind every restless, wandering or vagabond spirit that is causing me to feel restless, unsettled, and paranoid in my relationships, in the name of Jesus.
4. I bind the spirits that incite "fear to love," "fear to forgive," "fear to trust," "fear of betrayal", "fear of vulnerability," "fear of commitment," "fear of rejection," "fear of failure," and "fear of man," in the name of Jesus. I command them to release me right now, in the mighty name of Jesus.
5. I bind the argumentative spirits, in the name of Jesus.
6. I hold the blood of Jesus Christ against every power that wants to occupy my relationships and chase out those who are connected to me, in the name of Jesus.
7. Satan, you are the stranger and prowler in my relationships! I command you to leave right now, in the name of Jesus.
8. Blood of Jesus, nullify every generational curse that has kept us in demonic captivity, in the name of Jesus. O God, bless our familial line, in the name of Jesus.

9. Let the blood of Jesus cancel the evil patterns of adultery, divorce, conflict, immorality, rebellion, addictions, barrenness, perversion, idolatry, and sin (include all the problems that run in your family) that have been manifesting in my lineage and relationships, in the name of Jesus Christ.
10. Blood of Jesus, be transfused into our bloodline, cleanse and heal our ancestral foundation, in the name of Jesus.
11. Let the blood of Jesus Christ reestablish new patterns of holiness, obedience, peace, fruitfulness, faith, blissful marriages, the fruit of the Holy Spirit, household salvation, healing, deliverance restoration, repentance, and revival, in my bloodline, in the mighty name of Jesus.
12. Thank you, Mighty Deliverer, for doing more than I have requested in your precious name.

Make This Declaration.

- By the blood of Jesus, I will not utilize my own hands to scatter the godly relationships I have built over the years, in the name of Jesus.
- By the blood of Jesus, I will not stubbornly detach from those whom God has connected me to, in the name of Jesus.
- By the blood of Jesus, I refuse to buy into any lie or seduction of the devil, in the name of Jesus.
- Those in my relationships will not labor in vain concerning their families, children, ministry, business, career, and all that God has placed in their hands, in the name of Jesus
- By the power of the Holy Spirit, we shall reap the fruits of our labors concerning our relationships and the work of our hands, in the name of Jesus.
- I choose to release reconciliation into my relationships, in the name of Jesus.

CHAPTER 17

"How You Treat Others is How You Treat Me."

When we deny others what is within our power to give – acceptance, love, appreciation, validation or peace; we deny the Lord as well.

It is sad but true that many will end up in hell because they claim to love God but maltreat those connected to them. Often, we allege to love God that we have not seen but have only accepted by faith, but despise those we see and relate to daily. *"We love Him because He first loved us. If someone says, "I love God," and hates his brother, he is a liar; for he who does not love his brother whom he has seen, how can he love God whom he has not seen? And this commandment we have from Him: that he who loves God must love his brother also"* (1 John 4:19-21).

We need to take an inventory of how we treat people. What we do for others, we do for the Lord, and whatever good we withhold from them, we withhold from Him as well. Hence, we must be mindful of how we treat each other because the consequences of maltreating others are grievous. Would we want to disrespect, maltreat, verbally, or physically abuse the Lord?

Would we be angry, hostile or vindictive when we do not get our way? We might say, "Never!" However, these are acts of wickedness we exhibit against Him when we ill-treat others.

"Treat Them Right, Treat Me Right"

Let us examine the following Scripture and see how it relates to a relationship.

"Then the King will say to those on His right hand, 'Come, you blessed of My Father, inherit the kingdom prepared for you from the foundation of the world: for I was hungry and you gave Me food; I was thirsty and you gave Me drink; I was a stranger and you took Me in; I was naked and you clothed Me; I was sick and you visited Me; I was in prison and you came to Me.

"Then the righteous will answer Him, saying, 'Lord, when did we see You hungry and feed You, or thirsty and give You drink? When did we see You a stranger and take You in, or naked and clothe You? Or when did we see You sick, or in prison, and come to You?' And the King will answer and say to them, 'Assuredly, I say to you, inasmuch as you did it to one of the least of these My brethren, you did it to Me" (Mathew 25:34-40). In essence, this is what the Lord is saying: "Whatever you do for a neighbor, parent, boss, stranger, friend, colleague, sister or brother in Christ, siblings, spouse, and other relatives, you do for me."

Esteeming others is an indication that we are revering the Lord. Demeaning them means we are belittling Him as well. The acts of endearment we cheerfully sow into their lives are symbols of obedience and worship we offer to the Lord. Displays of affections, exhibitions of appreciation, tokens of forgiveness, affirmations of loyalty, illustrations of gentleness, gestures of empathy, and expressions of unconditional acceptance are oblations unto the Lord.

Deeds of tolerance show we cherish His mercy. Evincing gratitude reveals our indebtedness to Him. Personifying patience indicates we also need His forbearance. Commitment to people reveals our allegiance to Him. Sowing mercy means we recognize our fallibility and the need for leniency as well. Loving and accepting others prove our genuine love for a holy God who wholly loves and accepts us as we are. *"But do not forget to do good and to share, for with such sacrifices God is well pleased" (Hebrews 13:16).*

"Maltreat them, Maltreat Me"

It is imperative to note how the Lord feels about hoarding what we should be sharing freely with others. *"Then He will also say to those on the left hand, 'Depart from Me, you cursed, into the everlasting fire prepared for the devil and his angels: for I was hungry and you gave Me no food; I was thirsty and you gave Me no drink; I was a stranger and you did not take Me in, naked and you did not clothe Me, sick and in prison and you did not visit Me.' "Then they also will answer Him, saying, 'Lord, when did we see You hungry or thirsty or a stranger or naked or sick or in prison, and did not minister to You?' Then He will answer them, saying, 'Assuredly, I say to you, inasmuch as you did not do it to one of the least of these, you did not do it to Me.' And these will go away into everlasting punishment, but the righteous into eternal life" (Mathew 25:41-46).*

This is what the Lord is saying when we are selfish: "Whatever you do not do for a neighbor, friend, stranger, relative, brethren, coworker or others, you do not do for me." Are you hoarding or peddling what is within your power to *freely give*? This Scripture connotes that when we deny others what is within our power to give, we deny the Lord as well. When we withhold the *"fruit of the Spirit"* – love, joy, peace, and the like, we are selfishly *"stockpiling"* what we should be sharing liberally. We hoard love because we dread accountability, vulnerability, and rejection. We want others to earn our love. Also, withholding love is another way of punishing people and compensating for the frustrations of not being able to control them.

Based on Scriptures, whether we respond to others positively or negatively, we are relating to the Lord. When we disparage those, we are assigned to inspire, we are belittling the Lord Jesus.

When we badger people, we are nagging Him. The Israelites murmured against Moses and Aaron in the wilderness because they did not want to exercise their faith. Moses reminded them that their murmuring was not against him or Aaron but against God. *"Do all things without complaining and disputing, that you may become blameless and harmless, children of God without fault in the midst of a crooked and perverse generation, among whom you shine as lights in the world" (Philippians 2:14-15).*

Snubbing others to upbraid them implies you are penalizing the Lord with your silent treatment. When you are resentful at a parent, you are embittered at Him also. Think twice before you say anything because when you slander a brother or sister in Christ, you are insulting the Lord. You will be liable for your vilification and wrath directed at Him.

When you engage in physical abuse and strike a spouse, brother or sister, you are scourging the Lord, and you will take the rap for each lash! Can you handle the aftermath of lashing at the One who created you in His image and likeness? Unjustly pointing the finger at a Pastor, brethren or congregant signifies that you are imputing the Lord for your own shortcomings. Embracing fornication, adultery, pornography, dabbling into the demonic or galivanting from one Church to another without committing to one is indicative of your unfaithfulness to the Lord. When you impede reconciliation, you are snubbing the Lord to venerate your arrogance. Electing to stubbornly abscond a godly relationship on your terms unveils your apathy about Him. Lying or *"Sowing discord among brethren"* means you are dividing His body and are in direct opposition to His prayer in John chapter 17, verses 21 and 23.

Let's read the Scripture again. *"Then He will answer them, saying, 'Assuredly, I say to you, inasmuch as you did not do it to one of the least of these, you did not do it to Me."* This denotes that when we decline to meet others' needs, make them feel lovable, desirable, appreciated, celebrated or validated when it is within our power, we are shrewdly withholding loving deeds that would laud Him. He created us to give Him glory, pleasure, and to show forth His praise (Isaiah 43:7; Revelation 4:11).

Does God get the glory in how you relate to your relatives, friends, Pastors, neighbors or colleagues? Do your reflections, words, and responses show forth His praise? How we relate to others venerate or disparage Him. He is highly delighted by acts of kindness and deeply grieved by acts of hostility.

"Love and Submit to Me Through Others"

The Lord wants us to love Him through our connections. *"Assuredly, I say to you, inasmuch as you did it to one of the least of these My brethren, you did it to Me" (Mathew 25:40).* When others are yearning for our love, the Lord is craving our affection. The Lord wants to melt our hard-edged hearts so we can minister to Him through them. Therefore, when we deliberately suppress love and compassion, we are starving Him of the free gifts He gave us to share. However, when we show love, we are showering love on Him. There is nothing as fulfilling as magnifying the Lord when we demonstrate acts of kindness.

We are called to submit to the Lord through the people He has assigned to us. However, it is unbiblical to submit to sin, error or anything that dishonors Him. He wants to moisten our austere heart through others so we can be teachable and lovingly yield to him. Therefore, if you resist submission, you are rebelling against the Lord, not people. Nevertheless, submitting to authority, and each other implies we are yielding, ministering, worshipping the Lord with our obedience. We must esteem the Lord by yielding to each other.

God is the quintessence of love, benignity, and long-suffering. More than anything, He wants us to manifest His character so others will encounter Him through us. It has been said that "The apple does not fall far from the tree." We need to develop the *"fruit of the Spirit"* and starve the *"works of the flesh"* so we can become more like our heavenly Father. Behaving unlike Him is a display of egoism and disregard for Him and others. Not reciprocating His benevolence signifies that we are uncaring.

Abstain From What Causes Others to Sin

"Therefore, if food makes my brother stumble, I will never again eat meat, lest I make my brother stumble" (1 Corinthians 8:13). "Meat" or "food" is figurative of whatever will cause others to err or make them vulnerable to transgression. God will hold us accountable when we instigate others against Him or drag them through the mud. We must share love without strings attached to minister healing and alleviate others' burdens.

Are you deliberately provoking others to sin with your fury?

Are you doing things to exasperate their vulnerability?

Are you invoking distressful emotions to drive them further away from God? "And through thy knowledge shall the weak brother perish, for whom Christ died? But when you thus sin against the brethren and wound their weak conscience, you sin against Christ" (1 Corinthians 8:11-12).

Often, our behavior affects others. Reacting with arrogance will fan the flames of superciliousness in others. Exhibiting jealousy will intensify their paranoia and insecurities. *"Wounding their conscience,"* will cause them to erect emotional walls to wade us off. Withholding endearment will exacerbate feelings of rejection. Castigating them will coerce them to succumb to our immensely lofty expectations. *"But why dost thou judge thy brother? or why dost thou set at nought thy brother? for we shall all stand before the judgment seat of Christ.... So then every one of us shall give account of himself to God. Let us not therefore judge one another any more: but judge this rather, that no man put a stumbling block or an occasion to fall in his brother's way" (Romans 14:10,12-13).*

Exhibiting hostility will evoke their cynicism; verbally or physically abusing them will rend their souls, controlling them will tie them in knot, and Rejecting them will impel them to walk on eggshells in a relationship. Giving them the silent treatment will isolate them in a corner; shifting responsibility will rouse their self-righteousness; and trying to change them will not only harden their hearts but also keep them at bay. How we conduct ourselves can invoke either a positive or negative response in others. Hence, we must respond in ways that please God, not self.

"For even Christ did not please Himself; but as it is written, "The reproaches of those who reproached You fell on Me" (Romans 15:3). "Therefore let us pursue the things which make for peace and the things by which one may edify another. Do not destroy the work of God for the sake of food. All things indeed are pure, but it is evil for the man who eats with offense. It is good neither to eat meat nor drink wine nor do anything by which your brother stumbles or is offended or is made weak" (Romans 14:19-21).

"I Beseech You Brethren..."

Brethren, I appeal to all and sundry reading this book, especially leaders and workers in the Vineyard – Apostles, Teachers, Pastors, Evangelists, Prophets, Fathers, Mothers, business professionals, Musicians, Armor-bearers, Intercessors, Church workers, and anyone that serves in the body of Christ. I implore you in the name of our Lord Jesus, who counted us worthy to serve His people. Let us accept responsibility and personify His character in our homes, workplace, communities, relationships, Churches, not pass self-centeredness, self-righteousness, and lack of accountability to our children or the next generation.

Although we are human, God holds us to a higher standard. *"To whom much is given, much is required" (Luke 12:48b).* Our relationship with God defines our relationship with others. If we claim to love Him but detest those He has called to us, we are just as duplicitous as the Pharisees and Sadducees were. The only proof that we love Him is when we keep His commandments and do those things that are pleasing in His sight (John 14:15).

Often, we make all kinds of promises to God because we feel that is what He wants to hear. In reality, when it comes to obeying Him, it is a different ball game. We back out and make excuses to relieve our conscience. Obedience is the only evidence that we truly love Him, not our empty promises or acclamations of love and devotion. *"Now by this we know that we know Him, if we keep His commandments. He who says, "I know Him," and does not keep His commandments, is a liar, and the truth is not in him. But whoever keeps His word, truly the love of God is perfected in him. By this we know that we are in Him. He who says he abides in Him ought himself also to walk just as He walked" (1 John 2:3-6).*

If we claim to be His emissaries, we must not only love in words but also in deed and in truth (1 John 3:18). He is the embodiment of forgiveness, the quintessence of compassion, and the archetype of love. Though we have to buckle down, we must exhibit unconditional love to the fullest capacity to accurately represent Him

We Must First Drink Our Medicine

It is the greatest honor to represent Christ and minister to His people. If you are a believer or Minister of the gospel that has relationship challenges, use the word of God to resolve them. Please, harbor no grudge. Go easy on your kinsfolks, close and distant associates. Oh Please, let bygones be bygones and accommodate them for Christ's sake. Sometimes, God uses others' flaws to reveal our own weaknesses and intolerance. The fact that we are irritated at another human being is proof of our fallibility.

Every so often, we preach assertively on the pulpit while we do some "calisthenics jigs" to depict saintliness and staunch faith. We fervently tell others that Jesus saves and heals but will not allow Him to save or heal our alliances. We minister the gospel of restoration but remain emotionally broken and internally deformed. How can we herald a message of forgiveness but exhibit bitterness, propagate repentance yet manifest rebellion, and preach meekness but parade haughtiness? It is wrong to orate piety but display superciliousness or spread goodwill but then again exhibit intolerance in our relationships.

We profess that God detests noncommitment, yet swap relationships as often as we trade our cars. We prescribe and dispense the medicine of the gospel to humanity but refuse to imbibe it ourselves. Are we suggesting that the gospel will work only for others and not for us? Which gospel are we promulgating

– Christ's or a Seeker friendly and Seeker-sensitive adulterated doctrine that appeals to secular humanism?

It is a dual standard to "preachify" faith but exhibit fear, dish out the gospel of peace but have turbulent unions, use Truth to proselytize others but resist Truth, and teach repentance but shun genuine conversion of the heart. It is iniquitous to herald the love of God but exhibit antipathy in our interpersonal relationships. Our relationships are as dysfunctional as the unbeliever's because we know Truth but deliberately refuse to apply it. We natter and play like them and wonder why we have little or no victories. As Isaiah said, *"Why should you be stricken again? You will revolt more and more. The whole head is sick, And the whole heart faints. From the sole of the foot even to the head, There is no soundness in it, But wounds and bruises and putrefying sores; They have not been closed or bound up, Or soothed with ointment"* (Isaiah 1:5-6).

Is God not big enough to heal our lives and relationships? *"Is there no balm in Gilead, Is there no physician there? Why then is there no recovery For the health of the daughter of my people?"* *(See Jeremiah 8:22.)* Jesus is the only healing balm for human depravity. Until we begin to apply His truths, the world will always wonder why our lives and relationships are as maladjusted as theirs. We must heed the world's cry – *"Physician, heal thy self.... Drink thy own medicine."* Repentance, transformation, and revival must begin with us.

"If the LORD be God" Let's Serve Him in Truth

The Word of God sharply juxtaposes heaven and hell, faith and unbelief, light and darkness, carnality and spirituality, life and death, truth and error, righteousness and depravity, the fruit of the Spirit and the works of the flesh, the straight and the narrow path and the wide and the broad lane, and the blessings of obedience and the penalties of disobedience. It is sobering to note that there are no shades of grey between these biblical and worldly distinctions. It is either we are hot or cold, believers or infidels, expressing the character of God or evincing the traits of Satan, doing exploits for the kingdom of God or validating the kingdom of darkness, raising a paradigm of righteousness or compromising our *"most holy faith."* The days of practicing two sets of rules are over! *"If the LORD be God,"* then, let us repudiate idolatry, idols of the heart, rebellion, the lies we tell ourselves, and give all our devotions to Him.

To ignite the fire of revival in our homes, communities, marketplaces, and Churches, we must imbibe our own medicine before offering it to the world. Furthermore, we must know and apply truth to make us free. The devil is unredeemable because he is the author of sin. He knows and trembles at truth but cannot apply it (James 2:19). Others will embrace the Word only if there is proof that It is transforming our lives.

We must learn to forbear with each other even if we must suffer for righteousness sake, accept wrong when we are innocent, and sow ourselves as seeds for God to get the glory. The power of the gospel must influence our relationships so that unbelievers will be attracted to Him. If we are willing to receive and apply truth, it will dramatically revolutionize how we relate to each other. When we begin to treat others as we would treat the Lord, our relationships would be whole, and others would be drawn to Him by our way of living.

Those who are building covenant relationships and venerating God with obedience deserve Kudos for yielding themselves to Him. He will count your assiduous attitude as righteousness. However, those that are flaunting the works of the flesh in their relationships have the opportunity to tap into God's forgiveness and embrace change right now through the power of the Holy Spirit. Remember, we are called to laud and appreciate the Lord in our relationships. *"But ye are a chosen generation, a royal priesthood, an holy nation, a peculiar people; that ye should shew forth the praises of him who hath called you out of darkness into his marvellous light"* (1 Peter 2:9).

- **Scriptural Confession: Isaiah 50:4, Philippians 4:6-7, Philippians 2:3b**
- **Praise and Worship**

- **Prayer Points**

1. Oh God, may my life, relationships, and all that pertains to me bring you joy, praise, glory, and pleasure, in the name of Jesus.
2. Father God, let your holy name be glorified in my life and all that concerns me, in the name of Jesus.
3. Lord, let your power, glory, presence, anointing, and character that are manifested in my life draw others to you, in the name of Jesus.
4. The devil will not use my ignorance and stubbornness against the people assigned to me, in the name of Jesus.
5. The devil will not use the ignorance and stubbornness of those within and outside my inner circle against me, in the name of Jesus.
6. Lord God, give me "the tongue of the learned to know how to speak a word in season to him that is weary." Awake my ear every morning to hear you, in the name of Jesus
7. I "shall be careful for nothing, but in everything by prayer and supplication, with thanksgiving," I shall let my requests be made known to God; and the peace of God, which surpasses all understanding, will guard my heart, mind, and relationships through Christ Jesus.
8. Let the fire of the Holy Spirit torment all the powers that are assigned to discourage me from emulating the character of Christ, in the name of Jesus.
9. Let the blood of Jesus Christ scatter every evil altar speaking against the purpose of God for my life and relationships, in the name of Jesus.
10. Let the fire of God destroy anything on any evil altar that is been used against my loved ones, in the name of Jesus.
11. By the blood of Jesus, I nullify every conflict, confusion, anxiety, depression, rivalry, divorce or evil programmed into my life and relationships, in the name of Jesus.
12. I bind the spirit of confusion, in the name of Jesus.
13. Oh God, release love, peace, understanding, compassion, and the fruit of the Spirit in my associations, in the name of Jesus.

14. I choose to esteem others, in the name of Jesus.
15. Thank you, my Father, for the confidence that I have in You. You have heard me and will grant my heart desires, in the name of Jesus Christ.

CHAPTER 18

Who to "Fight" When in Conflict

Take the fight to the devil, not people.
He is the real villain and malevolent
intruder that must leave
your relationships.

In order to resolve disputes effectively, we must know who, how, and when to fight when there is discord. Disputes will be easily and quickly settled if we recognize who the real foe is. Neither you nor your kinsfolk, brethren, close or distant associates are the real enemy. Yes, some of them may behave like the devil or allow him to manifest his demonic traits through them. However unreasonable, unloving or insensitive each person in a relationship may feel the other is, neither is the real enemy.

Who is the Real Enemy in a Relationship?

Satan is! Mark him and learn to sniff him miles away. He incites people against each other so they can trade punches. Instead of fighting or firing at him, they combat or shoot each other. When the altercation intensifies and threatens the relationship, he sits back and gives his demons a high-five for accomplishing his goal to abate their solidarity. He has severed many significant alliances because we are combating each other instead of the real enemy.

Let us examine the following Scriptures: *"You have heard that it was said, 'You shall love your neighbor and hate your enemy.' But I say to you, love your enemies, bless those who curse you, do good to those who hate you, and pray for those who spitefully use you and persecute you, that you may be sons of your Father in heaven; for He makes His sun rise on the evil and on the good, and sends rain on the just and on the unjust. For if you love those who love you, what reward have you? Do not even the tax collectors do the same? And if you greet your brethren only, what do you do more than others? Do not even the tax collectors do so? Therefore you shall be perfect, just as your Father in heaven is perfect" (Mathew 5:43-48).*

The above truth may be a bitter pill for some to swallow. We would like to hang *"our so-called enemies"* in the nearest gallows or call fire from heaven to devour them as Prophet Elisha did to the youngsters who mocked his baldness. Often, the sad part is that those whom we refer to as enemies are not always the culprit.

It is imperative to note that the Lord will never endanger our lives or place us at the mercy of others. In His infinite wisdom, He knows that Satan is the ultimate enemy, not people. He is the source of all feuds, the real villain, and intruder that must flee from our relationships.

Take the fight to the real enemy and deal with him. Identify him and stop throwing punches at the wrong people. Attack issues, not people. Jesus identified the devil when he spoke through Peter, cautioning Him to avoid His main purpose on earth, the crucifixion. It is important to note that He did not rebuke him, but the devil that instigated him. Discern by the Holy Spirit when others are speaking out of their humanity and when the enemy is speaking through them.

"Who" to Combat When in Conflict

Demonic spirits toil tirelessly to bewitch people with strife. Rebuke the devil, not people for instigating chaos in your relationships. Destabilize him with truth and combat him with prayer, fasting, the word of God, and the blood of Jesus. Learn to separate loved ones and close associations from irritable conducts and bind the ungodly spirit that may be motivating them. Take authority and command the spirits of strife, fear, confusion, and other related demons to leave your relationships. Be sure that you are a born-again Spirit-filled believer that conforms to the Lordship of Christ or they will not obey you. Submitting to God emboldens us to resist the devil, and resisting him forces him to flee. When we obey God, the enemy is obligated to obey our command.

The devil is an egoistic demagogue who cunningly uses our hang-ups, blind spots, or debilities against our solidarity. He will use jealousy, misconceptions or gossip to incite you against others, so you will blame the disparities in your relationships on them and treat them like foes, but exculpate him. If you take the bait, your alliances will hardly co-exist as a team or trust each other. Don't let him use you to set up a conflict bomb that will blow up your affiliations.

Satan tempts people in deceptive ways to catch them off guard. Turn on your discernment and be alert. When you identify the adversary, you will be able to deal with him and reconcile your differences.

Vessel of Peace or Agent of Discord?

People in a relationship decide if they will be emissaries of peace or diplomats of conflict or if they will live a righteous or worldly standard. Their choice reveals either a spiritual or a carnal mindset. *"Ye shall know them by their fruits. Do men gather grapes of thorns, or figs of thistles?" (See Mathew 7:16.)*

"If my family is not my enemy, why do we clash every so often?"

We and our families argue incessantly because we have unrepentant hearts. Despite sitting on the pew week after week, reading the word of God, devouring restorative books, hearing impactive sermons by our Pastors, and the godly advice from those who care, our hearts remain obstinate, unrenewed, and unteachable. We are overly paranoid, sensitive, and easily irritated because our hearts are bleeding with real or imagined hurt.

The devil is the conduit for schism. He is a legalistic fugitive that roams about seeking whom to victimize and devour. Just as dead animals attract vultures, so do demonic traits like pride, anger, selfishness, unforgiveness, and jealousy attract him. If you are always at loggerheads with someone, it is because there is something in you that appeals to him. Until you rid yourself of all sinful behaviors that attract him, he will come vigorously for his goods. As long as those in a relationship are carnally minded, he will make them a channel of variance. He will utilize their frigid hearts to constantly spur discord and do his dirty job. He could not find anything in Jesus to use against Him (John 14:30). Until you repent of rebellion, renounce sinful attitudes, and shut the door of your relationships at his face, you will be at his mercy.

You may say, *"Well, Bridget, you don't really know some of the people I work with, live with, fellowship with! They lie, gossip, and act like heathens. I never know what to expect. They are all weirdos."*

Well, perhaps you are right. It does not matter how hideous we think others are. God's word is a holy mandate, not a recommendation. We must respond in ways that satisfy Him based on His directive and dependability, not on fallible people's unpredictability and eccentricity. We are just as culpable in His eyes when we are spiteful. Our responses must delight Him despite others' seemingly provoking conduct. We must decide if we would let Him use us as vessels of peace or authorize the devil to use us as agents of discord.

Using the Weakest Link

How does the devil use people to accomplish his goals? Unlike God, the devil is not omniscient. Nevertheless, to some degree, he understands our strengths and weaknesses and picks the most vulnerable person in a relationship to weaken it. He uses the susceptible one to push the other's *"irritation button"* to create chaos. In the Garden of Eden, he picked Eve because she appealed more to him. She was more vulnerable because she was the "weaker vessel" he could utilize to make Adam itch with rebellion. He could not get to Adam directly but indirectly through his wife. He knew that Adam would not listen to him but would listen to Eve. She was his wife, lover, and best friend. He would not accept the *"Tree of the knowledge of good and evil"* from him; but would from his wife, Eve – because he loved and trusted her.

Therefore, he used Eve as bait to get Adam to scratch with rebellion and bleed with sin. He utilizes the person that is most impressionable; the one that is easily offended, emotionally wounded, erratic, elusive, and distrustful to create friction to achieve his goals. Yes, he uses the weakest link; the one that is cantankerous, loves malice, takes longer to hold out the olive branch, and the one that is more susceptible to conflict to push a relationship up the creek. Hence, we must identify each other's strengths and weaknesses and extend more grace, prayers, compassion, tolerance, and love in areas where others are most vulnerable.

"But We Can't Stop Fighting!"

Yes, you can! Have you ever heard such a preposterous thing as the devil coercing people into a fight at gunpoint? People trade punches only because they elect to. Arguments will halt when you make a conscious effort to wash your heart and mouth with the word of God. Others will succeed in drawing you into a brawl only if you accept the boxing gloves they offer or if you agree to jump into the ring with them. However, if you shun conflict, they will have no choice but to take off their gloves and make peace.

Conflict does not have to cease for you only when others halt their hostilities. It fizzles out when you cease your own hostilities and dispose of your conflict ammunitions. *"But avoid foolish and ignorant disputes, knowing that they generate strife. And a servant of the Lord must not quarrel but be gentle to all, able to teach, patient, in humility correcting those who are in opposition, if God perhaps will grant them repentance, so that they may know the truth, and that they may come to their senses and escape the snare of the devil, having been taken captive by him to do his will" (2Timothy 2:23-26).*

Ask the Holy Spirit to help you confront your deficiencies. If you do nothing proactive to tackle them, they will come back and deal with your relationships. When we confront ourselves, we do not blame others for our personal struggles – regardless of their source. Rather we accept responsibility for our vulnerabilities and deal with what makes us predisposed to emotional pain, abuse, disappointments, low self-esteem, rejection, and the plethora of dysfunctions that trap us in captivity. When people traumatize us, unless we are underage, we need to recognize what is in us that appeals to their insensitivity and what makes them feel that we are prone to their victimization.

Also, we need to identify how we gave them access, close that door, and take back our authority. We must go through the process of change to wade off potential abusers and become whole.

"When Stella makes me very angry, I just blow a fuse!"
If so, then accept responsibility for what is unhealed in you that makes it so easy for Stella and others to push your buttons or make you blow a fuse. The devil will utilize people to stoke you in areas of weaknesses, so you will react in detrimental ways. Have you noticed that after the devil uses your unresolved wrath to get you into trouble, he is nowhere to be found when you are suffering the consequences of poor choices? Deal with your anger problem now so you will close that door against the enemy.

"Levi ticks me off all the time."

Deal with what is in you that easily rattles your cage. Many times, God uses other people's shortcomings or aggravating conducts to expose ours.

Often, people squabble partly because of the unrealistic expectations and undue burdens they place on others. They react to fear of rejection, apprehension to love, and the dread of losing control or being controlled. Fear produces torment. *"There is no fear in love; but perfect love casts out fear, because fear involves torment. But he who fears has not been made perfect in love" (1 John 4:18).* Fear induces interpersonal feuds. However, perfect love dispels fear. Perfect love is Agape love that transcends the fear of rejection, betrayal, vulnerability, timidity, and all the plethora of fears we exhibit in relationships. It refreshes and liberates us to be who we really are.

- **Scriptural Confession: Psalm 24:8, John 10:10, Psalm 24:7-10, Matthew 18:18.**
- **Praise and Worship**
- **Pray These Prayers by Faith.**

1. Father, help me to identify who the real enemy is whenever there is conflict in my relationships, in the name of Jesus.
2. "Satan," the word of God says, "You are a liar and a thief!" You are the intruder in my relationships! I bind and command you to get out now, in the name of Jesus Christ.
3. By the blood of Jesus Christ, Satan, carry your evil load on your own head and stay out of my relationships, in the name of Jesus Christ.
4. By the blood of Jesus Christ of Nazareth, let all powers that are warring against my loved ones and associations begin to war against themselves, in the name of Jesus.
5. Let all powers that want to entrap me fall into their own trap and entangle themselves in their own web, in the name of Jesus Christ.
6. Every power that has dug a pit for me and my loved ones, fall into your own pit, in the name of Jesus Christ.

7. By the blood of Jesus, let every power that wants to destroy my valued associations self-destruct, in the name of Jesus Christ.

8. Let all principalities and powers that want to destroy my dreams or the work of my hands, hang themselves in their own gallows, in the name of Jesus Christ.

9. Let all demonic agents, evil entities, and powers that want to bury the purpose and plans of God for me and my loved ones, bury themselves in their own graves, in the name of Jesus Christ.

10. By the blood of Jesus Christ, I command every plan of the enemy against my relationships to backfire, in the name of Jesus Christ.

11. All my divine relationships and I are in one accord in the natural and in the spirit realm; and we walk in the unity of the Holy Spirit, in the name of Jesus.

12. Let the thunder of God squash all eavesdropping spirits prying on my relationships, in the name of Jesus. Let their eardrums be crushed in the name of Jesus.

13. I bring the blood of Jesus against the peeping spirits that are spying on my household and interpersonal relationships, in the name of Jesus. Let their eyes be blinded by the fire of the Holy Spirit, in the name of Jesus.

14. By the blood of Jesus, I crush every head of Goliath standing in the way of my family and relationships, in the name of Jesus.

15. Thank you, Lord, for your faithfulness, unfailing love, and the blessed assurance that you will never leave or forsake us.

CHAPTER 19

When to "Fight" Amid Conflict

Never waste your time, energy or resources picking worthless fights. Know when to respond, back off or simply be quiet.

Pick Your Fights

We must learn when to fight and when to walk away because some battles are not worth fighting at all. Others are best left alone for the Lord to fight for you. Never waste your time, energy, and resources picking worthless fights with those you love. The devil uses quarrels to distract and keep relationships off course. Know when to respond, back off or be quiet when you have no favorable thing to relate to others. Unresolved issues that are hypersensitive should be handled prayerfully with wisdom, discernment, and understanding.

One primary reason for disagreement is that some people bottle-up ill feelings. They fail to converse on a deeper level and thus walk around fuming with subjugated feelings.

God created us as expressive beings. When we can no longer freely articulate our feelings, repressed emotions can clog the "arteries" that supply life to a relationship. Communication is the heartbeat of a relationship. Its collapse indicates a breakdown in all the vital organs that hold it together. A relationship without a good rapport is like an active volcano waiting to erupt.

Entrust Sensitive Subjects to the Holy Spirit

In hordes of relationships, some subjects are off-limits due to their sensitive nature. Often, these touchy areas are sealed off like a crime scene because we do not want to tread on delicate issues. Habitually, we peek in when we want to prosecute those who have hurt us and often end up swinging at them.

Entrust problematic subjects to the Holy Spirit, and He will help you convey them to others. There may be days you will have to pray; *"Holy Spirit, help me to be sensitive and patient with people. Help me to communicate and relate to them in ways that will let them know that I love and accept them unconditionally just as You love and accept me."* If you let Him answer in His time, it will haul needless burdens off your shoulders. Do not be tempted to go back and undo your prayer. Be patient… be patient – and be patient until He divinely intervenes. He knows those you love much better and will do an excellent job.

I am not advocating obliviousness or saying we should walk on eggshells, mask knotty issues or disguise them in a relationship. You can and should communicate them with the wisdom and understanding of the Holy Spirit. However, be mindful when dealing with complex issues because when wounds are raw, individual convictions are at stake, cherished traits are on the line, emotions run high, and people will fight relentlessly to stand their ground. Perhaps you may already be apprehensive, playing it safe, and not wanting to set off a conflict bomb – though the devil is eagerly waiting to find the right opportunity to launch a civil war in your relationship. The danger of trying to reconcile differences where people have strong convictions and are not willing to compromise is that it will lead to more mayhem. When they refuse to concede their position, the devil will utilize their doggedness to do cartwheels in the relationship.

Often, unresolved disputes in a relationship are like a brewing hurricane waiting to manifest. If you or anyone in the relationship decide to do battles in these areas, everyone will lose at the end of the day if none is willing to meet halfway. Let the Holy Spirit help you resolve these areas in His time so you do not grow further apart. Be proactive, transparent, teachable, and honest. Before you ask God to deal with others' heart, ask Him to thaw yours first. Choose your words carefully when dealing with "sticky issues," and you will be amazed at how it will launch your relationship to new heights. *"There is one who speaks like the piercings of a sword, But the tongue of the wise promotes health" (Proverbs 12:18). "Your words will either acquit or condemn you" (Mathew 12:37).*

Use Truth to Harmonize Your Differences

Apply "Truth" where you have sharp disagreements with others about biblical doctrines. For example, if you believe in tithing and others do not, state your convictions with respect, leave it alone, and let God deal with their hearts. Ask God to minister to them rather than whip them with your convictions. Just because we have a revelation about a biblical truth does not mean that others should become a whipping post or dumping ground. Those who feel too spiritually high and mighty to accommodate others are in la-la land. They are in a place of obliviousness and insubordination. We are in different seasons and spiritual levels. However, God is doing a progressive work in each of us.

It is all right to disagree with relatives, friends, business associates, neighbors or Church members as long as you do not allow your differences to sabotage the relationship. God elected you to be an integral part of that connection. Just like you matter, so do others matter as well. Biblically, you owe them love and respect regardless of how you feel about your Church members, parents, siblings, uncles, aunties, cousins, nephews, friends, grandpa, spouse, coworker, grandma, in-laws, and others. If you feel that some of your associations are discourteous or manipulative, do not erect protective barriers to segregate them.

175

As a substitute, establish healthy boundaries to disarm them from managing your life. Walls isolate and trap people. However, healthy boundaries not only check and balance their conduct but will also help you to embrace them in love. As an emissary of Christ, you must love them regardless of whether you feel that they deserve it or not. There is no such thing as a flawless family, friendship, Church, marriage or workplace because fallible people make up these relationships.

Work, business, weight, social, political, spiritual, financial, and other pressing issues that can incite conflict should be resolved prayerfully with wisdom through the guidance of the Holy Spirit. Do not sweep these unresolved issues under the relationship rug or use them as a yardstick to measure its value. At the end of the day, God is the final judge. Protect your relationships as long as you are not violating Scriptures. Our love for God and for each other must transcend cultural beliefs, race, gender, religious, and individual differences.

- **Scriptural Confession: John 14:26, Matthew 18:18**
- **Praise and Worship**
- **Pray These Prayers Sincerely From Your Heart.**

1. Holy Spirit of the Living God, You are my Teacher, Helper, and Counselor. Help me to discern when to talk about sensitive issues and when to be quiet, in the name of Jesus.
2. Lord, teach us how to resolve and harmonize our differences, in your holy name.
3. Father, help me to develop a sensitive and compassionate Spirit when relating to others, in the name of Jesus Christ.
4. By your power Holy Spirit, help me not to be overly sensitive to hurt, offenses or disappointments, in the name of Jesus Christ.
5. By your anointing Holy Spirit, minister to the people you have assigned to me. Help us to harmonize areas we have sharp differences, in the name of Jesus.
6. Holy Spirit, restore our souls. Heal our emotions. Heal painful memories in the name of Jesus.

7. Father, help me to love and accept others unconditionally regardless of their weaknesses just as you love and accept me, in the name of Jesus

8. Almighty God, help us to utilize our differences to enlarge our capacity to love, grow, tolerate, and forgive one another, in the name of Jesus.

9. I bring the blood of Jesus against the powers that want to use me to vex, spite, badger or belittle others' weaknesses or the powers that want others to vex, spite, badger or belittle my weakness, in the name of Jesus Christ. We shall not use our weaknesses against each other, in the name of Jesus. Together, we stand in solidarity and defeat the enemy in the name of Jesus.

10. By the blood of Jesus, I decree woe unto the power that wants to use me against others or that wants to use others against me, in the name of Jesus.

11. Almighty God, please give me divine strategies to know how to combat conflict in my relationships, in the name of Jesus Christ.

12. Lord Jesus, help me to crucify my flesh, sinful attitudes, and ungodly conducts, in your precious name.

13. Thank God for answers to your prayers.

CHAPTER 20

How not to Fight When in Conflict
(Wrong and Dangerous Conflict Arsenals)

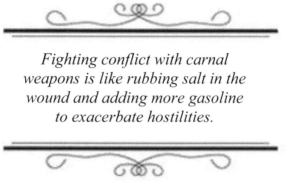

*Fighting conflict with carnal
weapons is like rubbing salt in the
wound and adding more gasoline
to exacerbate hostilities.*

The following factors are carnal and dangerous arsenals that mar interpersonal relationships and set them on conflict fire. No ambassador of Christ should ever use these weapons. Each time you fight with any of these ammunitions, you are rubbing salt in the wound and adding more gasoline to the conflict fire with your actions.

Christians that exhibit the following impious conduct will progressively build and detonate conflict bombs with their carnal behavior.

1). Unwholesome words
In the heat of fracas, people can use unsavory words to hit below the belt to score points. Injurious words are like snake venom. When injected into a relationship, it becomes toxic. Avoid ugly words that cut through the heart. *"Let no corrupt word proceed*

out of your mouth, but what is good for necessary edification, that it may impart grace to the hearers" (Ephesians 4:29).

2). Anger and intimidation

Often, we try to use anger to intimidate others when we cannot control them. Unresolved anger is like an active volcano waiting to erupt and devastate a relationship. *"An angry man stirs up strife, And a furious man abounds in transgression" (Proverbs 29:22). "He who has knowledge spares his words, And a man of understanding is of a calm spirit" (Proverbs 17:27). "A wise man fears and departs from evil, But a fool rages and is self-confident" (Proverbs 14:16). "A fool vents all his feelings, But a wise man holds them back" (Proverbs 29:11).*

3). Bitterness and resentment

Bitter people are contentious because they abhor peace and always want to get their way. Exhibiting bitterness is like firing *"bullets"* to spite others. *"And do not grieve the Holy Spirit of God, by whom you were sealed for the day of redemption. Let all bitterness, wrath, anger, clamor, and evil speaking be put away from you, with all malice. And be kind to one another, tenderhearted, forgiving one another, even as God in Christ forgave you" (Ephesians 4:30-32).*

4). Malice or silent treatment

Malice is like a hidden landmine waiting to ensnare those who fall into it. *"Therefore, laying aside all malice, all deceit, hypocrisy, envy, and all evil speaking" (1Peter 2:1). "Be angry, and do not sin": do not let the sun go down on your wrath, nor give place to the devil" (Ephesians 4:26-27). "Speak evil of no one, to be peaceable, gentle, showing all humility to all men" (Titus 3:2).*

5). Physical and emotional isolation

Often, we physically and emotionally detach from others when we are upset with them. When people in a relationship isolate each other to score a point, it backs them up in a corner and ensnarls them. The only way out is through reconciliation.

6). Control or Manipulation

Many formal and informal relationships are chaotic because of the devious ways we try to exploit each other. Manipulation demoralizes others. Those who use devious means to meet their needs will face God's judgment. Delilah used seduction to deceive Samson into revealing the secret of his strength. Jezebel used manipulation, lies, and deception to steal Naboth's vineyard. (See Judges 16: 4-31and 1 Kings 21:1-16.) They reaped the fruit of their deceptions.

7). Withholding love, affection, and other acts of kindness

It is egotistic, vile, and unbiblical to withhold good or geniality from a friend, colleague, neighbor, relative, brother or sister in the Lord simply because you are at loggerheads with him or her. NEW: The following Scriptures should keep us in check: *"Beloved, follow not that which is evil, but that which is good. He that doeth good is of God: but he that doeth evil hath not seen God" (3 John 1:11). "For he that will love life, and see good days, let him refrain his tongue from evil, and his lips that they speak no guile: Let him eschew evil, and do good; let him seek peace, and ensue it" (1 Peter 3:10-11). "Let every one of us please his neighbor for his good to edification" (Romans 15:2). "As we have therefore opportunity, let us do good unto all men, especially unto them who are of the household of faith. Knowing that whatsoever good thing any man doeth, the same shall he receive of the Lord, whether he be bond or free" (Galatians 6:10, 8). "And let us consider one another to provoke unto love and to good works" (Hebrews 10:24). "But to do good and to communicate forget not: for with such sacrifices God is well pleased" (Hebrews 13:16).*

Unwholesome words, anger, intimidation, bitterness, resentment, malice, manipulation, physical and emotional isolation, withholding love, and the like are Satan's favorite things. He uses them as arsenals of mass destruction to annihilate relationships.

Think about it! When you fight discord with any of the above weapons, you are authorizing Satan to hide his belongings in you and abetting him to express his demonic traits of wickedness and all his works of the flesh in and through you.

- **Scriptural Confession:2 Corinthians 10:4, 2 Corinthians 4:2, John 15:2, Luke 3:9**
- **Praise and Worship**
- **Ah! Pray the Following Prayers Aggressively.**

1. Father, I repent of all my sins before you. Cleanse me with the blood of your Son, Jesus.
2. Heavenly Father, I renounce anger, selfishness, malice, self-righteousness, envy, hatred, covetousness, and resentment, in the name of Jesus.
3. By the blood of Jesus, Satan, I absolutely refuse to let you hide your goods in me. I bind you, and I command you to take your sins and leave, in the name of Jesus.
4. I renounce Satan and his works, in the name of Jesus Christ.
5. By the power of the Holy Spirit, Satan, I refuse to let you manifest your demonic traits of anger, resentment, wickedness, and all your works of the flesh in and through me and my relationships, in the name of Jesus.
6. By the blood of Jesus, Satan, carry your evil load of sin and get out of my life and relationships, in the name of Jesus.
7. By the blood of Jesus, Satan, I take authority over you and bind all your activities in my life, in the name of Jesus.
8. By the blood of Jesus, I refuse to fight with carnal weapons. Therefore, let every power that wants to use these weapons to entrap me in bondage entangle themselves, in the name of Jesus Christ.
9. I use the blood of Jesus and the sword of the Spirit to pull down strongholds in my life, home, and relationships, in the name of Jesus.

10. By the blood of Jesus, let every demonic seed in me wither and die, in the name of Jesus.
11. I cast down imaginations and every high thing in my life, home, and relationships that exalt itself against the knowledge of God, in the name of Jesus.
12. I command every tree that is not bearing fruit in my life and relationships to be uprooted, in the name of Jesus.
13. Let the anointing of the Holy Spirit break every yoke of spiritual bareness, fear, hatred, limitation, conflict, division, rebellion, disobedience, and bondage in my life and relationships, in the name of Jesus.
14. Let the fire of the Holy Spirit consume whatever is not of God in my life and relationships, in the name of Jesus.
15. Precious Lord, I thank you for answering my prayers.

CHAPTER 21

How to Fight Amidst Conflict
(Right Arsenals to Fight Conflict Fires)

*When you become the
"water" that extinguishes
conflict fire, you glorify God
and defame the devil.*

The following are spiritual weapons and conflict fire extinguishers that heal relationships. Every representative of Christ should use them to put out conflict fire. You can never go wrong when you fight righteously. If you fight ugly – the devil's way, you and everyone interrelated will lose or suffer. But if you fight God's way, everyone will win, and the devil will lose. Let us examine the following "reconciliation weapons."

How do you quench conflict fire?
1). Extend love.
We cannot go wrong when we sow love seeds in others. Love can conquer and melt hardened hearts. Even the most stubborn and frigid people can be won over by love. Only true love can extinguish a blazing fire of conflict in any interpersonal relationship, strengthen and catapult it to new heights

2). Sow Forgiveness and kindness... reap the rewards.

One of the most significant spiritual weapons that extinguish conflict fire is forgiveness. *"For if you forgive men their trespasses, your heavenly Father will also forgive you. But if you do not forgive men their trespasses, neither will your Father forgive your trespasses" (Matthew 6: 14-15).*

"Therefore, as the elect of God, holy and beloved, put on tender mercies, kindness, humility, meekness, longsuffering; bearing with one another, and forgiving one another, if anyone has a complaint against another; even as Christ forgave you, so you also must do. But above all these things put on love, which is the bond of perfection. And let the peace of God rule in your hearts, to which also you were called in one body; and be thankful. Let the word of Christ dwell in you richly in all wisdom, teaching and admonishing one another in psalms and hymns and spiritual songs, singing with grace in your hearts to the Lord. And whatever you do in word or deed, do all in the name of the Lord Jesus, giving thanks to God the Father through Him" (Colossians 3:12-17).

"I will never forgive brother Dave, the choir director!"

Sometimes, we struggle emotionally, spiritually, physically, and financially because our relationships are defiled by resentments and unforgiveness. God does not honor the offerings of those who snub or despise His word. *"Therefore if thou bring thy gift to the altar, and there rememberest that thy brother hath ought against thee; Leave there thy gift before the altar, and go thy way; first be reconciled to thy brother, and then come and offer thy gift" (Matthew 5:23-24).*

"Bridget, why should I forgive those that do not deserve it?"

Do you deserve God's mercy? Yet He pours out His mercies on you daily because He loves you. Are you worthy of His love and forgiveness? Yet He forgives and loves you unconditionally. We do not deserve the goodness, mercies, and blessings of God. Yet,

He remains gracious to us. *"For we ourselves also were sometimes foolish, disobedient, deceived, serving divers lusts and pleasures, living in malice and envy, hateful, and hating one another. But after that the kindness and love of God our Saviour toward man appeared, Not by works of righteousness which we have done, but according to his mercy he saved us, by the washing of regeneration, and renewing of the Holy Ghost..." (Titus 3:3-5).*

As I indicated earlier, if He absolves you, why would you not pardon your relatives, colleague, boss, or brother in Christ? Forgiveness is more for you than for the wrongdoer. Without letting go, all efforts to snuff out conflict fire or reap the blessings of obedience will be futile. *"Finally, all of you be of one mind, having compassion for one another; love as brothers, be tenderhearted, be courteous; not returning evil for evil or reviling for reviling, but on the contrary blessing, knowing that you were called to this, that you may inherit a blessing" (1 Peter 3:8-9).*

It is hypocritical to ask God to *"forgive us our debts, as we forgive our debtors"* if in actuality, we do not intend to do so. The prerequisite for reciprocal forgiveness is to forgive first. *"For if you forgive men their trespasses, your heavenly Father will also forgive you. But if you do not forgive men their trespasses, neither will your Father forgive your trespasses" (Matthew 6:12, 14-15).*

We should confront, rebuke and correct in love when we are offended. However, when we "over punish," push our anger or resentment over the edge, it can backfire. Instead of winning back a brother, sister or friend, we can create a monster when we violate spiritual perimeters. We must stay within the healthy limits of corrective discipline so that transgressors would not be discouraged, overwhelmed with grief, and fall back into bondage. *"Sufficient to such a man is this punishment, which was inflicted of many. So that contrariwise ye ought rather to forgive him, and comfort him, lest perhaps such a one should be swallowed up with overmuch sorrow. Wherefore I beseech you that ye would confirm your love toward him......... Lest Satan should get an advantage of us: for we are not ignorant of his devices" (2 Corinthians 2:6-8,11).*

185

Do you want your prayers answered?

Turn the other cheek and hold out an olive branch. Forgive wholly, or you will be at the mercy of demonic tormentors that will plague your heart with trepidation and animosity. *"And when ye stand praying, forgive, if ye have ought against any: that your Father also which is in heaven may forgive you your trespasses. But if ye do not forgive, neither will your Father which is in heaven forgive your trespasses" (Mark 11:25-26).*

How Many Times should I forgive?

God expects us to forgive as often as we need to. *"Then Peter came to Him and said, "Lord, how often shall my brother sin against me, and I forgive him? Up to seven times? Jesus said to him, "I do not say to you, up to seven times, but up to seventy times seven" (Matthew 18:21-22).* There is a grievous repercussion for protracted acrimony. *"So My heavenly Father also will do to you if each of you, from his heart, does not forgive his brother his trespasses" (Matthew 18:35).*

Nail each other's offenses to the cross and leave it there. Bury the hatchet and do not go digging for bones. Will you be tempted to take back your forgiveness? Of course – but remind the devil that everything is under the blood of Jesus. Command him to get out of your relationships. He is the liar, thief, and conflict instigator! He is the stranger, the intruder that needs to be kicked out!

Remember, your conduct must move your relationships forward, not backward. You cannot go forward, looking back! Look ahead and move forward by faith. Instead of pointing fingers at others, ask the Lord to transform the relationship on His terms, not yours.

How do you quench conflict fire?

3). Become the "water" that douses conflict fire.

You cannot fight conflict fire with fire when you are dealing with human beings. You can only quench it with water. Our problem is we license others to control our responses and let them determine if we are going to be on the same wavelength or not. If they react, we react. If they respond, we respond. If they fly off the handle, we pay them back in the same coin.

"Rex, how you treat me is how I will treat you."

"Benjamin, if you are nice to me, I will be nice to you."

"Only if you respect me will I respect you, Esther."

"Genevieve, I will regard you only if you are considerate of my feelings."

"Hurt me, Ryan... and I will mar you as well."

The idea of loving only relatives who feel affection for us or doing good to only brethren who cherish us is archetypal of the world. If we minister to only neighbors who care for us, bless only colleagues who bolster us, extend kindness to only spouses who are thoughtful of us, what distinguishes us from the heathens? The mentality of giving a "tooth for a tooth" is unlike Christ! *"Do not say, I will recompense evil; Wait for the LORD, and He will save you" (Proverbs 20:22). "Do not say, I will do to him just as he has done to me; I will render to the man according to his work" (Proverbs 24:29).* Part of honoring God is caring in ways that are emblematic of Christ. Remember, freely, we receive love from Him; freely, we must share with others.

We can become *"the brook"* that drenches conflict fire when a relationship is blazing with hostilities. If we elect to be the peacemakers in our homes, workplaces, Churches, communities, and relationships, we would respond virtuously to laud God despite others' irrational behavior or the natural inclinations to gratify the flesh.

Each time we fight with biblical weapons, we become "water" that drenches the conflict fire with our Christ-like character. Our righteous temperament cools off the hot coals of conflict.

How do you quench conflict fire?

4). Become a "living epistle" of Christ.

Combating conflict fire with water connotes that we respond in ways that pleases God, and we become a *"living epistle"* of Jesus Christ encountered daily by others (2 Corinthians 3:2-3). Like the

Lord, we do not give *"an eye for an eye"* or mask offenses, but we *"overcome evil with good."* When we are cursed, we bless; when we are persecuted, we *"count it all joy;"* and when we are slandered, we answer kindly (1 Corinthians 4:12-13).

How do you quench conflict fire?
5). Respond, do not react.
Satan will constantly tempt you to react to people and situations. Endeavor not to act on his insinuations to irritate others. Always do the opposite of what he proposes. Utilize truth to expose, repel, and quash his lies.

Often, when we feel rejected or slighted, we recoil into seclusion for fear of getting hurt all over again and put up emotional fortifications to protect ourselves. We try to keep the other person at bay until we feel secure enough to share fellowship and communion again. Alternatively, make a deliberate effort to reach out with open arms and counter with empathy and absolution. As an envoy of Christ, shun your instinctive predisposition to withhold love to chastise others when they fall short of expectations. Instead, purposely release unconditional love to dispel fear, and your insecurities will melt away.

Trepidation coerces people to build mental barriers to insulate themselves. Instead of been cooped up in your own penal complex when you should be basking in the bliss of your relationships, establish healthy boundaries to check others' behavior as well as yours. Daily, we must cleave to God's truth, not other substitutes that will tear us apart.

Do not stiffen your pride muscles and say, *"Let's fight."* Alternatively, flex your love muscles and say, *"Let's make peace and heal."* It will be ruinous to lash out in anger or fan the flames of conflict when we can replace wrath with tolerance – and have much less to undo.

Do not shift blame, or you will make it so much easier for others to replicate your lack of accountability. Instead, accept responsibility and say, *"I am sorry." "Please, forgive me."* When you feel slighted, avoid malicious words that cut through the heart. Use wholesome words that will build, celebrate, and nurture others. Remember, we are representing Christ, always and everywhere. Wherever we are is *"Holy Ground."*

How do you quench conflict fire?
6). Attach issues, not people.
People are not your enemy. The devil is! When you attack people, you make it a personal war and empower them to become defensive and defiant. Also, you toss reconciliation out of the window and ruin any chance of getting your message across or winning them over. Instead, utilize your interactive skills to attack issues and separate others from their flaws just as Jesus separates our worth from our sin.

"How should I deal with infuriating people?"
Are you impeccable in your dealings with the people around you? I am quite sure that you react in exasperating ways that annoy others as well. We all do or we are liars! Exemplify tolerance in spite of their infuriating conduct. Rely on God's word to sculpt your riposte, not others' attitude. Base your obedience on God's faithfulness, not on people's conduct or imperfections. Respond optimistically because you love God, not because others merit your kindness.

The Lord expects us to accurately represent Him in how we think, speak, and act towards others regardless of whether they are considerate or not. *"He has shown you, O man, what is good; And what does the LORD require of you but to do justly, To love mercy, And to walk humbly with your God?" (See Micah 6:8.)* If we genuinely love the Lord, we will obey His mandate and *"turn the other cheek," "go the extra mile," and "sacrifice more"* as long as it glorifies God (Matthew 5:39-41).

How do you quench conflict fire?
7). Fight conflict fire with fire!
The only time to combat conflict fire with fire is when we engage in spiritual warfare through prayer, fasting, and the other ways prescribed by the Scriptures. By the word of God, the name, and

blood of Jesus, we renounce, nullify, and halt satanic intrusion and activities designed against the will of God for our lives and interpersonal relationships.

We should know that any entity that secretly and openly opposes the supreme God is deranged. The devil is demented and must be vanquished by the biblical weapons given to us.

Utilize your spiritual weapons to halt the enemy's onslaught rather than nag people and exacerbate hostilities. *Has the devil stolen your joy, peace or fulfillment? Has he infiltrated your friendships? Has he driven a wedge between you and your family? Has he created division among your parishioners? Are you on the threshold of giving up on a sister or brother in the Lord?* Fight fire with fire!

Like a narcissistic bully, Satan will not voluntarily release the relationships you care about without a fight. He is a self-exalted, perverted tyrant who wants to drag people through the mud. You have to force him out through warfare prayers, audacious faith, biblical responses, and steadfast compliance with the Lord. You can vanquish him only when you take your rightful place, put on *"the whole armour of God,"* and exercise your spiritual authority over him.

Wear your spiritual armor, become ruthless, and violent in the Holy Spirit. Let "holy anger" rise up in you! Roll up your sleeves, take the fight to the devil's terrain, and reclaim what he has stolen from you. Let him come and fight the Jesus Christ in you and get a black eye! Deplete him with praise and worship, prophetic declarations, the sword of the Spirit, thanksgiving, gratitude, the name, and blood of Jesus. Bombard him and his demonic forces with Truth, obedience, fruit of the Spirit, the sword of the Spirit, spiritual missiles, and all the biblical weapons available. You must *"pursue, overtake, and recover all"* that he has embezzled from you with biblical responses and fervent prayer.

Resolve to fight back with biblical ammunitions. Remember, we cannot combat conflict fire with fire when relating to people, or we risk contending with the Lord. We become *"water"* when dealing with people and *"fire"* when confronting Satan.

Make This Declaration

By the power of the Holy Spirit:

- I refuse to authorize the devil to destroy my relationships with conflict, in the name of Jesus.
- I will not ignite or fuel conflict fire with my words, thoughts or actions, in the name of Jesus.
- When there is conflict in my interpersonal relationships, I choose to be the water that extinguishes it. I am a peacemaker, a vessel of tranquility, a minister of reconciliation, in the name of Jesus.
- I yield my way to God's and accept responsibility for my behavior, not play the blame game.
- I choose not to use malicious words, retaliatory conduct to even the score, dig up old skeletons from old wounds; spew unrelated unresolved issues, utilize others' vulnerability and candor against them, in the name of Jesus Christ.
- I choose to use wholesome and uplifting words to respond to others, in the name of Jesus.
- I elect to align my demeanor, body language, and character with my Lord's, the Prince of Peace, and sow His peace, in His precious name.
- I choose to fight conflict with praise and worship, prophetic declaration, confession of God's word, intercession, the sword of the Spirit, the blood of Jesus Christ, the Name of Jesus Christ, and thanksgiving, in the name of Jesus.

Use These Seven Spiritual Ammunitions to Fight Conflict Fire with Fire

1) Targeted prayers of supplications and intercession (Philippians 4:6; Ephesians 6:18).
2) Faith and the sword of the Spirit, which is the Word of God (Ephesians 6:16-17).
3) The blood of Jesus Christ (Revelation 12:11).
4) The Name of Jesus Christ (Philippians 2:9-11).

5) Prophetic confession and declaration of God's word (Job 22:28)
6) Praise and worship (Psalm 145, 148).
7) Thanksgiving and gratitude (Philippians 4:6, Hebrews 13:15-16).

War in prayer with all the spiritual weapons available and your relationships will rise above the storm. When you fight God's way, conflict will not disintegrate your relationship but will make it stronger. The devil cannot touch you, your family, and relationships when the blood of Jesus and the fire of God overshadow your home.

- **Scriptural Confession: Isaiah 54:15, 2 Corinthians 5:15**
- **Praise and Worship**
- **Prayer Points**

1. By the blood of Jesus, I reclaim everything that the devil has stolen from my life and relationships, in the name of Jesus.
2. I choose to forgive those who have hurt me, (Mention each name) in the name of Jesus Christ.
3. I choose to be the water that extinguishes conflict fire, in the name of Jesus. I elect to respond in ways that please God, in the name of Jesus.
4. By the blood of Jesus Christ, I will not withhold from others what is within my power to do or give, in the name of Jesus.
5. I will not demand that others merit love, forgiveness, peace, mercy, that has been freely given to me by God, in the name of Jesus.
6. Freely I receive love, kindness, forgiveness, and peace from God. Freely I will share these divine benefits with others, in the name of Jesus.
7. Father God, help me to be a blessing to others, in the name of Jesus.
8. Let the thunder of God demolish every throne that God did not build in my home and relationships, in the name of Jesus.
9. Jehovah God, rule and reign in my relationships, in the mighty name of Jesus Christ.

10. I release confusion into every evil gathering assembled against my loved ones and other interpersonal relationships, in the name of Jesus.

11. Let all the powers that are assigned against my valuable relationships be paralyzed, in the name of Jesus.

12. Lord Jesus, destroy all the powers that want to sabotage my divine alliances, in your precious name.

13. Thank the Lord for answers to your prayers.

CHAPTER 22

Snuff out Conflict Fires Now!

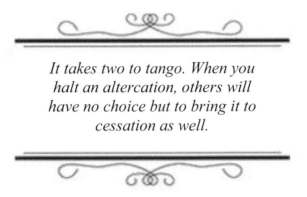

It takes two to tango. When you halt an altercation, others will have no choice but to bring it to cessation as well.

Responding scripturally to conflict ends hostilities swiftly. People in conflict must come to the solemn realization that the fire alarm in their relationship is blaring with urgency, demanding immediate attention. Each clang is a clarion call to heal and co-labor with the Lord to overhaul the relationship; unclog the jammed communication line, rekindle commitment, friendship, and emotional bond. Reconciliation is the choice to restore fellowship and communion so that the relationship will not go up in flames.

Who Should Initiate Reconciliation?

Trying to determine who should initiate reconciliation is like trying to ascertain who should do the right thing or put out the fire in a burning house. Because conflict is symbolic of fire, it must be extinguished instantaneously, so no one gets charred.

When a house is on fire, we do not analyze the fire or say, *"Let's debate on who should extinguish the fire," "Let's identify who and what started it,"* before we extinguish it. Instead, we douse it and ask the questions later. We need not deliberate who should obey God, do the right thing or put out a conflict fire. A burning relationship requires all hands on deck regardless of who is allegedly guilty or innocent – as long as God gets the glory. All of us are wrong. Only God is right! Take the initiative to do the will of God, be a peacemaker and a minister of reconciliation.

When Some or all Parties Snub Settlement

In situations when some or all parties in a relationship are unrepentant, those with the heartbeat of God must step in and help put out the conflict fire. God can use neighbors, friends, family, colleagues or even strangers to step up to the plate and intervene. However, we have to be led by the Holy Spirit so we do not sink in the quagmire or inflame the blazing conflict. While pumping fuel in a gas station, I observed a distressed couple squabble in front of their frightened young daughter, as everyone watched the drama in silence. I could not bear to see them tear each other apart while their little girl stared in sadness. Silently, I asked the Lord for wisdom and approached them. I do not remember specifically what I told them. However, I pleaded with them to resolve their differences – if nothing else, for the sake of their child. I believe it made all the difference.

When you do counsel those in conflict, always start and end with prayer. Do not take sides, show favoritism or whip them with guilt. Treat them with compassion and superimpose the word of God on their anger and bitterness. Remind them of their fallibility and the need to repent on both sides. Show them love, give them hope, and a reason to reconcile.

God will intervene in countless relationships when people with His heartbeat are willing to intercede, counsel, go the extra mile for others in conflict to be reconciled. We should work jointly to encourage each other in the physical realm and then also join spiritual forces and war against the kingdom of darkness on our *"knees."*

How long does conflict last?

Conflict lasts as long as you authorize it. Your reaction or response to discord determines how long your conflict fire will blaze. Responding to a conflict will put it out almost immediately. However, reacting to it will make it burn longer.

Often, some familial, communal, and national feuds last for months, years or even generations because many are deceived. They cling to their false perception of reality and insist that God must change His word to accommodate their superciliousness and animosity. The sad part is that somehow, they manage to recruit others, drag them into their war, and thus expose them to spiritual bondage. The devil loves to incarcerate folks in his prison.

When you have a chip on your shoulder and repudiate forgiveness, many generations will suffer for your transgressions. The devil will not only utilize your stubbornness as an access door to exploit others, but will ill-use them to reproduce your sinful acts just like he misused you. Some may be able to resist him. However, those who cannot will become his casualties because you enabled him in the first place.

The Best Time to Resolve Conflict

When is the best time to resolve conflict?

Now! Conflict is like a wild, uncontrollable fire. Its combustibility cannot be underestimated. Every conflict fire must be put out promptly or a distressed relationship could go up in flames. Whenever possible, resolve disagreements without further ado or schedule a reasonable time to settle it. This way, you will have a concrete plan to make peace. Because conflict is like a blazing flammable house fire, if reconciliation is deferred, a relationship could go up the creek without a paddle.

Do not put off forgiveness and reconciliation when you have the unction and grace to extend them now.

Surrender Your Conflict Ammunitions
"How do we end conflict?" It is easy!

- Yield to the word of God now!
- Concede to peace or reconciliation.
- Reach out to others in love.
- Stop Fighting mentally, physically, and verbally.
- Stop fanning the flames of conflict with malice, unresolved anger, real or imagined hurt, malicious attitude, negative body language, and unwholesome verbiage.
- Halt the whining and bickering.
- Cease pointing accusing fingers.
- Lay down your conflict weaponry.
- Relinquish your rights for peace.
- End the altercation now!

"Starting a quarrel is like breaching a dam; so drop the matter before a dispute breaks out" (Proverbs 17:14). Do not wait for the other person to cease his or her hostilities before you do. When you stop fighting, he or she will have no alternative but to discontinue as well. *"It takes two to tango"* but only one to untangle.

Do not clench your fists and say, *"Let's exchange blows!"* Instead, say, *"Let's reconcile and be friends again."* Remember, Satan is the *"real enemy,"* not people. Sometimes, the devil uses us to set our relationships on fire. Many have some fence-mending to do and some ground to recover from the devil. Go on, resolve the dispute now and venerate God.

Make These Confessions.

By the blood of Jesus Christ and the power of the Holy Spirit:

- I have control over conflict. Conflict does not rule in my home and relationships, in the name of Jesus.
- I resolve conflict speedily because I choose to stop fighting mentally, physically, and verbally now! At this very moment, I choose to sow tolerance and forgiveness.

- I halt whining, bickering, hostility and finger-pointing now. I confront my shortcomings. I lay down my conflict arsenal; relinquish my rights for peace; yield to the word of God and reach out to others in love. I choose to let go and let God. I choose reconciliation, in the mighty name of Jesus Christ. I seal this declaration with the blood of Jesus and the fire of the Holy Spirit.

- **Scriptural Confession: Job 22:28, Matthew 9:29, Matthew 18:18**
- **Praise and Worship**
- **Prayer Points**

1. By the blood of Jesus, I choose to relate to others in ways that please God, not self.
2. By the power of the Holy Spirit, the devil will not use me as a pawn to ignite conflict fire in my home and other interpersonal relationships, in the name of Jesus.
3. By the power of the Holy Spirit, I will not cooperate with the enemy to burn down my relationships, in the name of Jesus Christ.
4. By the blood of Jesus, I am a conflict firefighter, not a conflict fire-starter.
5. By the power of God, whenever there is a "conflict fire" in my life and relationships, I will not be the gasoline that will keep the fire ablaze! Instead, I will be the water that will extinguish it, in the name of Jesus.
6. I use the blood of Jesus Christ to bring a separation between my interpersonal relationships and conflict, in the name of Jesus.
7. I draw a Jesus Christ bloodline between my relationships and chaos, in the name of Jesus Christ!
8. I will not be utilized by the devil to sabotage my relationships, in the name of Jesus.
9. By the grace of God, I will not be a hinderance to others, in the name of Jesus.

10. By the grace of God, before any conflict fire starts in my life, home or relationships, I will co-labor with the Lord to avert it with truth, love, tolerance, compassion, forgiveness, in the name of Jesus Christ. Amen.

11. By the blood of Jesus Christ, the devil cannot scatter what God has built for me!

12. I refuse to collaborate with the devil. I cooperate with the Lord to build my relationships, in the name of Jesus.

13. Righteous Father, please help me to sow patience, tolerance, and forgiveness in my children, spouse, home, Church, community, and relationships, in the name of Jesus.

14. Oh Lord, help me to hide your word in my heart so that I will not sin against You. Give me understanding, and I shall observe your law with my whole heart. Your hands have made me and fashioned me. Empower me to obey You. May your word be a lamp unto my feet and a light to my path, in the name of Jesus (Psalm 119:11, 34, 73, & 105).

15. I seal these prayers with the blood of Jesus and the fire of the Holy Spirit.

16. Father, I thank you for answering my prayers.

CHAPTER 23

Biblical Guidelines for Reconciliation

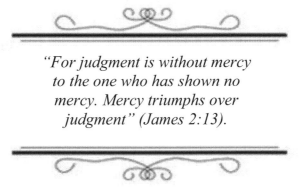

"For judgment is without mercy to the one who has shown no mercy. Mercy triumphs over judgment" (James 2:13).

The Collision of Conflict, Soul, and Spirit

The process of reconciliation can be trepidatious, intimidating, and yet refreshing because it confronts our flaws, but also gives us a sense of hope. It can be petrifying to lay our dignity on the line, walk bare to the foot of the cross, and surrender all our defenses for the sake of peace. It is a risk! Others may reciprocate our efforts or take advantage of us.

"Jacob was greatly afraid and distressed" when he wanted to reconcile with his brother, Esau. He was concerned about his family's safety and how Esau might respond to him *(Genesis 32:7)*. Still, he took the bulls by the horns and restored fellowship.

Often, when we are wrestling with making peace, we find ourselves in a place where faith and fear, the Spirit and flesh, the supernatural and natural, and divinity and humanity collide, and the one we yield to prevails. To attain the goals of reconciliation, fear must defer to faith, the flesh must kowtow to the Spirit, the natural must concede to the supernatural, and our humanity must conform to God. We must be willing to halt hostilities, realign fragmented ties biblically, unclog the lines of communication, restore fellowship, and apply the healing balm of forgiveness, so we can learn to heal, love, and trust again.

I have categorized the reconciliation process into 3 segments: "Before," "During," and "After." Jacob is our case study. (Study Genesis chapter 32 and 33.)

Section 1: Before Reconciliation

The Preparation

1). Seek the Lord: Reconciliation does not magically happen effortlessly without somebody actively engaged in co-laboring with God. Prior to your reconciliation meeting, involve the other party or parties if possible. Fast and pray so the Holy Spirit will take over, break up the fallow ground, and plant the seed of reconciliation. Intense fasting and prayer will lay the groundwork and give you a clear direction from the Holy Spirit.

Ask the Lord to *"renew the right spirit within you."* Often, God wants to heal our relationships, but the hidden idols of the heart can become a great impediment. For Jacob, he was a liar, supplanter, and deceiver. He came clean and wrestled with God because he wanted a new way of life. (See Genesis 32:24 - 32.) *What is holding you back from going all the way with God?* Do not let go until you have a divine encounter with Him. Like Jacob, we must be candid and penitent, so God will melt our taciturn hearts or reconciliation would only be momentary even if at all possible.

Discern how the Lord wants you to achieve the goals of reconciliation. He may instruct you to call, write, email, text, meet with the other person, take people as witnesses if the need arises or do some or all of the above depending on the situation. Also, He may lead you to do something entirely different. The bottom line is that you follow His leading so your actions will not be counterproductive.

2). Have a divine strategy: Jacob planned for every possible problem he might encounter before reconciling with his brother, Esau. He divided and arranged his family in columns to protect them in case a fight broke out. He coached them on how to greet him so they could soften his heart and Esau was highly impressed. *"And he lifted his eyes and saw the women and children, and said, "Who are these with you?" So he said, "The children whom God has graciously given your servant." Then the maidservants came near, they and their children, and bowed down. And Leah also came near with her children, and they bowed down. Afterward Joseph and Rachel came near, and they bowed down. Then Esau said, "What do you mean by all this company which I met?" And he said, "These are to find favor in the sight of my lord" (Genesis 33:5-8).*

Ask God for wisdom and a divine strategy to overcome the hurdles the enemy might throw at you before, during, and after reconciliation. Jacob told his servants to keep some space between the herds he wanted to present to Esau as a peace offering. Before proceeding to reconciliation, prayerfully prepare for any possibility and craft a contingency plan in place.

3). Send reliable representatives ahead of you if needed: Sometimes, people's hearts are hardened with bitterness. You may need to send trusted emissaries like elders, well-seasoned friends, relatives, colleagues or brethren ahead of you to help deliver your conciliatory message, plow the heart-soil of the other person, and get him or her ready for reconciliation. Special peace envoys play a pivotal role in the reconciliation process. They humanize you, convey your well-meaning intentions, take the heat off you, and soften the heart of the offended person you are in conflict with to become pliable and receptive. Before Jacob presented himself to his brother, Esau, he sent representatives to go before him to announce his intentions. Their job was to prepare Esau's heart to accept or receive him. *"Then Jacob sent messengers before him to Esau his brother in the land of Seir, the country of Edom. And he commanded them, saying, "Speak thus* to my lord Esau, 'Thus your servant Jacob says: "I have dwelt with Laban and stayed there until now. ... I have sent to tell my lord, that I may find favor in your sight" (Genesis 32:3-5b).*

.

4). Sow a peace offering if necessary: If you feel led, prayerfully sow a peace offering before, during or after the reconciliation in the life of the other person. Regardless of whether it pacifies the other person's anger or alleviates some tensions or not, it signifies your desire for harmony, goodwill, and adds more weight to your conciliatory approach.

Before Abigail became David's wife, she sowed a peace offering to appease David and his men. Her act of obedience prevented him from murdering her husband, Nabal. (See 1 Samuel 25:23-35.)

Jacob wisely utilized meaningful gifts to appease Esau and soften his heart for reconciliation, and it worked. *"And he commanded the first one, saying, "When Esau my brother meets you and asks you, saying, 'To whom do you belong, and where are you going? Whose are these in front of you?' then you shall say, 'They are your servant Jacob's. It is a present sent to my lord Esau; and behold, he also is behind us.'" So he commanded the second, the third, and all who followed the droves, saying, "In this manner you shall speak to Esau when you find him; and also say, 'Behold, your servant Jacob is behind us.'" For he said, "I will appease him with the present that goes before me, and afterward I will see his face; perhaps he will accept me." So the present went on over before him, but he himself lodged that night in the camp" (Genesis 32:17-21).* He hid behind his gifts and let them speak for him.

Like Jacob, you do not have to send some goats, rams, cows, bulls, donkeys, foals, camels with their colts, or other expensive gifts. Sending an inspirational Scripture or a simple *"thinking of you," "God bless you,"* or *"let's make peace and heal"* text, email or greeting card will do. God will definitely show you what to send that will be effectual. Genuine acts of kindness can mollify hardened hearts and grant us favor. This conciliatory approach will definitely make a difference.

5). Mind your tongue and body language: What you say or how you address the other person matters. Jacob called Esau *"My lord," "My brother,"* and *"Thy servant."*

If your mouth is speaking, *"peace"* but your body language is manifesting, *"war,"* the purpose will be defeated.

6). Mind your pride and humble yourself: When Jacob finally met Esau, he bowed himself to the ground seven times. (See Genesis 33:3.) He won his brother over with humility. He could no longer resist but yield to peace.

7). Take action and initiate reconciliation: If you are at loggerheads with others, God will constantly deal with your heart about your anger, resentment, and the need to forgive. The question is, will you listen to His tugging and obey Him? I am absolutely sure that God was dealing with Jacob's heart for the duration of 20 years he served his father-in-law, Laban. After he fled from him, He knew it was time to act and sent a message to Esau about his intention to meet him (Genesis 32:1-5). ***What was the message?*** *"….. and I have sent to tell my lord, that I may find grace in thy sight,"* Not *"let's meet so I can give you a piece of my mind. I' tell you how right I am and wrong you are!"* Discern what and how God wants you to say.

Section 2: The Reconciliation Encounter

The 3 Biblical ways to settle disputes are scriptural prescriptions for reconciliation. Whether you are settling with one or more people, you will find them very effective.

Method 1: Do it personally and confidentially

"Moreover if your brother sins against you, go and tell him his fault between you and him alone. If he hears you, you have gained your brother" (Mathew 18:15). Whether you choose to text, call, write or meet face to face with the other person, focus on the goal of reconciliation, which is restoring fellowship and communion.

Method 2: Take one or more witnesses with you

"But if he will not hear, take with you one or two more, that 'by the mouth of two or three witnesses every word may be established" *(Mathew 18:16).* Have others go with you as witnesses, buffers or a support system if need be. They will help prosecute your case for peace.

Method 3: Involve the Church

"And if he refuses to hear them, tell it to the church. But if he refuses even to hear the church, let him be to you like a heathen and a tax collector" (Mathew 18:17). The Church, as a corporate body, is fully anointed to settle disputes within and outside the Church if only, we are willing to be accountable.

"What should I say or do to enhance reconciliation?"

Sometimes, like Esau and Jacob, we do not need to utter a word, say too much, or do anything spectacular or we run the risk of ruining such a divine moment when love and hate collide, and love triumphs. We must be open-minded and led by the Holy Spirit. There have been times when I forgot my primed speeches and all the *thingamajigs* that I planned to do during reconciliation, and instead flowed with the Holy Spirit for the sake of peace. We come to a point in God where words become insignificant because love swallows up animosity, faith dampens fear, coldness gives way to empathy, caring engulfs indifference, serenity consumes discordance, and God gets the glory.

After Jacob prayed, had a divine encounter with God, dispatched envoys ahead of him, sent a peace offering to his brother, and executed the strategy God gave him, he was ready to meet his brother. Esau's heart was melted, overflowing with love, and was ready to meet Jacob also. *"But Esau ran to meet him, and embraced him, and fell on his neck and kissed him, and they wept" (Genesis 33:4). "But Esau ran..."* Why? He missed Jacob and could not wait to mend their broken bond, heal their fragmented souls, restore their communion, fellowship, and brotherhood. Faith subjugated fear. The Spirt brought the flesh to its knees. The natural caved in to the supernatural and divinity.

If you feel led to confront, confess, apologize, make restitution, talk about your hurt or other unresolved issues, do it wisely, honestly, concisely, and respectfully. Attack the issues, not the person. The outcome must be peace, not confrontation.

Points to Consider Amid Reconciliation

It is imperative to pray before and after resolution so your efforts will be fruitful. Consider the following biblical guidelines designed to help extinguish conflict fire explosions and embrace peace. Apply when necessary.

1). Pray and invite the Holy Spirit to your reconciliation meeting.

Jacob prayed that God would deliver him from his brother's wrath and He did. Ask Him to help you reach a fair and just resolution. He is the wisest Teacher, empathetic Helper, judicious Peacemaker, caring Counselor, greatest Mentor, and impartial Umpire of the universe. Each person must be willing to collaborate with Him to achieve the goal of resolving a dispute or the purpose will be defeated.

2). Each person must examine his or her own heart first and acknowledge any revealed sins or faults.

Each person must ask God to search his or her heart. *"I the LORD search the heart, I try the reins, even to give every man according to his ways, and according to the fruit of his doings" (Jeremiah 17:10).*

David prayed: *"Search me, O God, and know my heart: try me, and know my thoughts: And see if there be any wicked way in me, and lead me in the way everlasting" (Psalm 139:23-24).* If we are honest, He will reveal the part each played to create the conflict. We must judge ourselves first, not others (Matthew 7:3-

5). If we evaluate others with the same standard that we use to examine ourselves, we would be more forgiving.

3). Confess sin or faults to each other and accept responsibility for your part *(See James 5:16).* *"He who covers his sins will not prosper, But whoever confesses and forsakes them will have mercy" (Proverbs 28:13).* Be accountable for your contribution to the conflict fire.

"But I did not do anything wrong!"
That is self- righteousness*! "All the ways of a man are pure in his own eyes, But the LORD weighs the spirits" (Proverbs 16:2).* You may not have incited the conflict at hand, but your personal vendetta and other sinful dispositions are just as bad. *"Lying lips are an abomination to the LORD, But those who deal truthfully are His delight" (Proverbs12:22).*

You can state your innocence but also accept blame for participating in the feud – even if the other person does not. *Jesus, "when he was reviled, reviled not again; when he suffered, he threatened not; but committed himself to him that judgeth righteously" (1 Peter 2:23).*

"But I am not guilty!
Indeed! Did you keep loving, forgiving, and reaching out to those who allegedly hurt you? Did you try to win back their favor or earn their trust? Did you fast and pray for them? Did you involve the elders of the Church or trusted leaders to intervene and reconcile the relationship? *If* not, then you are equally as liable as they are. *"If we say that we have no sin, we deceive ourselves, and the truth is not in us" (1 John 1:8).* Perhaps those who hurt you may be as guilty as sin. They may have kindled the conflict fire, but your stubbornness is also fueling its flames. Certainly, you are not helping to extinguish it by your so-called innocence. Rather, the combustibility of your hostilities is keeping it ablaze.

We need to eschew self-adulation, false piety, and other self-serving braggadocious conducts. It always takes two to quarrel. We all have some degree of guilt. *"For all have sinned and fall short of the glory of God" (Romans 3:23).* Since we are all wrong and only God is right, repentance must begin with each of us. Our reflections and deeds must be aligned with the character of Christ.

4). Confront each other with love.

"But speaking the truth in love, may grow up into him in all things, which is the head, even Christ... Therefore, putting away lying, Let each one of you speak truth with his neighbor, for we are members of one another" (Ephesians 4:15 & 25). When you do confront, express your feelings and needs in the most courteous possible way. Use wholesome and affirmative words to articulate your perspective. Remember – it is only your perception, not the other person's. Give him or her the privilege to respond irrespective of whether he or she is right or wrong. Watch your body language, tone of voice, and attitude to ensure they align with your enunciations and desired expectations.

Jacob confronted his father-in-law, Laban, when he caught up with him after he fled with his wife and children. (See Genesis 31:36-42). His confrontation convicted him, which led them to make a peace covenant. Also, David confronted King Saul twice which led him to admit his sin and repentance. (See 1 Samuel 24:9-22; 1 Samuel 26:17-25.)

"What happens when others refuse to accept responsibility for offensive behavior?"
Certainly, there are folks who get irate with confrontation and will barely accept liability for their sin. Back off and trust God to deal with their hearts. Auguring will only exacerbate the hostilities. Exercise wisdom, self-control, and let the love of God come on-stream. Plug in your forbearance and let your compassion kick in also.

Remember; take on issues and do not attack people. Separate their uniqueness from their imperfections just as the Lord separate the sin from the sinner. Lay down your own conflict artilleries and temper justice with mercy. Let forgiveness mitigate the weight of offenses. *"For judgment is without mercy to the one* who has shown no mercy. Mercy triumphs over judgment" *(James 2:13).*

5). Find the middle ground and hitch horses together.

Your differences should strengthen your relationships, not shred them apart. The word of God must be superimposed on your distinctions. Two national presidents sat down to discuss their differences. The evasive one said, *"Let's forget our differences."* The wiser one retorted, *"No, let's respect them."* To avert conflict, we must strive to understand, appreciate, celebrate, and respect our differences, not try to utter, snub or abuse them. We must learn how to establish a good rapport with each other and utilize our interpersonal skills to polish the rough edges in our relationships.

6). Repent before God and each other.

Ask God and each other for forgiveness—even if you think you are innocent. Together, pray Psalms 32 and 51 for forgiveness. It takes humbleness and brokenness to admit wrong for the sake of peace. God honors a broken and contrite heart (Psalm 51:17). If nothing else say, *"I am sorry that we are in conflict." "I am sorry for the pain that our misunderstanding has caused you."* Sowing contriteness gives God the glory but shames the devil. In addition, it disarms the other person's defenses. Whether we are guilty or innocent, we need to sow mercy to acquire mercy. *"Blessed are the merciful, for they shall obtain mercy" (Mathew 5:7).*

"Bridget, it does not make sense! Why should I repent before someone that does not accept responsibility for his or her sins?"

Why would God step into your situation if you are as impenitent, troublesome, and egoistic as the other person? Repentance not only positions you on the right footing with the Lord, but also opens the door for divine intervention. God will utilize your penitence to thaw the other person's hardened heart. You are not accountable for others' choices but yours. One day, you will stand before God and give an account of yourself, not others.' Obey God based on His word, His faithfulness, and your reverence for Him, not on how imperfect people react or evade accountability.

Will an egocentric person take your act of contrition for granted?

Perhaps, a seemingly insensitive person may use your forgiveness to mask his or her behavior to resist change. However, this does not justify his or her blasé attitude. Your responsibility is to trust God, conform to His character, and leave the consequences to Him. He is fair, just, and knows exactly how to tenderize others. If He could till Nebuchadnezzar's hardened heart, get the thief on the cross to acknowledge his need for redemption, and transform Paul, the Apostle's heart, He can soften anyone's.

Remember, you cannot extinguish conflict fire with fire when dealing with people. If you "fight" His way, He will always protect you. If you fight your way, He has no obligation to safeguard your interest. He can only defend truth, obedience, and righteousness, not sin. He cannot go against His word or nature. Relinquish your hostilities and act in godly ways that will prompt Him to shield you. David continued to behave wisely despite Saul's ill-treatment and God protected His interest. (See 1 Samuel 18:12, 14-15 and chapters 18-29.)

"Overcome Evil With Good"

Tread in the Spirit, pay attention to whatever the Lord is revealing to you, and walk in love. *"Therefore If your enemy is hungry, feed him; If he is thirsty, give him a drink; For in so doing you will heap coals of fire on his head. Do not be overcome by evil, but overcome evil with good" (Romans 12:20-21).* You will be rewarded when you obey God because *"When a man's ways please the LORD, he maketh even his enemies to be at peace with him" (Proverbs 16:7).*

Joseph wholeheartedly forgave his brothers. *"And they sent a messenger unto Joseph, saying, Thy father did command before he died, saying, So shall ye say unto Joseph, Forgive, I pray thee now, the trespass of thy brethren, and their sin; for they did unto thee evil: and now, we pray thee, forgive the trespass of the servants of the God of thy father. And Joseph wept when they spake unto him. And his brethren also went and fell down before his face; and they said, Behold, we be thy servants. And Joseph said unto them, Fear not: for am I in the place of God? But as for you, ye thought evil against me; but God meant it unto good, to bring to pass, as it is this day, to save much people alive. Now therefore fear ye not: I will nourish you, and your little ones. And he comforted them, and spake kindly unto them" (Genesis 50:16-21).*

"Well, I am not Joseph!"
Right! However, you are still accountable to God. Do the right thing.

7). Conclude in prayer.
Pray for one another. Ask the Lord to give you the strength, grace, wisdom, and the anointing to continue to walk in love, truth, and obedience. Let your reflections, words, nonverbal expressions, and actions demonstrate the fruit of the Spirit – love, joy, peace, longsuffering, gentleness, goodness, faith, meekness, temperance (Galatians 5:22-23).

Section 3: After Reconciliation
Embrace Healing and Restoration.
Before and after any settlement, release your hurts to the Lord and let Him heal all the painful memories generated from the conflict or the reconciliation will peter out into nothing or a dead end. Often, conflict resolution will accomplish little or nothing for some people if they cling to unhealed emotional wounds. Tap into this divine solution: *"For I am the LORD who heals you" (Exodus 15:26).* We need to apply the balm of forgiveness to seal the cracks that conflict fire inflicted on the relationship walls,

utilize truth as a power hose to wash off the residue, move past all the emotional insecurities, and trust God to heal our broken hearts. Reconciliation brings us together so we can fellowship, commune, and trust again. If we do not embrace God's healing, reconciliation will only be momentary.

Will the devil tempt you to take back your forgiveness? What do you expect? It is his full-time job to make you feel bad for letting go. Tell him to go to hell and rot there with his acrimony and depravity. You are no longer going to help him do his dirty job or collaborate with him to penalize those you love.

When You Cannot Resolve the Entire Conflict

Sometimes, not all misunderstandings in a relationship will be resolved at the same time. When specific issues are too complicated to sort out, work with the ones that have been straightened out and be patient about the ones that are still up in the air. Be grateful for whatever the Lord has enabled you to decipher and trust Him with what has not been ironed out yet. If He intervened in working out the present conflict, there is hope that you will reconcile other seemingly intricate issues with time.

Nail all unsettled supersensitive matters to the cross and leave them there. Be patient, teachable, and allow God to deal with your heart as well as the other person's. Unless your situation is life-threatening, do not try to sever alliances just because others are not marching to your drumbeat. Often, how we react to others reveals our weaknesses. Perhaps God is using their shortcomings to showcase yours. Let Him use your differences to enlarge your capacity for tolerance rather than allow them to weaken the relationship. Remember, His grace is more than enough for you (2 Corinthians 12:9a).

- **Scriptural Confession: Mathew 5:7, Proverbs12: 22, James 5:16**
- **Praise and Worship**

- **Prayer Points**

1. Father Lord, enlarge my aptitude to be patient and tolerant, in the name of Jesus
2. I receive your grace and strength to deal with my own flaws and be tolerant of others' faults, in the name of Jesus
3. Holy Spirit, counsel me with your truth, in the name of Jesus.
4. Holy Spirit, help me to be kind to others, in the name of Jesus.
5. I choose to show mercy, forgiveness, and peace in my relationships, in the name of Jesus.
6. Let the blood of Jesus consume impatience, restlessness, resentment, pride, selfishness, rebellion, and all unChrist-like thoughts in my heart, in the name of Jesus.
7. By the blood of Jesus, I choose to count my blessings and name them one by one, in the name of Jesus.
8. Jesus, my Lord and my God, The only way, truth and life, The Pathfinder, The way maker, and Trailblazer. Please, go before my loved ones and other godly associations, and "make all the crooked places straight. Break in pieces the gates of brass, and cut in sunder the bars of iron," in the name of Jesus.
9. I rebuke the spirits of bitterness, anger, and malice, in the name of Jesus.
10. Let the blood of Jesus Christ be transfused into my system and flush out every residue of anger, hurt, fear, disappointments, rejection, and traumatized memories, in the name of Jesus.
11. Let the blood of Jesus heal every painful memory from past and present hurts, in the name of Jesus.
12. Oh Lord, heal me from the inside out, in your precious name.
13. Oh Lord, heal my body, mind, soul, and emotions, in your mighty name.
14. I receive healing in my emotions and soul, in the name of Jesus Christ.
15. Father, I thank you for your healing and restoration power.
16. Thank God for answers to your prayers.

CHAPTER 24

When Others Rebuff Reconciliation

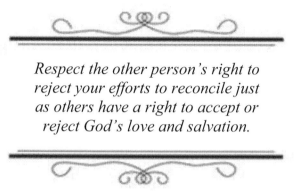

*Respect the other person's right to
reject your efforts to reconcile just
as others have a right to accept or
reject God's love and salvation.*

Sometimes, the person or people we disagree with may ignore, misconstrue or reject our good intentions for compromise. They may be too scared, livid, emotionally wounded or spiritually blinded to want to release their grievances. However, we cannot let the devil use their cold-heartedness to make us react in negative ways. Returning fire for fire or a tooth for a tooth will undoubtedly enchant him but displease God. Lauding God should be our focus.

"What should I do after I have done everything within my power to make peace, and the other person does not want to cooperate with me?"
Let us examine the following Scripture again. *"Moreover if your brother sins against you, go and tell him his fault between you and him alone. If he hears you, you have gained your brother. But if he will not hear, take with you one or two more, that 'by the*

mouth of two or three witnesses every word may be established. And if he refuses to hear them, tell it to the church. But if he refuses even to hear the church, let him be to you like a heathen and a tax collector" (Mathew 18:15-17).

Often, we are too quick to break relationships that are not in sync with our reality. There may be times when we need to disconnect from those who vehemently oppose peace. The following points will aid us to do things right.

1). As much as it hurts, don't take it personally.

Doing so will place you in a vulnerable situation. You will be tempted to become riled and malicious. Don't take the bait or turn it into a personal vendetta. Despite God's free gift of salvation, some people still reject Him. He does not force His own children to reconcile with Him. Despite your good intensions, respect the other person's right to repudiate reconciliation.

2). Prayerfully identify what the other person's "no" may imply.

Saying, "No" does not always denote that a person is totally apathetic about a relationship or wants to annul it. In some instances, saying, "no," may indicate, *"I need more time to process what has happened; sort out my feelings or identify where I am in this relationship, where I want to go, and how to get there."* It may simply indicate, *"Not now, I can't let Dave into my life now... maybe later...? I am not sure."* which suggests that reconciliation may be best at a more suitable time. "No" may also indicate, *"I need more time to hurt or heal."* Remember, people hurt and heal differently. Hampering reconciliation intensifies hurt, but embracing it induces healing and speeds up the restoration process.

Sometimes, saying, "No" may also connote, *"I am done with this relationship. I am no longer interested in it now or in the future."* If this is the situation, respect his or her decision and let the perfect will of God be done. You cannot impose harmony or coerce a relationship. However, you still have a divine obligation to respond biblically and forgive.

3). Refrain from nagging, condemning or pressurizing the other person.

Nagging causes others to recoil or become elusive. Reproving them desensitizes their hearts and spurs them to put up impenetrable barriers. Exacting pressure gives the other person 1001 reasons to remain apathetic and vindictive. Not everyone can perform under pressure. For some, pressure increases their insecurities, resistance, and insolence, and places an undue burden on them.

When too much pressure is applied, the other person may see reconciliation as a burdensome duty instead of a blessing or potential for growth. For a settlement to be a delight for the other person as it is for you, he or she must feel validated as a person and be able to communicate feelings without any fear of backlash. Only when a person feels valued will he or she have the incentive to embrace the benefits of compromise. Relax, and the other person will unwind and feel freer to forgive or communicate his or her feelings.

Give the other person a break! Give him or her the chance to reconcile out of love, not out of compulsion. Reconciling under duress brings only momentary and conditional peace. Reconciling out of love brings durable and unconditional harmony in a relationship.

4). Continue to respond with love despite what the other person's "no" may infer.

Bear in mind that every cloud has a silver lining. You have no other recourse than to be optimistic and trust God. We cannot extinguish fire with fire when in conflict with people. Choose to be the "water" that quenches it. Exhibiting love despite others' lackadaisical attitude disarms their anger, tears down their defenses, and demolishes the emotional strongholds they may have erected for protection. Also, it may cause them to become open-minded. It will pave the way for peace, and if nothing else, minimize their hostilities.

5). Wait, pray, and forbear.

Yes, it may not look fair, but like I said earlier, people handle conflict and heal differently. Sometimes, when one remains antagonistic or nonchalant about reconciliation, it is not always because he or she detests peace. It may be as a result of deeply embedded unresolved wounds that only God can define and heal.

Trying to impose harmony will only inflame the other person's trepidation. It may be too dicey to rattle his or her cage or expect a swift and peaceful resolution. Bide your time and re-approach subsequently when God gives you the grace to do so. While waiting for the other person to recuperate and analyze his or her feelings; halt your hostilities and maintain a cease-fire.

Lay down your conflict artilleries and walk in love. When you find yourself agitated about the other person's unresponsiveness, go back to the place of stillness and know that He is God (Psalm 46:10). He will be exalted in your situation, whether the other person reconciles with you or not. The devil will still be put to shame, in the name of Jesus.

6). Let go and let God!

After you have personally pursued peace, involved witnesses and the Church, and the other person does not want to resolve the conflict, you may simply disengage based on Mathew 18:15-17. Let God's purpose triumph. Accept the possibility that he or she may or may not want to reconnect with you.

Yield your will, fury, and hurt to God. Compliance indicates that you trust Him and are open to however He chooses to intervene. You cannot go wrong when you trust Him. The bottom line is that you have accepted responsibility. The ball is no longer in your court after you have repented and done everything within your power to sow peace in the relationship. You cannot force conciliation on others. Nonetheless, you can position yourself to be at peace with God, yourself, and expect His perfect will to prevail over the circumstance. You can pray others back into a relationship only if it is God's desire or if they choose to obey Him. If nothing else, your choice to bear no malice will glorify the Lord and emancipate you from demonic bondage.

The focus should be pleasing God, not whether others reach out to reciprocate your efforts to reconcile or not. *Have you truly forgiven them? Are you responding to those you are in conflict with in ways that glorify God? Do you trust the Lord with your concerns and with what you do not understand about their irritative behavior? Are you drawing your strength, joy, peace, and fulfillment from God or from people? Is your situation driving you away from Him or driving you into His safe arms? Are you unconditionally submitted to His perfect will for your life and situation or to only what you want?*

- **Scriptural Confession: 1 John 3:18, Ephesians 4:22-32; 5:1-11.**
- **Praise and Worship**
- **Prayer Points.**

1. Heavenly Father, I release those who have hurt me and every challenging situation to you, in the name of Jesus.
2. I yield my will, anger, and hurt to you, in the name of Jesus.
3. I choose to continue to respond with love regardless of others' reactions or responses, in the name of Jesus.
4. Father, I choose to be open to however You want to resolve the situation and heal my relationships, in the name of Jesus.
5. I choose to be open to your ways, timings, and due seasons, in the name of Jesus
6. Father, let the fire of the Holy Spirit ignite a new zeal, hunger, and love for You, in the name of Jesus.
7. Let the blood of Jesus begin to melt our stubborn hearts, heal our broken hearts and souls, in the name of Jesus.
8. Let the blood of Jesus melt my hardened heart and the hearts of those within and outside my circle, in the name of Jesus.
9. Let the blood of Jesus remove every barrier between our reconciliation, in the name of Jesus.
10. Let the resurrection power of the Holy Spirit roll away every stone that has been used to weigh down my relationships, in the name of Jesus.

11. Father God, step into our situation and help us to forgive each other and settle our differences, in the name of Jesus.
12. Let the blood of Jesus reconcile our disparities, in the name of Jesus.
13. I break and destroy every prison wall holding my household and relationships ransom in bondage, in the name of Jesus.
14. King of Glory, the Lord strong and mighty; The Lord mighty in battle; the Lord of host; *"break in pieces the gates of brass, and cut in sunder the bars of iron"* that have been used to cage my family, destiny, and relationships, in the name of Jesus.
15. Lord Jesus, "not my will; but let your perfect will be done" in my life and relationships, in your holy name.
16. Father God, thank you for our breakthrough and victory.

CHAPTER 25

Look Before You Break Divine Relationships

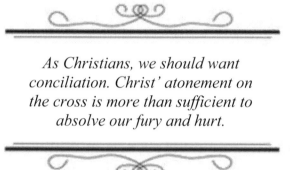

*As Christians, we should want
conciliation. Christ' atonement on
the cross is more than sufficient to
absolve our fury and hurt.*

Are all relationships ordained by God?
God does not endorse all relationships. Adulterous affairs, evil alliances, parasitic, obsessive, possessive, toxic, controlling or manipulative ties with hidden agendas are not divine but demonic relationships. They do not laud God. Such ungodly affiliations are orchestrated by people for selfish gain. He blesses only relationships that glorify Him, not the ones we stubbornly form out of egoism and rebellion.

What are divine relationships?
They are covenant relationships between relatives, friends, professionals, Pastors and parishioners, mentors and protégées, and other formal and informal ties that honor God. Sometimes, some of these ties can become ungodly and toxic when they stray

from God's original purpose for their connection and begin to pursue their agenda.

Covenant Relationships Matter

God ordained divine relationships for significant reasons. How would Joshua have led the Israelites to the promised land without Moses' mentorship? David would not have been king in Israel without the support of Samuel and the protection of his close friend, Jonathan. How could Queen Esther have assumed a position of prominence without her uncle, Mordecai's assistance? Would Ruth have attained greatness without her mother-in-law, Naomi? Who else would have imparted Elisha with a double portion anointing if not for Elijah? How could Timothy have overcome his insecurities without the counsel of the apostle Paul? Each of these people could have ended differently if not for the divine relationships that God used to accelerate their destinies.

Where would Lot have been without Abraham's protection? How successful would Laban have been without Jacob tending his flock? Without the wise counsel of Jethro, Moses would not have understood the importance of sharing the burden of the Israelites with the 70 elders. (See Exodus 18:17-24.) Would the disciples have transformed the world with the gospel without the empowerment of Jesus?

Nurture and Protect Divine Ties

Divine relationships matter a great deal. Many are in great distress partly because we have a soulish mindset like the unbelievers. How we think, communicate or relate to one another is hardly different. We should not be naïve about why God places us in certain relationships. He uses them to move us from where we are to where He wants us to be. Many destinies have been sabotaged, reframed or even terminated because people disconnected from significant relationships for the wrong reasons. There are hordes of distressed people who are frustrated because they disengaged from ties that would have catapulted them to their *Canaan*. These relationships may have been uncomfortable but would have shortened the distance to their goals. Often, we tend to run from people or relationships that infuriate, challenge, stretch, threaten or make us feel uneasy. Yet these are the people that God will use to sharpen us, enlarge our capacity, and take us through different seasons to new heights.

Imagine if Jacob had angrily detached himself from his children after He discovered their deception about Joseph, it would have taken a toll on their individual and collective destinies. Yet that is what many families do when they are in conflict. They rant about who gets to host the holiday dinner, divorce each other over earthly possessions, inheritance issues, and other irrelevant matters rather than settle their disputes. Jacob's deceptive children became the 12 tribes of Israel. Together, our families can attain unfathomable heights if only we set aside our disparities.

If Sarah had divorced Abraham for childlessness, she would have missed out on conceiving Isaac. What would have happened if Ruth had walked away from Naomi out of frustration? If David had stubbornly disconnected from Jonathan, Esther from Mordechai, Ruth from Naomi, Moses from Joshua, Elijah from Elisha, Paul from Timothy, Jesus from the disciples or verse visa, it would have deferred, redefined, or even aborted their destinies. Jesus understood the value of divine relationships; hence, He continued to love Peter and Judas even though he knew that the former would deny him and the later would betray Him. Divine relationships are in place to take us further than we can go ourselves and catapult us to greatness.

Relationship Hoppers

Some believers are habitual drifters. They gallivant from one relationship or Church to another, because they have allowed themselves to be influenced by a "vagabond spirit." Also, the fear of accountability causes them to float from one dysfunctional relationship to another. They are elusive, flighty, thrill-seekers, and relationship addicts. They crave new alliances because they feel that the next one may be better suited to meet their needs or expectations. Lo and behold, when they wake up and smell the coffee, they annul the relationship and meander to a new one. A new connection is like a new toy or paraphernalia they eagerly want to have fun with but will easily discard when they get bored. The euphoric feeling a new relationship offers quickly dissipates when confronted with commitment and accountability. Then comes the justification to seek a new one. They hardly associate long enough to cultivate healthy soul ties.

It is immature to bounce from one church to another, friendship to friendship, job to job, business to another, ministry to ministry, or change divine relationships as often as we do a wardrobe and expect to be fruitful. It is parasitic and demonic to use people as pawns, flee affiliations that require responsibility, and succumb to the control of a vagabond spirit when we should be giving the devil a black eye with Truth.

God wants us deeply entrenched in valuable ties, not uproot ourself when we cannot get our way or roam around like a little lost child. It grieves Him when we are not liaising with others. We need to settle down, grow, spread our wings where ever He has planted us, and invest in people to build trust.

Effects of Rending a Godly Relationship

Every legal contract or covenant has stiff consequences when violated. Default in a mortgage contract, car note, credit card, or medical bills will have one's name tattooed in the credit bureau. If humans have zero tolerance for those who violate societal standards, how much more will a holy God hold us accountable if we sever godly alliances.

God expects us to reverence Him more than we revere creditors. *"Do you not fear Me?' says the LORD. 'Will you not tremble at My presence, Who have placed the sand as the bound of the sea, By a perpetual decree, that it cannot pass beyond it? And though its waves toss to and fro, Yet they cannot prevail; Though they roar, yet they cannot pass over it. But this people* has a defiant and rebellious heart; They have revolted and departed. They do not say in their heart, "Let us now fear the LORD our God,......" (Jeremiah 5:22-24b). "It is a fearful thing to fall into the hands of the living God" (Hebrews 10:31). Let's discuss some of the ramifications.

1). Sin and disobedience can bring a curse.

Promising others to be there for them and breaching it intentionally is dishonesty. It can either evoke demonic attacks or curses if not properly addressed with repentance and prayers. *"Better is it that thou shouldest not vow, than that thou shouldest vow and not pay"* (Ecclesiastes 5:5). *"Offer unto God thanksgiving; and pay thy vows unto the most High"* (Psalm 50:14).

Often, we are too quick to make promises without considering the ramifications of breaking them on our terms. We yearn to start new relationships but also cannot wait to hop out when the honeymoon seems over. We may have legitimate reasons for discharging ourselves from valuable relationships during tumultuous times. However, the question is: *Is God releasing you from the relationship or are you releasing yourself?* Leaving on our stipulations still means disobedience if God did not release us from it.

We sin against God when we jump ship to evade commitment or accountability. Sin and disobedience bring curses. There are those who are walking around with the curse of disobedience, pride, and unbelief – and will account for their behavior. Our God is a covenant-keeper and will protect His integrity in a relationship regardless of whether we are faithful or not to those He has assigned to us. *"If we believe not, yet he abideth faithful: he cannot deny himself"* (2 Timothy 2:13).

2). Disobedience opens the door to unnecessary warfare.

If you undermine or desert a godly relationship without His approval, disobedience can open doors to various kinds of unnecessary warfare.

The prodigal Son deserted his devoted father because he felt he could do better without him. However, he learned the hard way when he could no longer withstand the warfare that disobedience brought into his life.

Joseph's brothers felt no use for him; hence they sold him to the Ishmaelites. However, when plagued with famine, the brother they once abandoned later became the cornerstone of the family when they needed him the most.

King Saul treacherously deserted David because of his soulish mindset. Instead of relating to him as a father figure, he became his adversary. Still, David refrained from taking matters into his hands but relied on God to deal with King Saul rather than murder him. While he waited for God's due season, Saul warfare intensified and fell by his own sword.

Let us not forget the warfare that Satan brought into Adam and Eve's lives because of their disobedience. Their disconnection from God exposed them to fear, guilt, shame, condemnation, and death.

3). Insubordination to God's word sabotages destiny.

We need friends and foes, benefactors and detractors alike. While allies cheer us on, opponents keep us alert and meek. When we stubbornly detach from those whom we are assigned to or are allocated to us, we cut off what we were divinely intended to sow in each other and prolong the distance to achieving our dreams. Likewise, we disrupt the blessings we would have garnered from one another and what we would have accomplished through that connection.

Often, we are too conceited to receive from those that should be stretching our faith muscles because of their flaws. We undermine their anointing and define them by their failings. When they correct us, we feel that they are controlling when all they are really trying to do is provoke us to repent. When others confront us with change, we feel that they are too hard on us when all they are doing is poking us with truth in areas, we are susceptible and noncompliant.

There are some *Moses'* that are ordained to help us confront our "Pharaohs," deliver us from bondages, and aid us to cross the *Red Sea*. But sadly, we have disconnected from them and missed a great opportunity. Equally, there are *"Joshuas"* designed to equip us to pull down strongholds and smash the *"walls of Jericho"* en route our *"Canaan"* that we may have regrettably detached from out of stubbornness. There are *"Davids"* assigned to embolden us to kill our *"Goliaths,"* and *"Nehemiahs"* that will galvanize us to rebuild the broken walls of our lives, families, Churches, communities, and other interpersonal relationships. The question is are we willing to remain in those valuable relationships long enough for divine impartation? Their experiences, anointings, and authority should qualify and make them matter.

God will link you with those that will: use truth to provoke you to change, insist you step up to the plate, give you the tools to confront your hang-ups, inspire you to tread by faith, hold you accountable when you are tempted to cut corners, compel you to walk on the straight and narrow part, motivate you to live by the Spirit, kick you out of your comfort zone, and squeeze you until the anointing oil of the Holy Spirit begins to ooze out of you. He will connect you to midwives that will help birth your vision, life coaches that will shorten the distance to your goals, and divine helpers that will catapult you to the throne. He will attach you to *"Mordecais,"* *"Ruths,"* *"Naomis,"* *"Deborahs,"* *"Jonathans,"* and *"Pauls"* that have the divine wisdom, anointing, and authority to prep you for your next season or Assignment.

Sometimes, they may seem hard on you because "the throne" is not for the weary, fearful or slothful. Cooperate wholly because you need their impartation and wisdom. Glean from their steadfastness, audacious faith, and other sagacious qualities until the purpose of God is fulfilled in your life.

There are those we must submit to because they are the *"Shepherds"* that will discern and appreciate our *"star,"* the *"Samuels"* *that* will anoint us as kings, the *"Ezras"* that will ignite a new spiritual hunger and thirst for God in us, the *"Good Samaritans"* that will pour in the oil and wine to heal our wounds, the *"Jonathans"* preordained to protect our calling, and the *"Elishas"* that would impart into us a double portion anointing. Regardless of how uncomfortable these relationships might be, we must cling to them like Ruth clasped to Naomi and Timothy allied with Paul, the Apostle until we get their impartation or their assignment or season in our lives elapse. While some of these divine relationships are temporal, others are permanent.

When you crave deliverance because you have wandered in the wilderness for too long, you will not be picky about how and who God will use to deliver you. You will be receptive even if He requires you to crawl, walk, run or hitch-hike to get to the Promised Land. Once, I submitted to a Mentor because the Lord wanted him to give me the tools to leave the *wilderness*. I was fed up with spiritual unfruitfulness and too angry at the devil to notice his flaws that could have hindered me from submitting to his tutelage. When the season was over, we parted ways, and God got the glory. I am grateful for how the Lord used him to impact my life and Ministry. Some of his flocks who let his deficiencies get in the way detached from him and forfeited what God wanted to impart in them through this imperfect Mentor. If you leave a divine relationship prematurely, your destiny will be at the mercy of your impulsiveness and disobedience. If you dissociate out of anger, pride or unteachableness, you may delay, divert, minimize, sabotage or even abort your blessings or destiny.

Just as we defend our rights to leave a covenant relationship when it is no longer meeting our demands, so must we also carefully ponder the ramifications of stubbornly abandoning it out of resentments.

4). Unresolved conflict generates hurt and grieves God.

All forms of break-ups – whether it is a Church, family, friendship or professional split come with pain, guilt, shame, and condemnation. It can take months or even years to overcome the trauma. Many never really get healed and are forced to deal with rejection and betrayal incessantly.

The devil is trying to sabotage many treasured relationships. Unresolved conflict has split -up hordes of Churches, families, businesses, and communities. It grieves God to see that the time, energy, and resources that should be invested in bearing fruits in these relationships are now diverted to battling one another.

Unsettled conflict weakens and divides the body of Christ. God wants us to be united, interdependent, and express His love, compassion, and character through the bond we have. We are the body of Christ. Like a cohesive family, we all rejoice, hurt, fall or rise together. Our solidarity is unequaled when united but frail when asunder. If you are looking for a perfect believer or Church to cultivate a healthy relationship with, stop wasting your time because you will never find one. The Church is made up of deficient people that must strive towards perfection and become more like Christ daily.

Satan is discombobulating us with his lies, abuse, intolerance, trepidation, worldliness, and antipathy. Yet we wine and dine with him and even sanction him to exhibit his impieties through us because we are unaware that he is the root of conflict in our homes, Churches, market place, and communities. Rather than accept responsibility and fall on our knees in contrition and cry out to God to restore us, we excuse our wickedness and blame each other. Living soulishly to please ourselves, resisting reconciliation, and rejecting those we should be loving should sadden us like it grieves God. The thought of unjustly isolating our relatives, friends, brethren, and associates should disturb our conscience. Which part of Mathew chapter 22; verse 36 to 40 do we not understand?

5). Unresolved conflict reduces a believer's credibility

It is so sad that some Christians go to secular or carnally minded half-baked counselors to resolve their disputes. It is no wonder that there are copious dysfunctional relationships in Christendom. *"Dare any of you, having a matter against another, go to law before the unrighteous, and not before the saints?" "... If then you have judgments concerning things pertaining to this life, do you appoint those who are least esteemed by the church to judge? I say this to your shame. Is it so, that there is not a wise man among you, not even one, who will be able to judge between his brethren?" (Look* up 1 Corinthians 6: 1, 4-5.)

"But brother goes to law against brother, and that before unbelievers! Now therefore, it is already an utter failure for you that you go to law against one another. Why do you not rather accept wrong? Why do you not rather let yourselves be cheated? No, you yourselves do wrong and cheat, and you do these things to your brethren!" (See 1 Corinthians 6:6-8.) Often, we rather go to unbelievers for counsel and accept their worldly solutions than repent. Many divine relationships are dissolved because of lack of contrition and reverential fear of God. We must choose His ways, not the world's

6). Unresolved conflict produces ungodly soul ties

As Christians, God expects us to cultivate godly soul ties with those within and outside our circle. As believers, our souls are supposed to bond on a deeper level than unbelievers. However, we are torn apart by antipathy and hurt.

Even divine relationships can turn sour or become toxic if people are contemptuous, indocile, and unaccountable. For example, King Saul was supposed to form a godly soul tie with David, mentor him like a father, and receive the blessings of obedience. Instead, he allowed jealousy and wickedness to get a better hold of him. The relationship that God would have used to enhance both of them turned sour because he could not handle his insecurities.

Sometimes, even in godly relationships, people develop demonic soul ties when they wallow in conflict or refuse to reconcile their differences. Parents can develop ungodly soul ties with their children if they have unresolved disagreements. Friends, neighbors, relatives, colleagues, Church members can also cultivate ungodly soul ties with each other if they choose to be unreconcilable.

To heal unhealthy soul ties in covenant relationships, we must accept responsibility and repent for the bad soul ties that were developed through anger, bitterness, and malice. When we repent, embrace forgiveness, and begin to respond in ways that glorify God, gradually, our souls will be restored. Every one of us will begin to bond on a greater dimension again.

7). Unresolved conflict has a negative ripple effect on the family and society.

People of all ages, races, gender, and beliefs are watching how we interrelate as Christians. When we distance from people that we should be ministering to, it becomes so much easier for those that would have embraced reconciliation to reproduce our sinful behavior. Our conduct should inspire, not dissuade others from yielding to God.

Life is not about how much we can get, but give, how much we can consume, but produce or how much we can reap, but sow in others. It is not about fueling our agenda to accumulate more but fulfilling the will of God. We must be willing to live and die for something greater than ourselves. We must superimpose the purpose of God on our aspirations and live exclusively to gratify Him. Doing the will of God must supersede everything else in a relationship.

Past generations have sacrificed everything to impart the present. What are we willing to do for future generations? We must sow godliness, faith, love, commitment, forgiveness, and tolerance in our relationships so that our sons and daughters will have a righteous standard to emulate. People are watching how we respond to issues of life. Our responses will either drive them into the hands of God or the web of the enemy.

Wrong Reasons to Exit a Divine Relationship

Many believers leave godly relationships for the wrong reasons. It is not biblical to detach from people because they are boring, old-fashioned, exasperating, parsimonious, egotistic, insensitive, complaisant, impoverished, lazy, imperfect, unlovable or inharmonious. Moreover, you cannot annul a divine relationship because of incompatibility issues or unmet needs that may be driving you and your allies further apart without considering if you have allowed God to use these challenges to enlarge your capacity to love and forgive. Due to hardness of heart, we choose to grow apart, have seemingly irreconcilable differences or develop hatred for others only because they are not kowtowing to our lofty expectations. So, when we feel threatened, we withdraw our love, pack up our "toys," and go play where we can have our way.

We should never leave a relationship because others are brutally honest or bold enough to confront, correct or rebuke us for sinning. We need allies that are not afraid to tell us the truth or hold our feet to the fire. Those who are provoking us to change, challenging us to wash our mouth because it stinks, and prodding us to maximize our potential are blessings in disguise and should be applauded.

Some of the other outrageous pretexts that people use to substantiate conflict or annul covenant relationships are unscriptural. Often, they are secular justifications used to evade repentance but gratify the self.

When to Detach From People

God requires more of us. *"To whom much is given, much is required."* As a believer, we know better because we have tasted the love, power, goodness, and mercies of God. Therefore, it is our responsibility to smear the fragrance of these divine encounters on others. We do not share love merely because we want others to respond in kind – although our humanity craves reciprocity. Sharing love transcends reciprocation from others. Fundamentally, we extend love to embody the character of God so others will encounter Him through us.

Based on Scriptures, we must exercise the fruit of the Spirit when dealing with people. However, there are times when we must walk away from an unwholesome relationship to protect ourselves and make concession for peace. At such times, we must disassociate to prevent abuse, strife, and the susceptibility to sin. Abraham had to separate himself from his nephew, Lot, for the sake of harmony when their herdsmen clashed. (See Genesis 13:5-

12.) Jacob severed himself from his brother, Esau, and later from his father-in-law, Laban, after serving him rigorously for 20 years and enduring his abuse. (See Genesis 31:1-55.) Initially, David used his craftsmanship in music to pacify king Saul's demons. However, when he persistently plotted to kill him, he dissociated from him to shield his destiny. Even Paul, the apostle, separated himself from Barnabas for a season after they had a "sharp contention" about John Mark. Later, they did work together as co-laborers in the Lord's Vineyard. (See Acts 15:35-40; 2 Timothy 4:11.)

Toxic relationships are unhealthy for our souls. When others try to lure us into the demonic, entice us with sin or turn us away from God, it is time to cut the umbilical cord! If people in a relationship are no longer conforming to His ways, they will become a distraction and stumbling block to spiritual growth. If they refuse to repent, then we can break away so that they will not taint us with their impiety and lead us into error. We need to decamp from ungodly alliances that will distort our focus, make us backslide, wane our thirst for God, hamper our goals or abort our divine Assignment for their selfish gains. We must establish healthy boundaries and love some people from a distance until they are willing to repent.

What about people that leave divine relationships the wrong way?

Have you disconnected wrongly? Every so often, God will require you to make amends if your circumstances allow it. He did in the case of Hagar. He commanded her to go back and submit to her mistress after she ran away from Sarah's harshness. Jacob could not reverse his wrong against his brother, Esau. However, he humbled himself and made amends.

Onesimus robbed his master, Philemon, and ran away. However, he came back and made restitution after he became a believer through Apostle Paul's ministry. There have been a few times when I disconnected for the wrong reasons, and I had to repent and crucify my pride. I went back and submitted to the relationships because the Lord compelled me to do so. However, if you cannot recompence, genuinely repent and ask God for forgiveness. He will forgive and bless you if you endeavor to make your new relationships work.

Disconnect Biblically When Necessary

We need to be mindful that we do not break up relationships recklessly, apathetically or soulishly. I worked with a talented Woman of God; I'll call Evangelist Anna. Every personal and general discussion we had were related to the *"news media."* I didn't like that because I respect confidentiality and expect those around me to do the same without having to pull my teeth out. To make matters worse, I had to relate every single thing I conversed with other circles of friends and Ministry leaders to her like we were all conjoined in the hips. The problem was not only the constant clash of our distinctive personalities, but the high maintenance required to pacify her and maintain our fleeting friendship. It was grueling and time-consuming, but the Holy Spirit enabled me to continue to walk in love and understanding.

I begged the Lord several times to release me from the relationship. But He didn't because He was using her to enlarge my capacity to love and tolerate. Each time, I tried to end it, something would happen that would require me to minister to her. Though I had seemingly justifiable reasons to detach, I resisted the urge because I knew better and decided to ride it out. I realized that I couldn't just walk away without the Lord's approval. So, I continued to manage the relationship. However, it was an enormous relief when He finally released me on His terms. Everything fell in the right place and the timing was perfect. There was no drama, ill feelings or schism when we went our separate ways. Whenever we meet, we can still hug and talk like old times with no hard feelings. May the Lord be praised!

Sometimes, relationships that are supposed to be divine connections can turn toxic because some people can be cruel – such as in the alliance between Esau and Jacob and King Saul and David. If there is no repentance or change, the Lord may *"permit"* a disconnection. Remember, *"God's perfect will"* is different from *"God's permissive will."* Just because He allows something does not mean it gratifies Him. His *"perfect will"* is that we fellowship, commune, and dwell in perfect unity. However, there are times He will allow the severing of a valuable relationship either temporary or permanently only because the people that are allied vehemently oppose reconciliation or His will.

We should be exhibiting interpersonal skills and enhancing divine relationships, not absconding from them. However, if you feel that you must leave a relationship, ask yourself: *Am I disconnecting out of pride, anger or rebellion? Is the Lord releasing me or am I releasing myself from the relationship? Will my "staying" or "leaving" laud God?* Be honest with yourself. Sometimes, like Paul, the apostle and Barnabas, it may be only a temporal disconnection. Regardless, prayerfully, contritely, unassumingly, and quietly do it the right way without any drama or hard feelings. Do not flaunt your ego or cause problems. Lay down your conflict weapons and let God get the glory.

How we enter or exit a relationship matters to God. One must bear the responsibilities of entering, remaining or withdrawing from it. Do everything you can to esteem God and everyone connected. However, when you feel that you must disaffiliate, ensure that you approach it with intense prayer, fasting, and counseling from matured believers. We must enter or leave peoples' lives based on God's stipulations, not ours. It is a grievous sin to enter or exit relationships out of rebellion or for selfish gains.

Chase Satan Out, not People.

Enough of Satan's bedevilment! He has no legal right to drive you out of the lives of those whom God has assigned to you. He is the trespasser that must be booted out, not those you love. If God forgave you, why would you not exonerate them? If you believe that His word delivers, let It liberate you and your loved ones. Yes, you may be hot under the collar right now because of their wrong. However, do not *"split the baby into half," "throw the baby out with the bathwater"* or "build a conflict bomb" that will blow up a relationship just because you want to have your way. Emotions may flare-up. However, take a breather and find healthy ways to resolve your seemingly irreconcilable issues. When you have a bee in your bonnet about conflict you will be blind to other possibilities that God is presenting to you. Let your love for Him bring you to your knees in complete surrender. He understands your situation and knows how to fix it. Let His word steer you in the right direction, let character defend you, and gentleness mature you.

Regardless of the degeneration of a relationship, God is a restorer and can make all things beautiful again. He can turn a disintegrating alliance into a scenic paradise if everyone is willing to collaborate with Him. He cares because He is the Originator of all godly associations. We form a *"three-fold cord that cannot easily be broken"* due to our covenant with Him. (See Ecclesiastes 4:12.) *"With one mind and one mouth, we glorify God, even the Father of our Lord Jesus Christ" (Romans 15:6).*

Again, we must *"look"* carefully before divorcing godly alliances because of the deleterious aftermath of disobedience. The implications of stubbornly dissolving relationships that are ordained by God should alarm us. The physical, emotional, and spiritual toll can be noxious. It is always better to explore other efficacious options before crossing the Rubicon.

Indeed, as a loving Father, God will eagerly forgive us if we abandon those, He has called us to minister to – if we repent. However, disobedience will stifle the blessings and possibilities that such alliances would have produced.

- **Scriptural Confession: 1 John 3:18, Ephesians 4:22-32; 5:1-11**
- **Praise and Worship**
- **Prayer Points**

1. Oh God please help me to forgive myself and those you have assigned to me, in the name of Jesus.

2. Oh God, save me from the trap and pollution of the enemy. Deliver me from the hands of the devil, in the name of Jesus.
3. I hate everything that God hates and love only what He loves, in the name of Jesus.
4. Conflict is not my portion. My portion is fruitful relationships with those I love, in the name of Jesus.
5. By the blood of Jesus Christ, I refuse to be cantankerous or whine about others, in the name of Jesus. Instead, I choose to appreciate and celebrate them, in the name of Jesus.
6. Let every serpentine spirit mocking and taunting me with "Ye hath God said...." Be paralyzed, in the name of Jesus.
7. I hold the blood of Jesus against the spirit of strife assigned to turn me against others, in the name of Jesus.
8. By the blood of Jesus, I command all the powers that have been assigned against my relationships to turn against themselves, in the name of Jesus.
9. I command every arrow of strife and divorce fired at my relationships to go back to the sender, in the name of Jesus.
10. Let God arise in my divine relationships and let all His enemies scatter by fire, in the name of Jesus (Psalm 68:1.)
11. By the blood of Jesus, I reclaim everything that the devil has stolen from my life and relationships, in the name of Jesus.
12. Let every valley in my life, household, and relationships be exalted, every mountain and hill be made plain, the crooked places be made straight, and the rough places be plain to the glory of God, in the name of Jesus. (Isaiah 40:4).
13. I reverse and nullify every evil decree pronounced against my family and relationships, in the name of Jesus.
14. Thank you, Lord, because only your will and purpose will prevail in our lives and relationships, in the name of Jesus.
15. Thank God for answers to your prayers.

CHAPTER 26

"Do not be Unequally Yoked..."

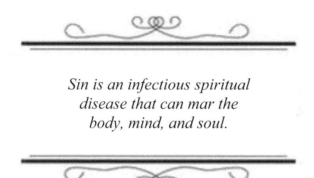

*Sin is an infectious spiritual
disease that can mar the
body, mind, and soul.*

"*D*o not be unequally yoked together with unbelievers. For what fellowship has righteousness with lawlessness? And what communion has light with darkness? And what accord has Christ with Belial? Or what part has a believer with an unbeliever? ¹⁶ And what agreement has the temple of God with idols? For you are the temple of the living God. As God has said: "I will dwell in them And walk among them. I will be their God, And they shall be My people." Therefore "Come out from among them And be separate, says the Lord. Do not touch what is unclean, And I will receive you." "I will be a Father to you, And you shall be My sons and daughters, Says the LORD Almighty" (2 Corinthians 6:14-18).* We cannot live a double standard anymore. It is either we are holy or impure, heaven or hell bound, on the straight and narrow path or the wide and broad lane, and liaising with God or the devil. We cannot have it both ways.

"Come Out From Among Them…"

Let us examine three types of ungodly people or relationships, when, why, and how we should avoid them.

1). The Hardened Sinner With a Reprobate Mind

People with a reprobate mind are carnal, lawless, and habitual sinners. They are addicted to sin and wittingly err against God to gratify their flesh. Often, people develop a degenerate mind when they incessantly ignore the nudging of the Holy Spirit to repent. Gradually, their hearts harden even more with every resistance to repentance until they have no consciousness of sin. Eventually, sinning becomes a way of life because their conscience has been *"seared with a hot iron"* (1 Timothy 4:2; Romans 1:28). Impenitence can desensitize one's conscience. Beware of unrepentant sinners and consider the dangers of closely associating with them.

a). Sin is contagious, like leprosy. *When you lie with the dogs, you get the fleas.* If sin is not dealt with, it can spread and contaminate innocent souls. *"Know ye not that a little leaven leaveneth the whole lump?" (See 1 Corinthians 5:6b).* Just as Miriam was placed outside the camp of the Israelites when she contracted leprosy through disobedience, so should we keep habitual sinners at bay until they show fruits of repentance or change. (See Numbers 12:1-16.) Like a pandemic, if sin is not nipped in the bud, it can infect us and become a stronghold.

Even David did not want to dignify idolaters by mentioning their names. *"Their sorrows shall be multiplied that hasten after another god: their drink offerings of blood will I not offer, nor take up their names into my lips" (Psalm 16:4).* He did not want to be associated with "dissemblers" because of their evil influence. *"I have not sat with vain persons, neither will I go in with dissemblers. I have hated the congregation of evil doers; and will not sit with the wicked. I will wash mine hands in innocency: so will I compass thine altar, O LORD" (Psalm 26:4-6).*

We must detach from people that are in cahoots with Satan to defile us with sin. *"Now we command you, brethren, in the name of our Lord Jesus Christ, that ye withdraw yourselves from every brother that walketh disorderly, and not after the tradition which he received of us" (2 Thessalonians 3:6).*

The Israelites sank into idolatry and sacrificed their children to idols because they embraced the heathenistic nations that lured them into it. They intermingled with them, adopted their paganistic cultures, and sin became *"snares, scourges in their sides, and thorns in their eyes." (See Joshua 23:13.)*

We cannot be complacent about sin or succumb to repulsive conducts as norms. Sin is an infectious disease that can corrupt and ravage relationships if proper perimeters are not in place to check others. Korah, Dathan and Abiram's sin of insurrection not only polluted the camp and destroyed 250 people, but it also incited the anger of the Lord and a plague that obliterated 14,700 Israelis. (See Numbers 16:1-50.) The only cure for this spiritual malady is genuine repentance.

b). Temptation to sin: Satan is an enchanter! He can use others to seduce us. If we stay too close to habitual sinners, we may be tempted to adopt their errant ways. We can interrelate with them only if we are influencing, transforming, and imparting them with the gospel, not the other way around. Also, we need to impose limits, so they do not drag us through the mud. Those who feel that they are immune from falling should heed this warning: *"Wherefore let him that thinketh he standeth take heed lest he fall" (1 Corinthians 10:12).*

c). It weakens relationships and exacts undue burden on others: Condoning or excusing one with self-defeating habits can weaken a relationship. If a friend that is a *"sin addict"* refuses to come clean, it will place an undue burden of guilt on you because you may have to keep lying for her. If her conduct is left unchecked, you may have to bear that albatross around your neck. The devil can sow the same seeds of addiction in your life because you are masquerading her. When you help people to hide their sin, you will form a demonic soul tie with them and open yourself up to demonic exploitation as well.

d). Sin generates unnecessary warfare: King Saul and the Prodigal Son had sin related warfare due to their disobedience.

The mariners had enough discernment to unmask Jonah's sin of rebellion and acted wisely. Once they discovered that his defiance against God induced their storm, they had to throw him into the tempestuous sea or continue to suffer the repercussions. It saved their lives and that of Jonah's (Jonah 1:1-16). Many of us would have continued to enable and defend him. We must stand up against iniquity.

e). Sin hinders victory and breakthroughs: The Israelis could not defeat their enemies because of sin in the camp. *"... Neither will I be with you anymore, unless you destroy the accursed from among you. ...There is an accursed thing in your midst, O Israel; you cannot stand before your enemies until you take away the accursed thing from among you" (Joshua 7:12-13).* Achan stole the Babylonian garment and weakened their hands. Sin dilutes one's spiritual authority and standing with God.

f). It may well save the sinner's soul: Paul, the apostle, addressed this important issue: *"It is reported commonly that there is fornication among you, and such fornication as is not so much as named among the Gentiles, that one should have his father's wife... To deliver such an one unto Satan for the destruction of the flesh, that the spirit may be saved in the day of the Lord Jesus" (1 Corinthians 5:1,5).* Sometimes, we need to let a hardcore sinner face the music to save him or her from self-sabotage. We must shield ourselves from possible sin pollution.

g). Risk of liaising with the sinner and the devil to defile the name of Jesus: *"I wrote to you in my epistle not to keep company with sexually immoral people. Yet I certainly did not mean with the sexually immoral people of this world, or with the covetous, or extortioners, or idolaters, since then you would need to go out* *of the world. But now I have written to you not to keep company with anyone named a brother, who is sexually immoral, or covetous, or an idolater, or a reviler, or a drunkard, or an extortioner—not even to eat with such a person. For what have I to do with judging those also who are outside? Do you not judge those who are inside? But those who are outside God judges. Therefore "put away from yourselves the evil person" (1 Corinthians 5:9-13).*

We are to love, but distant ourselves from worldly believers so their sin will not defile us. We must hold their feet to the fire and demand accountability. *"For we hear that there are some which walk among you disorderly, working not at all, but are busybodies... And if any man obey not our word by this epistle, note that man, and have no company with him, that he may be ashamed. Yet count him not as an enemy, but admonish him as a brother" (2 Thessalonians 3:11, 14-15).* Certain boundaries must be in place before reconnecting so we do not become liable to sin as well. We must protect the sanctity of divine relationships.

2). The Physical, Sexual, Verbal or Emotional Abuser

I realize that I am treading on a delicate terrain when it comes to the issue of verbal and emotional abuse. What one may call verbal or emotional abuse may mean something entirely different to another. What may be disparaging to one person in a relationship may mean something else to the other. In my extensive years of counseling, what some people may delineate as verbal or mental abuse does not always connote denigration. Some perceive it as mistreatment because they have an unhealthy self-concept, brittle emotions, and an overly sensitive wounded spirit.

Sometimes, we feel maltreated when others confront us and disparaged when we cannot have our way. People that have the spirit of rejection manifesting through them are at risk of feeling rejected when things go awry. Those that have fragile emotions are more inclined to feel derided when they clash with others. A little or no attention from their friends, family or acquaintances may make them feel ill-treated or injure their overly delicate emotions.

Some people who complain about verbal or emotional abuse indulge in abuse themselves. Their supposedly pejorative situation is a direct or indirect replication of their scathing invectives. Perhaps, there are only a few relationships that are untarnished by verbal and emotional abuse. Just as others say or do things to belittle us knowingly and unknowingly, so are we just as guilty. This does not excuse abuse at all! It is just that when we claim to be victims when we are not, the real victims suffer tremendously. They may not be taken seriously or get the help they desperately need. It takes spiritual maturity to distinguish between real and imagined abuse and refrain from treating people with cruelty as well.

When people in a relationship engage in verbal, emotional, sexual or physical abuse, hold off on reconciliation until they are willing to change their injurious behavior. When you honestly feel that your life is endangered, then lingering in an abusive environment will not help. Any form of abuse or violence is unhealthy and unlike God – and should never be condoned. Tolerating abuse makes you an enabler. As long as you allow yourself to be a whipping post, you are abetting aggression. You are a child of the King of kings, not a punching bag. Immediately remove yourself from that precarious situation to a safe place until the other person or people are willing to act decently. God will not get the glory if the devil uses people to destroy you.

In situations where one or more abusive people refuse to repent, prayerfully remove them from your inner circle or the relationship altogether. Depending on the type of alliance, disconnect to protect yourself if they refuse to leave. People that insist on deprecatory conduct have a negative concept of self and others. Hold them accountable and kept them at bay pending their repentance. Although we need to allow others to change, we must also live by a holy standard to inspire them to follow suit. It is so much easier and less stressful to work with a broken, contrite, teachable, and repentant transgressor than with an egoistic, obstinate, and evasive one with a seared conscience. It is one thing to fall into sin but another to wallow in it because one has no conscience, convictions, godly sorrow or restraint. There is nothing as distressing as relating to a *"sin practitioner"* who relishes in self-indulgence and harum-scarum ways. Until a habitual sinner sees the repulsiveness of iniquity just as God sees it, he or she will never accept responsibility.

Demons control abusive and hateful people. Until they are penitent, go through deliverance, and expel the spirits of hatred, violence, lust, greed, pride, and other related spirits, they will continue to be in bondage and exploit others.

While guarding against abuse, forgive those who hurt you and cease your hostilities. Ask God for wisdom to know how to review the issue and respond if they repent. Tread cautiously by the Spirit and do not fall into a demonic trap.

3). "Evil, Wicked or Diabolical People"

Throughout this book, I have accentuated the need to love and forgive each other just as Christ loves and forgives us. However, you may have some nagging questions like the following:

"How should I respond to people who want to hurt me and my family because they are evil?" "How should I deal with loved ones or associates who are involved in witchcraft or are trying to destroy me?" "Should I associate with wicked or diabolical people?" These are common but logical questions.

Stay away from heinous people and pray against their evil influence and deeds. They can bewitch, entice or lure one into error or bondage. There are biblical ways to handle diabolical relatives, friends, foes, employers, employees or neighbors that have deliberately made themselves enemies of God but friends of Satan.

Besides demonic spirits, Satan has some human agents working undercover for him to willfully oppose God, "steal, kill, and destroy" people. The Bible calls them: **Antichrists** (*1 John 2:18-23, 2 John 1:7-11, 1 John 4: 3*). **Workers of Iniquity** (*Luke 13:27, Psalm 5:5, Psalm 14:4, Psalm 28:3, Psalm 53:4, Psalm 59:2, Psalm 64:2, Psalm 92:7&9, Psalm 94:4 &16, Psalm 141:4& 9, Job 34:22, Proverbs 10:29, Proverbs 21:15*). **False**

Prophets and Teachers *(1 Timothy 4:1-3, 1 John 4:1, 2 Corinthians 11:4, Galatians 1:7-8, Matthew 7:15, Matthew 24:11&24-26, Mark 13:22, 2 Peter 2:1, Jeremiah 5:31, Jeremiah 14:14-15).* **Fake Pastors** *(Jeremiah 2:8, Jeremiah 12:10-11, Jeremiah 22:22, Jeremiah 23:1-40, Micah3:5-7).* **Evil Doers** *(Micah 2:1-2, Psalm 37: 9, Psalm 26:5, Psalm 140:1&11).* **Eaters of Flesh and Drinkers of Blood** *(Psalm 27:2, Micah 3:3).* **Witchcraft, Magic, those with a Familiar Spirit** *(2 Chronicles 33:6, Isaiah 8:19, Leviticus 19:31, Leviticus 20:6 & 27, 2 Kings 21:6, 1 Chronicles 10:13).* **Idolaters** *(Deuteronomy 13:1-18, Galatians 5:20, Revelation 21:8).* **The Wicked** *(Psalm 7:11, Psalm 9:17, Psalm 10:13, Psalm 11:5-6, Psalm 34:21, Psalm 36:1, Psalm 140:4, Psalm 145:20, Proverbs 5:22, Jeremiah 23:19, 30:23, 2 Peter 3:17).* **Enchanters** *(Exodus 7:22, 2 Kings 17:17, 2 Kings 21:6, 2 Chronicles 33:6, Isaiah 47:12, Jeremiah 27:9-10, Isaiah 47:9-14).* **Diviners, Psychics, Spiritualists, Clairvoyants, Mystics, Mind Readers, Necromancers, Telepathists** *(2 Kings 17:17, Deuteronomy 18:10-14, Jeremiah 14:14, Ezekiel 13:6-7& 23, Isaiah 44:25, Micah 3:7, Jeremiah 29:8-9, Zechariah 10:2).* **Sorcerers, Mediums** *(Jeremiah 27:9, Revelation 21:8, Malachi 3:5, Acts 13:6- 11).* **Murderers** *(Revelation 21:8, Revelation 22:15, Isaiah 1:21).* **Astrologers, Stargazers, Prognosticators** *(Daniel 2:2&27-28, Isaiah 47:13, Daniel 5:7).* **Soothsayers** *(Micah 5:12, Acts 16:16)* and all forms of **Satanism and Occultism** not listed here for lack of space. Until they truly repent, renounce Satan and his works, and submit to the lordship of Jesus Christ, they are God's enemies. "Do *not be unequally yoked"* with them." Stay far away!

Just as God is constantly looking for ways to bless His children so is the devil exploring ways to debauch them. Do not take people who are fiendish for granted or define them with your natural mind. They may look normal or innocent in the natural, but are atrocious in the spirit. Do not try to reason with *"the wicked."* They are irrational like their father, the devil. If they will not reason with God their creator, why do you think that they will reason with you?

Extinguish Interpersonal Conflict Fires!

Dealing With Heinous People

a). Pray for their salvation and deliverance so that: *"Their eyes will be open and they will come to the knowledge of truth." "In meekness instructing those that oppose themselves; if God peradventure will give them repentance to the acknowledging of the truth; And that they may recover themselves out of the snare of the devil, who are taken captive by him at his will" (2 Timothy 2:25-26).* Intercede for the redemption of their souls, but keep them at bay – whether they are close or casual acquaintances. We cannot trust people that are colluding with Satan. Instead, we must use our spiritual armaments to halt their fiendish conducts.

b). Deal with the spirit and power behind their acts of evil against you: Satan recruits demons and people to work for him. You do not have to offend them to incite their mischief. We cannot be careless, clueless or indifferent about evil surrogates that are helping him to achieve his malevolent ambitions.

We cannot deal with demonic agents soulishly or combat spirit with flesh. Confront devilish people by the Spirit, not flesh (Zachariah 4:6). Ensure your spiritual armour and antennae are on. (See Ephesians 6:13-18.)

Refrain from attacking people. It is unscriptural to pray against people. We should pray only against our spiritual enemies, not individuals *(Ephesians 6:12)*. Deal with the spirit that is controlling and using them against you. The evil entity behind a person's fiendish behavior rouses him to act and lash out in monstrous ways. Bind the evil spirit that is influencing and manipulating him, not the person, in the name of Jesus.

Peter tried to dissuade Jesus from going through the cross. However, the Lord bypassed him and attacked the devil behind his statement. He did not bind Peter but the devil. *"But he turned, and said unto Peter, Get thee behind me, Satan: thou art an offence unto me: for thou savourest not the things that be of God, but those that be of men" (Matthew 16:23).*

245

Use the word of God to go aggressively after the spirit that is inciting and empowering others against you with a vengeance. Jesus confronted Satan directly when he tempted Him. *"And Jesus answered and said unto him, Get thee behind me, Satan: for it is written, Thou shalt worship the Lord thy God, and him only shalt thou serve" (Luke 4:8).*

c). Fire for Fire: The devil is unrepentable, unchangeable, and unredeemable because he is the author of sin. We have a divine duty to use our spiritual weapons to bind and force him out of our lives and relationships.

Develop a praying spirit and make anywhere you are a war room. Pray in and by the Holy Spirit to hit the right target. Like I elucidated earlier, we must become water that douses conflict fire when we are relating to people. However, we must return fire for fire when dealing with Satan and his demonic entities because that is the only language they understand. Like the Psalmist and other biblical folks, we must pray imprecatory prayers against God's enemies, invoke judgement on their devilry, renounce their seductions, foil their schemes, crush their demonic gadgets, dilute their power, scatter their convocation, rain calamity on their parade, fire back their arrows, and reverse their curses, hex, jinx, bewitchments, divination, and enchantments, in the mighty name of Jesus Christ. Psalms 35, 69, 83, 94, 140, and many other Scriptures portray fire for fire prayers.

d). Close open doors that can give them access to you: Samson invoked the demons in Delilah through lust. King Saul gave entrée to evil spirits through jealousy and disobedience. Gehazi welcomed the devil through greed and it had a ripple effect on his life and future generations. Miriam gave entrée to leprosy when she murmured against Moses. Lot's wife became a pillar of salt because she embraced insubordination. Achan ushered in untimely death through the accursed things he stole. Within moments, the ground caved in and swallowed him up. His destiny vanished into thin air – all because of a Babylonian garment, two hundred shekels of silver, and a wedge of gold weighing fifty shekels.

We must bolt all outlets so Satan cannot access our lives through sin, negligence, curiosity or ignorance. If we close the door, he cannot come in to exploit us. All his curses and evil plans against us will backfire, in the name of Jesus. *"As the bird by wandering, as the swallow by flying, so the curse causeless shall not come" (Proverbs 26:2).*

e) Hand your "enemies" over to God: *"For the battle is not yours, but God's,"* and He will fight for you (2 chronicles 20:15). David handed Saul over to God to judge him. *"The LORD judge between me and thee, and the LORD avenge me of thee: but mine hand shall not be upon thee. As saith the proverb of the ancients, Wickedness proceedeth from the wicked: but mine hand shall not be upon thee. After whom is the king of Israel come out? after whom dost thou pursue? after a dead dog, after a flea. The LORD therefore be judge, and judge between me and thee, and see, and plead my cause, and deliver me out of thine hand" (1 Samuel 24:12-15).*

David was considerate but also distrustful of Saul. He continued to honor the green-eyed King as the Lord's anointed, but also ran for his dear life. Paul, the apostle, handed some folks to Satan. *"...Having faith and a good conscience, which some having rejected, concerning the faith have suffered shipwreck, of whom are Hymenaeus and Alexander, whom I delivered to Satan that they may learn not to blaspheme" (1 Timothy 1:19-20).*

Loving our enemies does not mean we should condone their malevolent deeds. We must call out evil and halt them biblically. We are obligated to love people, not trust them unless they earn it. God loves, but does not trust everyone. He trusts only those who obey Him. We must ask for the grace to love and forgive the seemingly unlovable and unforgivable. However, we must set boundaries to distant ourselves from sin and war in the spirit against the satanic powers that are fueling evil. The enemies of God are also our adversaries. Because they abhor God, they also abhor us and must be put in their place. We cannot become their doormat or target practice. God wants us to rise up, take a stand, and exercise our spiritual authority over them. *"Who will rise up for me against the evildoers? Who will stand up for me against the workers of iniquity?" (See Psalm 94:16.)*

- **Scriptural Confession: Psalm 140**
- **Praise and Worship**
- **Prayer Points**

1. Let the anointing of the Holy Spirit break the yoke of bareness in my life and relationships, in the mighty name of Jesus.
2. Oh God, give us the wisdom to discern your will, purpose and plan for our lives, in the name of Jesus.
3. Deliver me, O LORD, from evil men; Preserve me from violent men, Who plan evil things in *their* hearts; They continually gather together *for* war. They sharpen their tongues like a serpent; The poison of asps *is* under their lips. *Selah*

   Keep me, O LORD, from the hands of the wicked; Preserve me from violent men, Who have purposed to make my steps stumble. The proud have hidden a snare for me, and cords; They have spread a net by the wayside; They have set traps for me. *Selah.* I said to the LORD: "You *are* my God; Hear the voice of my supplications, O LORD.

   O GOD the Lord, the strength of my salvation, You have covered my head in the day of battle. Do not grant, O LORD, the desires of the wicked; Do not further his *wicked* scheme, *Lest* they be exalted. *Selah*

   "*As for* the head of those who surround me, Let the evil of their lips cover them; Let burning coals fall upon them; Let them be cast into the fire, Into deep pits, that they rise not up again. Let not a slanderer be established in the earth; Let evil hunt the violent man to overthrow *him*." I know that the LORD will maintain The cause of the afflicted, *And* justice for the poor. Surely the righteous shall give thanks to Your name; The upright shall dwell in Your presence" (Psalm 140).
4. Thank God for answers to your prayers.

CHAPTER 27

Jesus Christ Crusaders for Relationships

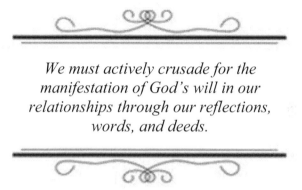

We must actively crusade for the manifestation of God's will in our relationships through our reflections, words, and deeds.

P eople who exhibit *Agape* love have the mind of Christ. They are ardently crusading for the manifestation of God because they believe in something greater than themselves. Regardless of the iniquitous state of humanity and the immense number of dysfunctional relationships in Christendom, there is still a remnant who lives exclusively for God. A vast number of them may not be television personalities or household names. However, God applauds their unusual sacrifices.

Sacrifices of Obedience

Hordes of believers are utilizing prayer and obedience to weather financial, marital, spiritual, and health storms in their alliances. Many are affluent materially but are also loaded with love and empathy. Others are destitute but rich in love and mercy.

Several are forced to endure ill health, abstain from the good things in life or cope with circumstances beyond their control. Nonetheless, they eagerly find innovative ways to connect with others on a deeper level. We need to be more sensitive and appreciative of kingdom warriors who are exemplifying the character of Christ amidst tumultuous times. It is our responsibility to honor and minister to them.

Making Bricks Without Straw

Many in unwholesome relationships ask for nothing and are content to love others and obey God. Some are connected to people that are apathetic, evasive, and egotistical. Others that are *"persecuted for righteousness sake"* readily forfeit certain pleasures in life to partake in *"the fellowship of Christ's sufferings"* and contend for their faith. They would rather *"deny themselves and take up their cross"* in obedience than rescind their divine relationships. Armed with God's grace, they readily habituate themselves to what they cannot change. They acclimatize themselves to their circumstances, learn to make bricks without straw, and are grateful to be alive to serve others. Despite their challenges, they remain steadfast because they draw their joy, strength, and fulfillment from the Lord, not from people.

One may wonder if such conscientious believers are real. Yes, they are ordinary intelligent people who do not feel that life must revolve around meeting their needs. You can find these unassuming believers in both developed and developing nations. God delights in how they respond to others' bolshie attitudes. They are chaste, grounded, and dyed-in-the-wool believers despite temptations to falter. In the face of pressures, they continually *"press toward the mark for the prize of the high calling of God in Christ Jesus."*

Someone might say, *"Oh no! I don't think I can live like that! No one gets in the way of meeting my needs."* We say things like that because we are egoistic, unteachable, and carnally minded. We feel that we know everything and are smarter than the omniscience God who created us when we are finite braggarts. We can learn a thing or two from those who collide with our sense of reality.

For those who are going through any pain or suffering right now in their relationships, meditate on how Paul, the apostle, responded to difficulty. *"Concerning this thing I pleaded with the Lord three times that it might depart from me. And He said to me, "My grace is sufficient for you, for My strength is made perfect in weakness." Therefore most gladly I will rather boast in my infirmities, that the power of Christ may rest upon me. Therefore I take pleasure in infirmities, in reproaches, in needs, in persecutions, in distresses, for Christ's sake. For when I am weak, then I am strong" (2 Corinthians 12:8-10).* Receive God's enabling grace and strength to overcome and fire back arrows of affliction at the enemy, in the name of Jesus.

The "Remnant" Believer

Are you a remnant believer? God has a remnant of men and women of integrity. They live biblically to validate their faith and foster His will. They are audacious divine helpers, confidantes, and facilitators intensely driven by faith, love, and obedience. They give all of themselves so others will encounter God through them. Their benevolence and loyalty should give us the impetus to care, give, and love more than ever before. Their unmovable faith, peerless devotion, extraordinary sacrifices, and godly approach to life should set us on holy fire and drive us into the presence of God.

The unprecedented ways they personify servanthood should melt our hearts with contrition, compel us to rededicate our lives to the Lord all over again, and replicate the same meekness in our relationships. God is calling everyone to a life of consecration and service so we can use our relationships to crusade for Him and fulfill His ambassadorship mandate. Consistently, He expects us to minister to those within and outside our circle in ways that will augment their thirst for righteousness and reproduce the nature of Christ. We must remain in the frontlines and be a buffer against conflict, a trailblazer for peace, and the spiritual gatekeepers of our interpersonal relationships.

As Christ's ambassadors and ambassadresses, we are called to utilize our sacred mantle to transform and heal humanity. We are the yardstick that others use to measure and define God's love. We ought to be a safe harbor, prototypes, pacesetters, nurturers, ambiance regulators, heart-tenderizers, peacemakers, mood-setters, and the face of the Lord in our alliances. We must become a catalyst for hope, use our gifts to enrich others, and be the impetus for their personal and spiritual growth.

We need to cultivate *"a meek and gentle spirit,"* live boldly by the "Truth" in uncharted territories, love God through people, and bend over backward to minister to those who cannot reciprocate us. We should be warmth, bounteousness, and inspiration on display in our relationships. Personifying altruism, amiability or empathy will inspire those we encounter to duplicate the same virtues in their associations.

Everyone of us must use our leadership as a bully pulpit to evince humility, brokenness, and the character of God in our homes, Churches, market places, and communities. When we comply with the Lord's standards, others will have no choice but to act in accordance with His will. Loving others wholly validate our total surrender to the Lord.

The Lord Says, "Thank You."

We need to appreciate the multitudinous believers who are leaving no stone unturned to exalt Christ in their relationships. A colossal thank you from the Lord to all loving parents that do not feel appreciated by their children and caring children that do not feel validated by their parents. He treasures neighbors, relatives, bosses, professionals, parishioners, Ministers, friends, and spouses that do not feel cherished by others – though they go to great lengths to show love and empathy. There were days you could have cut corners or bailed out of your relationships, but you did not! Instead, you jumped through hoops and clutched to God. The Lord appreciates your faithfulness and will *"reward your labor of love."* He is counting on you to continually be His standard-bearer.

The Lord highly esteems kingdom warriors that are down in the trenches interceding for marriages, businesses, families, and Churches. They are in the combat zone or ground zero liberating communities and nations from the clutches of Satan. Thank you for your steadfastness. It energizes my faith and sets my heart ablaze for God. Just as you are standing in the gap, so will He send others to pray for you and your relationships. As you are fighting for others, the Almighty God will fight for you. You will never labor in vain, in the name of Jesus.

Ah, wonderful readers, you have been so patient! The Lord delights in you! Thank you for championing His cause in and outside your home. Just as you are watering your family and others, He will also water and prosper you in His name. He will count all your acts of love as righteousness and reward you for the time and efforts invested in reading this book. I pray that He will reveal Himself to you as never before, empower you to conquer every obstacle, and fulfill His divine purpose, in the name of Jesus. His mercies, favor, and presence will always overshadow you, in His precious name.

God's Will, Our Will

May the Lord be exalted! Yes, we are a part of the remnant. We are imperfect ordinary believers who were battered, demoralized, suppressed, harassed, emotionally maimed, and spiritually deformed by the devil. We roamed in the wilderness and floundered in demonic captivity for years. Once, we were the casualties of devilish exploitation, but in His mercy, Jesus delivered and set us free.

We are fed up with spiritual bareness, the high rate of dysfunctional relationships in Christendom, and are determined to make a difference. The devil has been wreaking havoc in godly relationships and we see it as a divine duty to halt him. By the power of the Holy Spirit, we are coming out swinging at him - his lies, deception, selfishness, bitterness, unbelief, unforgiveness, pride, fear, and conflict. We are disgusted by the present state of the family, Church, community, and are determined to utilize truth, obedience, love, forgiveness, the sword of the Spirit, the name and blood of Jesus, and all the spiritual weapons available to raise a standard.

We recognize the importance of adopting the mind of Christ and yielding to Him to buffer those we love. Consequently, His will has become our will, his purpose, our purpose, and His counsel, our counsel. What grieves Him aggrieves us. Only what pleases Him, gratifies us. Daily, the zeal to *"seek first His kingdom...."* and become more like him consume our hearts. Because we are so attuned to His Spirit, we communicate only what we hear Him say and do only what we see Him do in our relationships. Doing His will has become greater than life and the burden to obey Him, burns daily in our hearts. The joy of expressing His love through obedience far supersedes the daily struggles of life.

Intermittently, our ignorance reverberates meaningless sounds like empty barrels. Often, we *"wrestle"* with God because of our deficiencies, but continually abide in Him. Without His guidance, we are like a short-winded whale looking befuddled outside the ocean, barely clinging to life. *"In Him we live, move, and have our being."* He is our natural and spiritual oxygen, heartbeat, significance, identity, hope, daily bread, peace, strength, purpose, joy, fulfillment, and the essence of our being. Our lives, marriages, children, career, family, future, interpersonal relationships – and everything revolve around Him. He is the nucleus and driving force of our lives.

We realize that we are *"living epistles,"* the conveyors of His glory, replica of His character, vessels of peace, agents of transformation, and kingdom emissaries, mandated to regulate the spiritual temperature in our environment. Therefore, we yield our will to Him, and He skillfully circumcises our desiccated hearts so the life of Christ will be made manifest in us. Daily, our *"flesh becomes dead to sin, and our spirit becomes alive unto God."* We gladly *"crucify the flesh,"* *"turn the other cheek,"* esteem others as better, *"mortify the deeds of the flesh,"* and *"buffet the flesh"* to renounce the old nature and its susceptibility to rebellion. We fight *"the good fight of faith," "not by might, nor by power," but by the Holy Spirit.*

"We are troubled on every side, yet not distressed; we are perplexed, but not in despair; Persecuted, but not forsaken; cast down, but not destroyed" (2 Corinthians 4:8-9). We can do all things through Christ who strengthens us (Philippians 4:13*). "Not that we are sufficient of ourselves to think anything as of ourselves; but our sufficiency is of God" (2 Corinthians 3:5). "His grace is sufficient and His strength is made perfect in our weaknesses" (2 Corinthians 12:9).*

Furthermore, our life rises and falls on God. When we rise, we rise on Him, and when we fall, we fall on Him. Whether we rise or fall, we conform to Him. We gleefully bask in the splendor of His omnipotence, holiness, and omniscience. His unmerited love intoxicates us, His faithfulness enthralls us, His grace captivates us, His mercies enchant us, and His sovereignty stupefies us. We are enraptured by His forgiveness, flabbergasted by His blessings, entranced by His longsuffering, invigorated by His beauty, and astounded by His perfection and Almightiness. We cannot help it – we are addicted to Him.

We are willing to toe the line, care for, share with, commit to, forbear with, forgive, tolerate, inspire or love others because it pleases God. Are we perfect? Of course, not! However, our utmost goal is to become more like Him every day.

For us, sin or disobedience is not an option, not because we have perfect relationships, but because we love God too much to grieve Him. He loathes sin! We cannot desert a sibling, relative, colleague, neighbor, brother or sister in Christ or leave him or her in the cold. We have created too many casualties and abandoned too many wounded soldiers on the battlefield to die. Not again! No, we can't and won't, in the name of Jesus! We are in this together because we are one body of Christ. *When one member hurts, we all hurt, and when one member rejoices, we all rejoice.* We have one Master, *"one faith, and one baptism."* Loving one another is the only proof that we genuinely love Him.

Daily, we are in the frontlines serving others, fighting for the Lord's cause, and exemplifying His gospel. Stride by stride, our indomitable General, Jesus Christ, gives the command and we obey. He leads, and we follow. When He says, *"Love,"* we love, *"Forgive,"* we forgive," and *"March,"* we march! No questions asked! By His grace, we love, forgive, march in obedience, and will never retreat or raise the white flag because we have reached the point of no return.

The Lord luxuriates in our obedience and grins with pleasure whenever we exhibit His character. He rejoices when we rhapsodize about His love because others are empowered to taste the bliss of heaven on earth. When we show humility, tolerance, and forgiveness, He beams proudly and gives His Son, Jesus, a high-five for exemplifying them on the cross. He scents the aroma of our oblations – sacrifices of righteousness, well-pleasing to Him. Our total submission to Him sends His feet tapping for the thrill of creating us. Oh, how much He loves His children! Oh, how much we love Him! *For the Lord is good and His bounteous mercies endure forever (Psalm 136:1-26).*

Enlist to Heal Relationships

Are you not appalled by the demonic exploitation of interpersonal relationships? Families are turning against each other, our sons and daughters are traumatized by a heathenistic culture, Churches are striving with one another, the devil is hauling many marriages to divorce court, and our business and communities are in distress! We are divided and exploited by our insecurities.

The Lord is asking: *"Who will manifest my character and raise a godly standard in relationships? Who will stand up for truth and righteousness? How many more divorces, broken homes, barren Churches, traumatized children, corrupt businesses, and dysfunctional communities will prompt you to evince my glory in your relationships? What will it take for you to swallow your pride to forgive others? Why won't you trade your anger and intolerance for understanding? What matters more to you – my way or your way, my will or your will? Which weighs more – your love for me or your love for self? Are you living to please Me or please yourself?"*

Enlist in the crusade to heal our children. Blow the trumpet of salvation and deliverance for our communities. Join us to rebuild the foundation and broken walls of our families by living holy. Ring the bell of transformation and revival for our Churches. Proclaim God's love on the rooftops and in your relationships. Be a part of God's soldiery of warriors who are Holy Spirit *"armed and dangerous,"* fighting for His kingdom. Will you enroll and help bear the burden of the Lord?

We are ordinary people desperate for God. We want Him as much as we need Him! Like the Psalmist, *"As the deer pants for the water brooks,"* so our souls pant for Him. *Our souls "followeth hard after" Him."* Our *"heart and flesh crieth out"* for Him to deliver our offspring, reconcile our marriages, fortify our homes, resuscitate our communities, revive our Churches, and heal our relationships. Because of our fallibility, we may not always measure up to His standard of prayer, fasting, and rugged faith. However, we will always long for a contrite heart, crave a new move of God, and grasp the hem of His presence until His glory manifests.

What are You Willing to Restore?

What is your cause? Until you are willing to live radically for the Lord or for something greater than yourself, you will never move beyond meeting your needs or basking in your comfort zone. David walked in love despite challenging times. The Prophet, Hosea, risked his reputation and extended unconditional love to his licentious wife, Gomer. Esther risked her life to save the Jewish generation. What are you willing to risk to save your bloodline? What are you willing to rescue in your environment? What problems are you called to solve in your profession? What are you assigned to transform in your relationships? What are you willing to sacrifice to heal your Church, family, community or generation?

"Oh Bridget, you don't understand. I have been hurt many times. I don't trust people." "I don't have time." "I have my own problems!" Fair enough! Except that when life rotates solely around you, other people suffer. The truth may be a bitter pill to swallow. However, your life will greatly improve – if you renounce narcissism. Many have walked on the *"straight and narrow"* path and sacrificed for the counsel of God to manifest in your life. It was grueling, but they were addicted to gratifying God, not self. You can and should emulate them.

God did not place us in relationships for exhibition, competition or personal gain. He divinely positioned us to live by example so that the budding generation will be primed to reproduce and bear good fruits as well. Like a magnet, our character must draw them to God, not repel them. Our lifestyle should be the impetus that propels them into His arms. It is our divine obligation to blaze the trail, groom our children to be kingdom warriors, and pass the baton of holiness to them. Why? So, they too will be empowered to live virtuously, raise a higher standard for their offspring, and maximize destiny. We cannot swap their future for transitory pleasures or fan the flames of past generational bondage. The kingdom of God must come into every aspect of our lives. His purpose must prevail in our children, in the name of Jesus Christ.

Our faith must have no shadow of turning and be propelled by the will of God, not selfish desires. We must be driven by truth, not by illusion, compelled by love, not emotions, prompted by the Spirit, not flesh, possessed by faith, not fear, and impelled by stanch Scriptural convictions, not flimsy excuses. Until the burden to obey God becomes greater than our rationalizations, we will always find duplicitous ways to justify disobedience.

Treat Others as You Would Want to be Treated

The fundamental rule for building covenant relationships is, *"Treat others as you would want to be treated" (Luke 6:31). "And whatever you do, do it heartily, as to the Lord and not to men, knowing that from the Lord you will receive the reward of the inheritance; for you serve the Lord Christ" (Colossians 3:23-24).*

Envision the challenges in your relationships as stepping-stones to your healing, opportunities to stretch your faith, and occasions to trust God. One of the proven ways to avoid, manage or resolve conflict is when we adopt the mentality of the Psalmist in the following prayer and make it a lifestyle.

Pray this prayer:
Almighty God, "Who can understand his errors? Cleanse me from secret faults. Keep back Your servant also from presumptuous sins; Let them not have dominion over me. Then I shall be blameless, And I shall be innocent of great transgression. Let the words of my mouth and the meditation of my heart be acceptable in Your sight, O LORD, my strength and my Redeemer" (Psalm 19:12-14).

The fear of God is the panacea for all relationship maladies. We can build healthy interpersonal relationships only if we cultivate the fear of God and respond to each other biblically as a way of life.

- **Scriptural Confession: Psalm 51, 25, 86, 119, Ephesians 1:17-23; 3:16-21**
- **Praise and worship**
- **Prayer Points**

1. Create in me a clean heart, O God, and renew a steadfast spirit within me, in the name of Jesus (Psalm 51:10).
2. Lead me in Your truth and teach me, For You are the God of my salvation; On You I wait all the day (Psalm 25:5).
3. Teach me Your way, O LORD; I will walk in Your truth; Unite my heart to fear Your name, in the name of Jesus (Psalm 86:11).
4. Let integrity and uprightness preserve me, For I wait for You (Psalm 25:21).
5. "Teach me, O LORD, the way of Your statutes, And I shall keep it to the end. Give me understanding, and I shall keep

Your law; Indeed, I shall observe it with my whole heart" (Psalm 119:33-34).

6. "Incline my heart to Your testimonies, And not to covetousness. Turn away my eyes from looking at worthless things, and revive me in Your way" (Psalm 119: 36-37).

7. "Your hands have made me and fashioned me; Give me understanding, that I may learn Your commandments" (Psalm 119: 73).

8. "Direct my steps by Your word, and let no iniquity have dominion over me, in the name of Jesus" (Psalm 119:133).

9. I pray Oh God of our Lord Jesus Christ, the Father of glory, that You may give unto my family and alliances the spirit of wisdom and revelation in the knowledge of You: That the eyes of our understanding being enlightened; that we may know what is the hope of Your calling, and what the riches of the glory of Your inheritance in the saints, And what is the exceeding greatness of Your power to us-ward who believe, according to the working of Your mighty power, Which You wrought in Christ, when You raised him from the dead, and set him at Your own right hand in the heavenly places. Far above all principality, and power, and might, and dominion, and every name that is named, not only in this world, but also in that which is to come: And hath put all things under his feet, and gave him to be the head over all things to the church, Which is his body, the fullness of him that filleth all in all (Ephesians 1:17-23).

10. Father God, perfect what is lacking in our faith. Make us increase and abound in love towards one another, so that You may establish our hearts blameless in holiness before You, in the name of Jesus. (See 1 Thessalonians 3:10-13).

11. Heavenly Father, I pray that You would count us worthy of this calling, and fulfill all the good pleasure of Your goodness and the work of faith with power; so that the name of our Lord Jesus Christ may be glorified in us, and we in Him, according to the grace of our God and the Lord Jesus Christ (2 Thessalonians 1:11-12).

12. Almighty God of hope, fill my family and other relationships, with all joy and peace in believing, that we may abound in hope, through the power of the Holy Ghost (Romans 15:13).

13. Almighty God, I pray that you will grant us according to the riches of your glory, to be strengthened with might by your Spirit in the inner man; That Christ may dwell in our hearts by faith; that we may be rooted and grounded in love; that we may be able to comprehend with all saints what is the breadth, and length, and depth, and height; and to know the love of Christ, which passeth knowledge, that we might be filled with all the fullness of God. Now unto You O God that is able to do exceedingly abundantly above all that we ask or think, according to the power that worketh in us, Unto You be glory in the church by Christ Jesus throughout all ages, world without end. Amen (Ephesians 3:16-21).

14. I seal my prayers with the precious blood of Jesus Christ.

15. Almighty God, I thank you for the breakthroughs and testimonies.

A Special Prayer for You

Dear Purpose-driven Reader,

May God give you the grace, wisdom, patience, and the anointing to always avoid and resolve conflict; embrace reconciliation; cultivate great communication and listening skills, identify and function in interpersonal relationship roles, and utilize your relationship to worship Him, in the mighty name of Jesus Christ.

This I pray, that your love may abound more and more in knowledge and all discernment; that you may approve the things that are excellent, and be sincere and without offense till the day of Christ. May you be filled with the fruits of righteousness which are by Jesus Christ, to the glory and praise of God (Philippians 1:9-11). Now may the God of patience and comfort grant you to be like-minded toward one another, according to Christ Jesus, that you may with one mind and one mouth glorify the God and Father of our Lord Jesus Christ (Romans 15:5-6).

May the grace of our Lord Jesus Christ, the unfailing love of God, and the sweet fellowship of the Holy Spirit be with you and your relationships. Wishing you all of God's best.

Together, every day, every moment, create, sculpt, and paint your own paradise with those around you.

Championing the will of God for relationships,

Bridget

Special Invitation

Dear Friend, God exclusively and uniquely made you. However, do you have a personal relationship with Him? I invite you to accept the Lord Jesus Christ into your heart now. "Today is the day of Salvation." If you want your life transformed, repeat the following prayer:

Dear Almighty Father, I come to you in the name of your Son, Jesus Christ. I acknowledge that I am a sinner. Please forgive me for my sins and cleanse me with the blood of Jesus. I accept Jesus into my heart. Thank you for saving and cleansing me, in the name of Jesus. Amen.

If you genuinely repented and accepted Jesus as your Lord and Savior, you are born again! Welcome to the family of God. Now begin to walk in victory, emulate the character of Christ, live in the Spirit, walk by faith, and experience an exhilarating, adventurous way of life through Christ.

To become a mature Christian, connect with a Bible based Church that can mentor you. Daily, study, meditate on the Bible to feed your spirit, and develop a consistent prayer life. May God bless you abundantly.

"Set Free" Biblical Counseling

"Set Free" Biblical Counseling (On-site, live/virtual sessions) Our counseling regime is based on the Bible. This divinely inspired "God-breathed" sacred book produces faith, hope, joy, and lasting peace. It is the only antidote for all infirmities, distresses, societal ills, and all human maladies. No other book written by finite and fallible humans can genuinely deliver or set people free. I have seen marriages restored, hurts healed, lives transformed, and horrendous situations reversed through the power of the Holy Spirit when people applied truths in Scriptures. If you willingly obey God, you will overcome your problems regardless of how seemingly insurmountable they may be. Call or email for information about:

- Marriage/Relationships
- Premarital Preparation Course/Counseling
- Depression/Grief/loss
- Fear/Anxiety/Panic Attack
- Emotional wounds/Trauma
- Ministerial Issues
- Discovery of life Purpose, Birthing/pioneering dreams or vision
- Deliverance from Sexual Perversion, Addictions, Destructive habits, deep-rooted strongholds
- Life Recovery and much more.

Schools of the Spirit

School of Ministry Boot Camp: Answer the call of God. Get the tools to start your ministry. 15 months of accelerated courses. Only 6hrs/weekly in the virtual classroom/Teleconference line. Ordination available.

Marriage and Family Institute Premarital Preparation Course: A State of Florida certified; 4hr on-site, online or virtual classroom. Couples who have a certificate of completion get a discount on their marriage license.

"Set Free" Marriage Boot Camp: A three, five or seven-day bliss of self-confrontation, conflict resolution, forgiveness, healing, and reconciliation for couples.

Bachelor/Spinster Institute: Get the practical tools and resources to build a loving, fruitful, and long-lasting relationship.

Churchology Institute: Equip your leaders, ministry of helps, and congregants and ignite the fire of revival in your territory. Empower them to accelerate to the next level or prepare for the move of God.

For current conferences, seminars, workshops, and for more information, call, email or log into our website: www.JesusChristUniversity.org
Info@JesusChristUniversity.org

Weekly Ministerial Sessions

Global Ministerial Network/Empowerment
For Ministers, leaders, and those who feel called to ministry. "Iron sharpens iron."
Day: Tuesdays. Time: 8pm – 8:30pm (EST).

Weekly Marriage/Relationship Tune-up
A relationship clinic that empowers marriages and other interpersonal relationships. Get the tools to resolve your relationships' challenges.
Day: Tuesdays. Time: 8:30pm – 9pm (EST)

"Oh God Save And Heal Our Children" Intercessory Prayer
A weekly prayer/intercession for our sons/daughters. Join a global network of parents and those with a burden for children.
Day: Tuesdays. Time: 9pm – 9:30pm (EST)

Attend A Live or Virtual Session
To attend a live or virtual session, send us a text or email and a link will be sent to you to join the session.

Email:
bridget@bridgetbazunu.org or
info@JesusChristUniversity.org

Contact

To contact Bridget Bazunu or invite her to minister in your church, event or conference or for any information:
Call, Email or Log into:

Websites
www.bridgetbazunu.org
www.JesusChristUniversity.org

Emails
bridget@bridgetbazunu.org
info@JesusChristUniversity.org

Phone
407-443-5393
Please, include your testimony or help received from this book when you write.

"Blessed be the LORD for evermore. Amen, and Amen"
(Psalm 89:52.)

Hallelujah!

Made in the USA
Columbia, SC
02 October 2020